Organisations & Management in Social Work

Organisations & Management in Social Work

Everyday Action for Change

Mark Hughes and Michael Wearing

3rd Edition

Los Angeles | London | New Delhi
Singapore | Washington DC | Melbourne

Los Angeles | London | New Delhi
Singapore | Washington DC | Melbourne

SAGE Publications Ltd
1 Oliver's Yard
55 City Road
London EC1Y 1SP

SAGE Publications Inc.
2455 Teller Road
Thousand Oaks, California 91320

SAGE Publications India Pvt Ltd
B 1/I 1 Mohan Cooperative Industrial Area
Mathura Road
New Delhi 110 044

SAGE Publications Asia-Pacific Pte Ltd
3 Church Street
#10-04 Samsung Hub
Singapore 049483

Editor: Kate Wharton
Editorial assistant: Lucy Dang
Production editor: Katie Forsythe
Copyeditor: Sharon Cawood
Proofreader: William Baginsky
Indexer: Elske Janssen
Marketing manager: Camille Richmond
Cover design: Wendy Scott
Typeset by: C&M Digitals (P) Ltd, Chennai, India
Printed and bound by CPI Group (UK) Ltd,
Croydon, CR0 4YY

First edition published 2007. Reprinted 2009, 2010, 2011 and 2012
Second edition published 2013. Reprinted 2014, 2015

This 3rd edition first published 2017

Library of Congress Control Number: 2016938472

British Library Cataloguing in Publication data

A catalogue record for this book is available from
the British Library

ISBN 978-1-4739-3451-1
ISBN 978-1-4739-3452-8 (pbk)

Contents

List of Figures

List of Practice Examples

About the Authors

Dr Mark Hughes is Professor of Social Work in the School of Arts and Social Sciences, Southern Cross University, Australia. He has worked as a social worker in health, aged care and mental health settings in both Australia and the UK. He has also worked as a social work academic at the University of Queensland, the University of New South Wales, and Goldsmiths College London. Mark's research interests centre on organisational practice, social work with older people, and lesbian and gay ageing. Mark is co-author of six books, as well as a range of journal publications.

Dr Michael Wearing is a Senior Lecturer in the Social Work Program, The School of Social Sciences, University of New South Wales (UNSW), Australia. He teaches in a range of areas of theory, policy and practice in social work and criminology, notably on organisational practice, human and health service delivery and working in youth justice and related areas. He trained as a social worker and sociologist at UNSW and maintains a strong research and publishing career in social policy and applied sociology in Australia and internationally.

Acknowledgements

We would like to acknowledge the support provided to us by the Faculty of Arts and Social Sciences and the School of Social Sciences at the University of New South Wales, as well as the School of Arts and Social Sciences at Southern Cross University. In particular, we wish to thank Richard Hugman, for his assistance while Head of School, and our colleagues Karen Heycox and Lesley Hughes in their support of the book. Thanks also to John Healy and Elizabeth Saunders for their assistance with the first edition of the book. Special thanks go to family and friends who have encouraged us along the way. Mark would like to give special thanks to Yugo Shiozuru and Peta Hughes. Michael thanks Megan Edwards, Robert Urquhart, Rod Smith, John Healy, and Aron and Ellen Wearing. Thank you also to Kate Wharton, Lucy Dang, Katie Forsythe, Sharon Cawood and their colleagues at SAGE Publications for their support of the book and their expertise and invaluable advice.

Many of the ideas in this book have emerged and been clarified through our teaching experiences and conversations with students. So we hope that the book matches their expectations and assists them in becoming more active and reflexive organisational operators.

Introduction

Social Workers in Organisations

When talking to people about social work as organisational practice, we frequently get responses like: 'Is that about filing and administration?' or 'Paperwork is so boring'. Well, we can't honestly say that organisational practice is not about administration, filing or paperwork – because it is – but we can say that there are ways of doing administration, filing and paperwork that are in line with social work's values and that promote clients' and communities' interests.

We can also say that organisational practice in social work is more than these three things. It is also about teamwork and developing organisational skills, such as mediation and negotiation. It is about knowing how to plan, implement, manage and evaluate projects that meet community needs. It is about leadership, accountability and professional supervision. Organisational practice also involves understanding and working with managerial concepts and processes, such as strategic planning and risk management. Social work organisational practice involves understanding and participating in decision-making processes and taking action to improve service users' experiences of our own and other organisations. We argue that the fine detail of such practices is commonplace in everyday work but needs to be elevated in the consciousness for an active and engaged reflexive social work to be effective in the myriad of social contexts that require professional intervention – from individual and family work to public advocacy and political lobbying.

This book examines the detail of these different organisational practices to encourage active, participatory and reflective practice. It also examines a wide range of social work practices within their organisational contexts – ranging from micro-level individual work to macro-level community development. Without organisational activities, those social work practices that may be stereotypically seen as more 'real' or more exciting social work – perhaps an assessment of a child's needs, or a counselling session, or a meeting with a community group – simply could not occur. We encourage social workers to engage actively in the everyday politics of organisational life to promote better practice, more equitable treatment of service users, greater respect for colleagues, and increased enthusiasm for change in the workplace.

When we hear accounts of social work in practice, the organisational dimensions of that practice are not always apparent. But, if we work to uncover the 'behind the scenes' activity, organisational and management functions become explicit and appear essential to any action that is taken. In Practice Example 0.1, a real situation, a voluntary sector worker talks about her practice supporting a family in crisis, beginning with a family interview jointly conducted with the local statutory social workers.

Supporting a family in crisis

Her father proceeds to say basically [his daughter] was pathetic, useless, there was no point, he'd tried everything, who the hell do we think we were giving her a service when it was a waste of time. It was extremely abusive. Anyway I started challenging him about his framing of her in the meeting, gently saying things like, 'Well, I guess you know she's your daughter so if you're here you must have some concerns about her safety and well-being.' [He responded] 'Nope, I think she's pathetic and I don't know why you're wasting your time.'

Really what it got down to was me saying to him, 'How might you be feeling if you were sitting in a room with your family and other people saying to you that you were pathetic?' I repeated everything back to him. This made an enormous shift in the room because all these people who were being abused by him had never spoken up to him. They would never lift their eyes off the table when he spoke. [The statutory social workers] … were having the same perception of what was happening in the room. So they were exploring this, and challenging his behaviour too, saying 'Well you know, I think there is some hope', and 'this girl has particular skills and strengths, that is why we're working with her'. We couldn't participate or collude with the abuse [of] this girl in the room, nor would we do it at any other time. Anyway, the most remarkable thing happened where the mother said, 'I can't go home with you. This is too abusive and I've been hostage in this house for x number of years.'

So we took her into another room. She started disclosing the sexual abuse and violent behaviour in the house with everybody in the family. We had to take the girl into another room, obviously distressed and affected by what was happening. We tried to extricate her from him. He was hanging on to her arm saying, 'She wants to stay with me'. We called the police. Basically a [protection order] was applied for on that day. [The statutory social workers] set the woman up in a hotel because the girl couldn't return to her house once this disclosure had happened.

There's a whole range of things that happened around that, but the outcomes, in terms of protection for this family, were that we then built on the strengths of her mum and generally went through what they were going through and their experiences and disclosures. We got housing for them in a week. We got [a protection order] taken out on the whole family. We set them up in counselling. (Cited in Wearing and Edwards, 2003: 1–3)

This is a powerful account of active social workers in practice, promoting the rights and welfare of members of society and achieving change. Effecting change such as this is why we are employed in human service organisations and why social work is valued as a professional endeavour. And this change could not occur were it not for the everyday organisational and management systems supporting the practice.

In this case, critical factors included the professional supervision and ongoing training that enabled the social workers to confront the father's abusive behaviour and model appropriate behaviour. Organisational procedures provided guidance on how to respond to the situation, including strategies to promote the safety of family members and workers. Organisational resources were made available by managers to provide the necessary staffing to respond to the situation and provide appropriate levels of follow-up work. The allocation of resources to this work would have been balanced with other competing priorities. Effective inter-agency teamwork enabled the joint interview to occur and provided a basis for liaising with the police and local services. Information management systems both within and across the organisations enabled accurate record keeping and completion of documentation (such as legal documents) to facilitate the assessment of and intervention in the family's situation.

These are just a few of the organisational and management systems and processes needed to engage with the complex family situation that confronted the social workers. Without a good knowledge of these organisational dimensions and without an ability to work effectively with them, the outcomes for the family may have been quite different.

So, to be an effective social worker it is necessary to be an effective organisational operator (Thompson, 2003). At times, this is an uncomfortable reality. How often do we feel constrained by the organisation in our professional endeavours? How frequently do we need to stand up to managerialist practices and advocate on behalf of clients or communities? Sometimes it is tempting to see social work as an alternative to the oppressive practices of human service organisations and to see social workers as pitted against managers, administrators and bureaucrats. Yet, to position social work as ethical professional practice – against organisations as monolithic impersonal structures – is simplistic and undermines our usefulness to those who seek our services. Moreover, it denies the human and relational qualities of the organisations that employ us and that we are required to exercise active membership of and help construct.

In this book, we see human service organisations – such as social service departments and not-for-profit organisations – as essential vehicles for social work practice. What social workers do on a day-to-day basis is bounded by the organisation that employs them. It is often our position and authority within an organisation that determines our usefulness to service users; for example, by facilitating access to needed resources. However, human service organisations are not just containers for social work activity; they are also necessary for putting into effect social work's professional enterprise. By working within organisations, social work's commitment to its core values – such as self-determination, care and safety, and social justice – can become real in the relationships formed with service users and communities, and in the outcomes achieved. Organisations are essential to achieving – or at least to pursuing – social work's virtues and ideals as a profession.

This doesn't mean that social workers should become driven by organisational or managerial agendas. For social workers to be effective organisational operators, they not only need to be able to work competently within existing arrangements, but they also need to be able to critique these arrangements, and be able – and willing – to work strategically and tactically to change them. Developing a detailed analysis of such things as organisational systems, structures, processes and cultures provides a basis from which to work strategically to effect change and work through the everyday challenges that face us. In our book, we hope to assist you in developing this capacity to critique organisations. We also want you to develop your understanding of how to work competently within existing organisational arrangements as an active member and employee to the benefit of clients and communities and in line with social work values. This involves thinking and acting strategically and ethically.

What Can Organisational Theory and Analysis Offer Social Work?

In this book, we bring social work practice literature and organisational theory literature together to highlight the potential of organisational analysis in social work and to support the development of social workers as competent, strategic and ethical organisational operators.

Payne (1997) claims that theory is a social construction, and for social workers it is 'defined by what they do' in the reflexive awareness that develops from interaction with clients, agencies and the social context. Social work 'theory' – sometimes known as practice theory or a kind of practical meta-knowledge – also reflects 'the histories of theoretical, occupational and service contexts' (Payne, 1997: 25). Payne is careful not to confuse this theory with general social theory, of which the sociology of organisations is one dimension. It is important to acknowledge the diversity of theory and practice across countries, and particularly when the western-centric English-speaking and European countries are compared with the rest of the world, especially developing countries. Social work needs to be particularly aware of non-white approaches to the analysis of organisations if it is to take the political struggle against racism, discrimination and violence seriously.

Reed (1999) argues that since the nineteenth century we have lived in an 'organisation society' that has seen the triumph of the rational, including planned management and change, over the irrational in the social world. Organisations mediate real human conflicts between collective needs and individual wants. Some theories legitimate the social order by de-politicising – via scientific and rational means – social conflicts. However, there are other theories, some of which we examine in this book, that draw attention to the wider political and social context of organisational practices and how they might support prevailing ideology or discourse.

There are three propositions we want to make about organisational analysis for social work and for management in the social services. First, organisational analysis is best understood as an activity of 'politics from below' that enables fine-grained interpretations of various cultures as they interact with the structure of organisations. Consequently, a central component of organisational analysis is an analysis of change, both within the organisation itself and within society. Studying organisational change as a front-line practitioner or manager will be assisted by use of different perspectives on how organisations work and change in the wider social and political context. Thus, our book is broader than a discussion of the managerial or organisational processes that lead to outcomes as determined by managers or organisational elites. It is not a book about the technicalities of such a narrowly defined organisational practice. From our perspective, a concept such as organisational change is not only about 'top-down' decisions from senior management. Change in organisations is also influenced by the internal activities of front-line staff and clients, as well as by line managers and senior management. It is influenced by volunteer management boards and by internal actors acting as advocates and whistleblowers. It is influenced by external actors, such as community activists, government officials, politicians and others, who allocate funds to human service organisations. And it is influenced by the media, political ideology and the effects of policy change.

A second proposition is the need to guard against the de-politicisation that organisational analysis can potentially encourage. There is a strong theme in the political science literature, following Reed (1999) and Wolin (2004), that organisational theory has distracted attention away from mainstream politics, critical policy analysis and policy change. This is an issue that social work needs to address if it is not to be captured by the technical and de-politicised language of business-oriented organisational analysis. Part of the explanation for the rise of organisational analysis, especially in American social science, relates to disillusionment with the political arena and the public sphere. One consequence of this in the last two decades is the managerial efforts to try to solve social problems and deliver social welfare through technical, managerial and market-driven means (Wolin, 2004). We are very conscious in this book of the need to be sensitive to social work in organisations as political action.

The third and final proposition is that there is a pervasive political amnesia in social work and social work education in liberal Anglo democracies about the politics and sociology of organisations. Social workers find much of their work in large organisations or bureaucracies, such as social services departments. Similarly, social workers in non-government agencies rely heavily on large government organisations because much of their agency's funds are tied to government programmes. So the practice of social work is attuned to the nuances of these bureaucracies, but this does not mean the rules or formality of such organisations should be accepted and remain unchallenged by professional identity, values and knowledge. From our position, it is important for social workers to make use of the literature on the sociology of organisations in their work, not to be constrained by organisational structures simply because 'that's how they've always been', and to seek alternative organisational forms in line with social work values.

Social workers are located in many different kinds of organisational contexts and an understanding of the theory, purpose, goals, culture and structure of these organisations is central, among other understandings, to practice in human service areas. Social work also intervenes at various levels of society and social interaction – from the micro practice of counselling and family work to the macro practice of community development. This requires a sophisticated knowledge of processes and structures in human service organisations. In particular, understanding the effect on staff, clients and communities of organisational power and authority should be central to the daily work activities of social workers, managers, health and social care professionals, community workers, case managers and clinicians alike.

Overview of Chapters

In this book, we examine some of the tensions social workers experience as organisational operators and as skilled, thoughtful and professional practitioners. This third edition has been further updated to reflect the contemporary conditions of social work practice, and to bring new knowledge to bear on the arguments previously developed. In addition to providing a grounding in important organisational theories and concepts and in developing capacity in organisational analysis, we aim to offer strategies for active, ethical and reflexive organisational practice. In this edition, we place greater emphasis on the relational dimensions of organisational practice and the potential of a focus on relations to counter the individualised tendencies in managerialist practice. Crucially, we see social workers as more than bystanders in human service organisations. We see them as having the ability to engage actively and work strategically with different aspects of organisations to produce change in line with social work values, and in many instances to provide leadership on change. Another theme within the book is around service user participation, although we recognise the constraints on this given social workers' organisational contexts and, in particular, their statutory responsibilities with involuntary clients. We introduce practice examples – including a number of new ones for the third edition – to illustrate issues and strategies in organisational work.

The focus in Chapter 1 is on the relationship between social work and organisations, and the tensions social workers experience in their organisational roles. Part of the challenge for social work is how the profession is reconfiguring itself in light of labour market changes, such as the increased casualisation of the workforce, and more 'outsourcing' of work to the private sector. A critique of managerialism is a theme in various sections of the book. In this chapter, we address managerialism as a dominant theme and as sets of discourse in human service organisations in the early twenty-first century. We conclude with a discussion of knowledge and learning in social work for organisational practice. This includes but is not restricted to strategies such as evidence-based and best practice.

In Chapter 2, we continue our discussion of knowledge for organisational work. Specifically, we introduce and discuss some of the key schools of organisational theory in relation to metaphors. These metaphors reflect different ways of knowing and studying organisations and are derived from different paradigms, traditions and histories in organisational theory. We argue that while these metaphors and theories often provide competing ways of understanding organisations, they can be seen to be coexisting in organisational life and analysis. In particular, we present four 'downstream' metaphors that represent conventional or traditional theories as offering useful, albeit limited, understandings of human service organisations. We also highlight metaphors that challenge conventional ways of viewing organisations and that highlight their complexities and contingencies. Following Chia's (1996) lead, we frame these as 'upstream' metaphors.

Social workers often feel they are subject to constant change in their organisations. Whether it's a new set of guidelines, an internal restructure or a new strategic plan, everything always seems to be changing. So, in Chapter 3, we turn our attention to organisational change and social workers' experience of such change. We highlight the impact of environmental change and examine two key responses: planned change and emergent change. We also highlight the emotional and psychological dimensions of organisational change and the challenges social workers face in maintaining a sense of integrity in the face of large-scale organisational change, such as managerialist reform.

As in other areas of practice, social workers need to be effective communicators in their organisational practice. We discuss some key areas of organisational communication in Chapter 4. These include managing conflict and responding to emotions in organisational settings. An important part of organisational communication is facilitated through the use of information and communication technology, which involves negotiating computer-based client systems and the ubiquitous social media platforms. Increasingly, social workers are required to work across disciplinary and organisational boundaries. In this chapter, we explore issues in working effectively together through, for example, collaboration, partnership and teamwork strategies.

Chapter 5 examines issues of risk and decision making within human service organisations. We consider some of the different approaches to decision making, including rational decision models and the ways in which these can be bounded by everyday realities. We critique the individualisation of risk (e.g. through cultures of blame and personal liability) and the challenges facing social workers in assessing possible negative outcomes of risk decisions. While risks are often presented as negative, risk-taking is fundamental to an expression of autonomy and human agency, and, we argue, is a necessary part of organisational life. Risk discourse, including risk identification and assessment, is central to debates about social work and social policy today (Kemshall, 2002; Webb, 2006).

In Chapter 6, we examine some different approaches to leadership in the organisations and management literature, particularly highlighting the potential of transformational and distributed leadership approaches. We highlight the latter as particularly relevant to building learning organisations and to social work, given its focus on self-determination and empowerment. The chapter also looks at one of the common ways social workers exercise leadership in organisations: through supervision. We consider different approaches to supervision and some of the key issues facing supervisors and supervisees.

In Chapter 7, we explore social work's range of responsibilities and how these can be affected by organisational roles. We argue that while social work does have a responsibility to the organisation and to the profession, it also has a commitment to society and to the people who are constructed as its clients or service users. Two different forms of responsibility are examined in detail: passive responsibility or being held to account for past actions, and active responsibility or being more responsible to ensure future behaviour is appropriate (Bovens, 1998). In order to be accountable to communities and service users, we argue that participatory and empowerment strategies and evaluation are needed within human service organisations. In particular, these are discussed in relation to anti-racist social work.

Chapter 8 explores various levels of experience in human service organisations. We offer ways in which staff can experience and deal with workplace stressors, notably arising from managerial processes and the impact of change. Strategies for enabling clients or service users to assert their humanity and agency in organisations are considered. The chapter also includes an exposition of various levels of experience as our 'life-worlds' in organisational work: the client and individual level, the group and networking level, the intra-organisational level, the inter-organisational level, and the community and society level.

Chapter 9 brings together some of the themes of the book and looks, in particular, at the ethical context for organisational practice. A starting point for addressing some of the dilemmas that face practitioners is to develop an understanding of one-self, learn about organisational practices and create a practical ethic for working in organisations. We need to see beyond the mirage of the organisation as impenetrable structure and recognise the organisation as human, reflective of our own agency and thus changeable. The chapter considers strategies for active and reflexive learning and ethically based organisational change.

Conclusion

In bringing together some of the key themes, concepts and issues in organisational theory and from the practice literature on social work and organisations, a rich and complex understanding of how to study organisations as real and 'live' relational entities emerges. We suggest that culture and structure interact in determining organisational inputs, processes and outcomes. In particular, social workers can learn the art of studying organisations on the ground and use their knowledge and experience to make sense of change processes and the positive or detrimental effects caused by such change.

We hope that this book encourages students and practitioners to develop a broader and more politically aware approach – which we frame as an active and reflexive approach – to understanding and working in human service organisations. This involves developing an awareness of the position of social work, as a profession, in both organisational contexts and the labour market. This is the focus of our first chapter.

1 Social Work in Organisations

In this chapter we overview

- social workers as active participants in organisations;
- social work as a professional occupation;
- key players in human service organisations;
- labour market reform and managerialism;
- social work knowledge in organisational practice.

Introduction

Social work is a profession that is practised within the confines of an organisation and the tasks that social workers carry out are defined by the nature of this organisation. Thus, a social worker employed in a voluntary sector family centre may be engaged in more individual and family counselling work than a social worker in a hospital setting. Similarly, the knowledge that social workers use in their daily work may also vary: the family centre social worker may have specialist knowledge of particular therapeutic techniques, while the hospital social worker may have specialist knowledge of particular illnesses and their impact on individuals' capacity to live independently. Some social workers may feel that they have little wider professional identity outside of their particular job role or simply that the nature of their job results in more identification with the organisation than with the profession.

Nonetheless, social work does have something unique to offer human service organisations. Our argument here is that social work is a socially active and engaged profession within organisations. We have an accumulated body of knowledge that helps us understand individuals and communities within their wider social and political contexts. We promote certain values and take political stances in order to defend these values. We apply our knowledge and values through our skills in critical thinking, research, policy development, counselling and networking. In this sense, social workers bring a unique awareness and capacity to organisational practice. We argue throughout this book that social work is an active, engaged and reflective profession that skilfully uses interpersonal communication, interaction, ethical and political tactics and change strategies to initiate and sustain positive social processes and outcomes for clients of human service organisations. In this sense, we see social workers as active rather than passive change agents, as engaged in decision making and taking risks rather than being 'fence sitters', and as motivated by their professional community of shared practices, knowledge and core values.

Negotiating the Ideals and Realities

If we conceptualise social work as incorporating knowledge, values and skills generated through professional education, socialisation and experience, it is possible to see that social work extends beyond the confines of a particular job or organisation. The challenge for social workers is negotiating the slippage between the potential or the ideals of social work as a professional activity and the reality of social work as organisational work (Lymbery and Butler, 2004).

The work environment will always limit the potential of social work. There is no one job that can facilitate the meeting of all the profession's aims and aspirations. With social work skills, the potential of 'I can do this' can easily slip into 'I do this', as the capacity to exercise a wide range of skills is undermined by the lack of opportunities to practise these in daily work. Similarly, the confidence of 'I know this' can be reduced to 'I know this to do this job'. Even more challenging is the slip from 'I believe this' to 'I believe this to do this job'. This results in social work losing its distinctiveness and its purpose – 'social work without a soul' – and may result in external political and economic agendas – such as neo-liberalism and managerialism – determining a social worker's role.

It is social work's values and, in particular, its commitment to social justice which set it apart from other occupations. While it is recognised that there are different interpretations of what social justice means, typically practitioners point to equality and fairness as being important (O'Brien, 2011). According to Bisman (2004: 115):

> Without this emphasis on social justice, there is little if any need for social work or social workers. ... [I]n practice, social workers draw from the same knowledge base in human behaviour and social systems as do psychiatrists and city planners. It is the application of knowledge and skills towards moral ends that imbues the profession with meaning and defines the role of the social worker in society.

These values are not exhaustive. We would include alongside social justice, core values such as respect for others, especially those marked as disadvantaged, different or marginalised, and self-determination for our clients (see Chapter 9). It is understandable, then, that social workers may experience tension and uncertainty in the gap between what they know and believe and what they do in their day-to-day work. Similarly, they may fear the reduction of what they know and believe to only what they need to know and believe in order to do the job. Later in this chapter, we explore this tension in relation to debates about evidence-based and best practice.

For some social workers, this sense that their professional identity is limited by their organisational role comes as a surprise. Their social work education had been not just about instilling in them the skills, knowledge and values of social work, but also about socialising them into the profession. That they are not able to fulfil all of the potential of their professional identity in the organisation that now employs them challenges many people and may lead them to question the adequacy of their education to prepare them for organisational life. The newly qualified worker is confronted with the following questions:

- How is what I do different from what other employees do?
- What contribution does social work make to the organisation and to its service users?
- How do I apply my social work knowledge, values and skills to the work of the organisation?
- What happens when organisational practices conflict with my social work values?
- Should I seek to influence the organisation in line with social work values, and, if so, how should I go about this?
- How can I survive, maintain competency and integrity, and flourish, as a social worker and as a person, in this organisation?

For many social workers, the challenges of organisational practice are managed by engaging (and re-engaging) with the profession, its knowledge, values and skills. Importantly, this should not be an abstract enterprise or one that solely helps manage the stress of social work, but rather it should facilitate the reformulation of the self in relation to an unfolding professional identity. In this context, self-care would not be an isolated process but directed towards improving practice (Miehls and Moffat, 2000: 346). Central to this would be developing a greater sense of integrity as a person, and as a professional and organisational operator. For Banks (2010: 2181–2), this involves:

A *commitment to a set of values*, the context of which relates to what it means to be a 'good person in a professional role' and/or a 'good professional'.

An *awareness that the values are interrelated to each other and form a coherent whole* and that their interrelationship is what constitutes the overarching goals or purpose of the profession.

A *capacity to make sense of professional values* and their relationship to the practitioner's own personally held values.

The ability to give a coherent account of beliefs and actions.

Strength of purpose and ability to implement these values [emphasis in original].

There may be organisational systems and supports to enable you to do this. For example, newly qualified social workers may be directly responsible to a social work educated supervisor, who, in addition to providing advice on the handling of specific cases, may also assist in integrating professional learning and personal practice, spending time helping workers to acknowledge the dilemmas of practice. While other supports, such as mentoring schemes and seminar groups, may be found within the organisation, it is likely that many social workers will need to look for these beyond the organisation so that they can continue to explore their emerging identity as a social worker. Many social workers engage in ongoing professional development activities run by the professional associations, post-qualifying consortia and universities. While, for some, these activities are the first to go when things get really busy, their benefits in facilitating reflexivity and an integrated social work identity should not be underestimated.

For individual social workers, the challenge is to 'work critically within the world *as it is* while seeking change, and to work within agencies *as they are* while being able to promote positive change' (Hugman, 2001: 329, our emphasis). For us, this is fundamental to critical, ethical and reflective practice within human service organisations: to be able to stand both inside and outside the organisation, and, using this knowledge, to work strategically to change the organisation. We must recognise and engage with management and professional agendas in organisations, but we must also be critical of them, consider their impact on service users and their social and political situations, and seek to alleviate this impact. In Practice Example 1.1, a social worker seeks to engage with and extend her professional identity.

PRACTICE EXAMPLE 1.1

An unfolding social work identity

Christiana is a newly qualified social worker employed in an intake team of a statutory child protection agency. During her social work studies, Christiana became very interested in anti-racist and critical reflective practice. She is of African heritage, having left Sierra Leone in the mid-1990s following the civil war in that country. She lives in a city with an increasing African refugee community, with many people arriving from Sudan in recent years. There have been some negative media reports about this increasing group in the population – both in terms of perceived pressures on health and social services, and in relation to 'gangs' of young African people roaming the streets at night.

In reflecting with her supervisor on her first year in the job, Christiana described having gone through a 'culture shock'. She explained this in a few ways. The first culture shock related to her experience commencing with the child protection team – everyone was very busy, it was difficult to see work though to a meaningful end on the intake team and child protection notifications and high-risk situations took priority, while preventative work seemed minimal. Christiana didn't have a child protection placement during her degree so she felt quite unprepared for working in this setting. A second culture shock related to working with so many people who do not come from a social work background and who do not seem to share the same perspective on social justice (or even the same language about social justice) that she does. Another culture shock related to the disproportionate number of African families the organisation is responding to, and about whom child protection notifications have been received. Together with the negative media reporting, she has become increasingly concerned about the unfair ways her own African culture and heritage are being represented in the agency and society more broadly.

As she expressed to her supervisor, Christiana has been left wondering what it is she does as a social worker that makes a difference in people's lives, how she manages the authority in her statutory role with her commitment to social justice and empowerment, and how to work collaboratively with people who don't share the same professional values. In conversation, Christiana's supervisor helped her recognise that not all of the potential of social work as a profession can be realised in one job, but that nonetheless there are ways that her commitment to anti-racism and social justice can be put into practice in her work. These include supporting her colleagues to challenge the negative attitudes of other staff and community members towards African people, doing some background research on some of the reasons why African migrants may become over-represented in child protection notifications, and encouraging local community groups to develop strategies to address these factors. She has increasingly recognised that not all of this can be done in her regular job and so she has engaged with the local branch of her professional association to work on these issues, including writing a submission and discussion papers on the needs of African refugee communities. While these initiatives have raised questions for her – including a feeling of discomfort in being seen as an 'expert' on issues for African people – in recent months she has felt more in control of her work (both inside and outside the organisation) and how this connects with her emerging social work identity.

The Nature of Social Work Organisations

We speak and hear of them so often that it seems strange to ask: what are organisations? They feel like a real and solid presence in many aspects of our lives, from sporting to educational organisations, from retail to government organisations. However, if we strip away the bricks and mortar – which really are simply containers for organisations – then we can begin to uncover the complex web of human relationships and interactions that comprise them. How we come to understand these relationships and interactions has been shaped by a wide range of theoretical ideas. Thus, different conceptualisations or definitions of organisations emerge from different theoretical perspectives and traditions. We overview some of these theories in Chapter 2 and discuss their implications for understanding and analysing organisations. However, at this point it is useful to identify two alternative ways of defining organisations.

The first and most common definition of organisations emphasises their rationality and goal-directed nature. There is a sense that people come together to pursue a common purpose and create structures and processes that are best suited to achieving that purpose. According to Etzioni (1969: 3), 'organisations are social units (or human groupings) deliberately constructed and reconstructed to seek specific goals'. Forming an organisation and working together is thus seen as more efficient than working separately to achieve the agreed goals. Working together as an organisation involves creating structures and technologies that are suited to the pursuit of these goals. For many, the rise of the modern organisation in the nineteenth and twentieth centuries embodies the 'inexorable advance of reason, liberation and justice and the eventual eradication of ignorance, coercion and poverty' (Reed, 1999: 25).

An alternative to this modernist and functionalist definition of organisations derives from a range of social constructionist, critical and postmodern ideas, and emphasises not the rationality of organisations but their irrationality, or, at least, their frequent irrationality. While organisations are often intended to be rational and goal directed, the people within them often act in contradictory ways. At the centre lies the exercise of power through the creation of structures, technologies and language, meeting a wide range of human needs which are frequently unrelated to the formal or espoused goals of the organisation. Casey (2004: 303), in summarising the trajectory of critical and postmodern views of organisations, identifies organisations as 'sites of action' and as comprising 'contested and negotiated rationalities'. For Chia (1996: 150), organisations are 'loosely emergent sets of organizing rules which orient interactional behavior in particular ways'. Thus, those operating from this position are actually not so much interested in defining or theorising *organisations* (as completed entities) as they are in defining and theorising the processes of *organising*.

The agencies social workers work in are commonly referred to as 'human service organisations'. This term signifies their purpose to be the production of services to meet human needs, rather than the production of material goods. Garrow and Hasenfeld (2010) go further than this, however. They claim that human service organisations 'engage in moral work, upholding and reinforcing moral values about "desirable" human behavior and the "good" society' (2010: 33). The legitimacy human service organisations have in working with people is gained from their wider institutional environment and social policy arrangements. However, their outcomes and effectiveness are more determined by the everyday small-scale interactions between service users and workers (Garrow and Hasenfeld, 2010). We agree with this orientation and would take it further to identify cause and effect chains in our field of awareness for everyday practice. Most importantly, social workers can become skilful at identifying and acting on the external and internal forces that precondition decision making, and the informal and formal ways in which leadership and collegial effort with user-led inputs take effect and drive organisational change and change cultures. In order for social work to do this, it must remain connected to the experiences of service users and attuned to the intricacies of everyday interaction and communication in and around the organisations they work in.

Key Players in Social Work Organisations

Human service organisations employ many workers in a range of capacities and job roles. Sveiby (1997) identifies four main players in complex organisations: the professional, the manager, the support staff, and the leader. His categorisation is based on an understanding of the power plays that occur in those organisations that employ highly skilled people and that rely on the transfer of information and knowledge. It classifies each of the players in terms of professional and organisational competence. This categorisation produces archetypal roles that are present within social work organisations, at least in people's minds and within organisational culture, if not in actual practice.

If we recognise the area of community competence, we can also incorporate into the schema two additional players: the volunteer, and the client or service user. These players are not (usually) employees of the organisation, although they may receive some benefits from being involved in the organisation, such as receiving services or gaining skills. The important players in social work organisations include both paid employees and those present and active in the organisation in other ways.

It is also worth noting another common distinction made in the social work and community services literature: that of being on the 'front-line'. Front-line workers are typically seen as being at the 'coalface' of human service delivery. These are the people who have most contact with service users and who may consequently have considerable community competence. For those working or managing on the front line, there are dangers that, if they are not properly supervised and supported, they may easily become burnt out or may end up acting defensively. In Chapters 5 and 8, we examine these dangers in more depth.

The Professional

The professional is characterised as having access to specialised knowledge that can be applied in understanding and responding to situations within the organisation's remit. That is, professionals are concerned with delivering the organisation's services and providing expert advice. Stereotypically, they are seen to be highly committed to their job (to the extent that they frequently work long hours), to have a high degree of professional pride and confidence, to subdivide themselves into increasingly narrow ranges of specialisation, and to dislike routine and bureaucracy (Sveiby, 1997). Further, the professions are characterised by:

- control over abstract and formal knowledge;
- considerable autonomy, especially in terms of task decisions;
- authority over others, including clients and other workers; and
- a commitment to altruism in professional behaviour, often embodied in codes of ethics and monitored by professional bodies. (Hodson and Sullivan, 1995; Noordegraaf, 2007)

Each of these can be seen on a continuum, so that some professions – such as medicine and law – may be identified as having more and a higher level of these attributes than others – such as social work and nursing. Their community competence may be seen as emerging mainly from their contact with clients, to whom they provide professional services, and their subsequent understanding of clients' needs and concerns. While it is easy to see how the interests of professionals might conflict with those of the organisation, it is important to recognise that organisations provide an institutional resource for the professional project and that professionals can significantly influence the organisations in which they work (Suddaby and Viale, 2011).

We will discuss issues for social work in the human services labour market below; however, it is important to note that social work has experienced some conflict and ambivalence over its identity as a professional occupation. Some have argued that social work is not fully professionalised and have characterised it as a semi-profession (Etzioni, 1969). Others have seen its claim to professional status as working against the interests of service users and communities who are themselves the real experts (Bamford, 1990). According to this argument, the more professional the worker becomes, the less likely they are to have high levels of community competence.

Despite these debates, social work has evolved in western nations as a professional occupation, and it is possible to recognise, to some degree, the stereotypical professional attributes in social work roles. At the same time, social workers strive towards greater community competence, and working with and understanding the issues of people within communities is not necessarily seen as antithetical to professional practice.

The Manager

Sveiby (1997) argues that managers have high levels of organisational competence and, because they have less contact with service users, we suggest that they can be seen as having less community competence than professionals. Regardless of any prior career or academic specialisation, managers are usually employed in that capacity because of their organisational skills. In their managerial role, they focus on maintaining organisational functioning in line with the organisation's goals (Bryman, 1999). In human service agencies, their role is not so much in delivering services, but in ensuring an organisational context that enables others to provide services.

Managers are frequently involved in activities such as staff recruitment and supervision, managing resources and finances, coordinating information systems, and reporting to higher levels within an organisation (such as to a senior executive or to a management committee). Managers are often less involved in immediate task decisions than they are in medium-term planning, which commonly involves decisions about how resources will be allocated to particular organisational goals or programmes. The power of managers rests in their control over financial resources (Hodson, 2001), as well as in their symbolic authority.

The Support Staff

Support staff include a range of employees – such as secretaries, administrators, office workers, clerks, receptionists – whose role is to support the work of the manager and, often to a lesser extent, that of the professionals (Sveiby, 1997). Their role is focused on the needs of the organisation, and, although Sveiby classifies them as relatively low in terms of organisational and professional competence, the longer they are employed in an organisation the more they are likely to be valued for their organisational knowledge. Additionally, specialised skills, such as note taking, word processing or spread-sheeting, can often be seen as an important resource. Many support staff are also front-line organisational workers in that they are often clients' first point of contact with the organisation.

The Leader

According to Sveiby (1997), leaders display high levels of both professional and organisational competence. We would argue that, at least in human service organisations, they should also have high levels of community competence. Thus, leaders are characterised as having expert and in-depth knowledge across the whole organisation.

An organisation's leader would most obviously be the person in the most senior executive position within the organisation: the person who is seen to exercise the most authority. However, sometimes others can emerge as leaders within organisations, although it is likely that they too would be able to exercise considerable authority and autonomy in their role. It is often noted that the difference between managers and leaders is that while managers seek to preserve the status quo – the healthy functioning of the organisation – leaders will often seek change and innovation so that the organisation can grow and adapt to changing community and societal needs (Kotter, 1990). Leaders are stereotypically seen as risk takers and as motivating others through their own charisma. In Chapter 6, we examine some different approaches to leadership.

The Volunteer

In human service organisations, the volunteer role may range from stuffing envelopes during a fundraising initiative, to providing in-home respite to someone living with a terminal illness, to sitting on an organisation's management board. Volunteers are often drawn from the organisation's 'community'. They may espouse a desire to redress the social problems or fulfil the community needs that are within the organisation's mandate. This may sometimes emerge from personal experience. For example, volunteers with the various Alzheimer's disease societies and associations are frequently carers, ex-carers, partners, relatives and friends of people with dementia. Thus, volunteers may often be prized for their community competence: their connection to and knowledge of the communities the organisation provides services to.

Depending on their background, volunteers may also have considerable professional and management knowledge. However, apart from those on management committees, they may have less opportunity than they wish to implement this knowledge in their volunteering role. Inevitably, everyday organisational life revolves around those in paid capacities, and volunteers can sometimes feel unsupported and unacknowledged in their work. Thus, volunteers frequently experience tensions around their status, role and level of inclusion in the life and culture of the organisation (Netting et al., 2004). This is often particularly acute when community organisations grow from being 'grass-roots' (with volunteers often instrumental in setting up the organisation) to funded service-providing organisations (where volunteers may have a more marginal role).

The Service User

Another important organisational player – and perhaps the most important – is the person or group constructed variously as the client, service user, patient, consumer or customer. Without these people, the organisation would not exist. Service users can be seen as having high levels of community competence, at least in their knowledge of their own experience within communities. Service users may be typically seen as lacking professional and organisational competence in the organisation from which they are seeking services. This does not mean that they necessarily lack professional or organisational knowledge and skills generally or within other organisations (such as those that employ them). And in some sectors, service users' community competence – in terms of their lived experience – is being more formally recognised. For example, in the mental health sector, service users are being employed as peer workers to provide support to other service users, although, as with volunteers, there are challenges in negotiating a meaningful role within the organisation (Gillard et al., 2013).

In Chapter 8, we examine issues in service users' experience of social work organisations in some depth. It is, however, important to acknowledge here the wide variation in people's experiences and in the level of their involvement in organisational life. Some clients may visit the organisation only once, while others may receive regular services and support over many years. Despite increased rhetoric around greater client involvement in both statutory and non-statutory settings, the experience of user involvement strategies is not always positive, especially if they are poorly resourced or seen as tokenistic. For non-voluntary clients, such as those being investigated for child abuse or neglect, there is unlikely to be any motivation for further involvement in the life of the organisation.

Inevitably, the distinctions made here between organisational players are caricatures, albeit ones that remain persistent in organisational cultures. In addition to their inability to reflect the diversity of personalities and activities within organisations, these caricatures fail to account for the considerable overlap between tasks regardless of the specific role designation. For instance, all members of the organisation are likely to be involved in administrative or secretarial work. Most employees would do their own typing of letters and reports and many would do their own photocopying. Similarly, different employees may participate in management functions, for example by taking responsibility for leading a sub-committee of the staff meeting.

In Practice Example 1.2, a social worker struggles to understand the way in which role boundaries are demarcated within her organisation.

PRACTICE
EXAMPLE 1.2

Inclusion, exclusion and organisational roles

Chris recently joined a social services team working with young people with disabilities and their families. The team comprises social workers, welfare officers, administrative staff, an occupational therapist and a team manager. Also involved with the team are volunteers who contribute to a visiting programme, and representatives of service users and parents/carers.

The annual team planning day is held off site and involves team building and strategic planning activities, such as discussing changes in community needs. One issue to be addressed is the availability of administrative staff to carry out tasks (e.g. photocopying documents, taking phone messages) required by volunteers and service user representatives. There has been debate within the team as to whether or not it is appropriate for administrative staff to be doing this work, especially as resources are currently stretched. Some administrative staff feel that the parent/carer representatives are taking advantage of their generosity by asking them to photocopy articles.

During her induction, Chris met with some volunteers and representatives who expressed concerns that they had not been invited to the team planning day. They argued that they were best placed to advise on changes in community needs and should be involved if they were to have a meaningful role in the organisation.

Chris took the matter to the next staff meeting and was surprised at the level of concern expressed about the idea of involving the volunteers and representatives in the planning day. Some staff argued that they would not be able to discuss the issue of the administrative staff's workloads, because they would feel too uncomfortable raising this in front of volunteers and representatives. Others felt that it was inappropriate because it would restrict their ability to discuss particular clients and their families during the meeting. Underneath it all, Chris suspected that the staff may also have felt some resentment that a special day set aside for the team could be taken over by 'outsiders'. It left her wondering about the boundaries of social services teams and the marginal status still experienced by volunteers, service users and carers.

Social Work in the Labour Market

While in the past social work may have been seen mainly as a voluntary or charitable activity, today social work is constructed as paid labour. The use of a social work qualification to gain employment and the subsequent use of social work knowledge, values and skills in that employment are central to how social work is defined. This is the case even though social work as a professional identity extends beyond organisational and job boundaries. Social workers compete in the labour market and assert themselves (not always very well) as best placed to occupy a particular job.

The labour markets of western industrialised nations have undergone considerable change over the last few decades. One shift that is often noted is that from a Fordist to a post-Fordist labour market. Fordism emphasises a modernist production-line approach, with workers having specific job roles and little wider organisational knowledge. The post-Fordist labour market is more delineated by workers experiencing overlap between job roles, referred to as multi-skilling, having to constantly update their skills and having to be more flexible in their career paths (Carey, 2015). Other labour market reforms include:

- shifts from industrial to service and information modes of production;
- increasing casualisation of the workforce and consequent effects on employee benefits such as sick pay;
- more individuals having to change occupations with consequent periods of unemployment and re-training;

- increasing demand for specialist qualifications to be competitive in the labour market;
- more instability in the role of unions in setting the terms of employer–employee relations;
- greater reliance on the 'outsourcing' of public sector work to private or voluntary sector workers; and
- more emphasis on demonstrated job competence for employment, education and training. (Carey, 2015; Perrons, 2000; Shapiro, 2000)

The globalisation of the labour market also significantly impacts on social work. For example, in the UK staff shortages in social work have led to a heavy reliance on overseas-trained practitioners. This results in ethical questions, not just about their capacity to work in Britain, but also about the impact of 'poaching' qualified staff from other – sometimes poorer – countries (Welbourne et al., 2007).

An important implication of these labour market changes has been the proliferation of professional turf wars where professional groups compete in terms of status and expertise to resolve human problems. The last century saw a five-fold increase in professional occupations in advanced economies: from 4 per cent to over 20 per cent (Hodson, 2001). Competition is fierce as to which professional group will dominate in different service settings and in determining what the specific areas of its expertise are. According to McDonald (2006), social work's professional project involves attempts to exercise authority over others as well as strategies to align the profession with the power of the state (e.g. by being registered or being empowered by the state to intervene in people's lives). Social work also exercises authority in non-government organisations that are autonomous from the state and commonly have their own cultures and hierarchies involved in non-state social policy.

One way to monopolise is through social issue construction, a strategy which medicine and law have been particularly good at. This involves the profession identifying a social issue that needs redress and then setting about defining the nature of the issue, framing the possible responses and then claiming the expertise to deliver these responses (Jamrozik and Nocella, 1998). A further way in which a profession can promote itself as best equipped to frame and respond to a social issue is through science and the language of science. As a result, the professions align themselves with research activities, and most have recently adopted the assumptions and practices of evidence-based practice (McDonald, 2006) (to be discussed later in this chapter).

Like other professional groups, social work has been profoundly affected by these developments. It has asserted its professional status by claiming expertise in particular service areas (e.g. child welfare), by demanding professional registration, by asserting the importance of a university qualification for entry into the profession, and by aligning the profession with scientific discourse and evidence-based practice.

In English-speaking countries, the alignment of social work with the state and the existing and potential turf wars between social work and other professions are an important backdrop to understanding multi-disciplinary practice in human service organisations. While emphasis is placed by governments on collaboration between professionals within and across organisational boundaries (e.g. Farmakopoulou, 2002), the reality of the labour market is such that these professionals are also competitors.

While the proportion of the labour market comprising professions is likely to continue to increase overall (Hodson, 2001), there are particular factors within the human service sector which are holding back the growth of social work, in particular, as a professional occupation. We discuss below the effects of neo-liberal and managerialist policies and practices on social work. For now, it is important to note that these reforms have led to an opening up of a range of social-work-type positions that are not designated specifically for social workers. Many social workers – those with a social work qualification and eligible for membership of social work associations or registration as a social worker – do not have jobs entitled 'social worker'. Some are called care managers, project workers and childcare officers. Increasingly, jobs have been opened up to a range of qualified and non-qualified staff who are able to demonstrate the appropriate competence and experience to carry out the job tasks (Carey, 2015). The underemployment of social workers in para-professional work, where 'their qualifications are neither required nor fully utilized', contributes in part to a deprofessionalisation of social work (Healy and Meagher, 2004: 245).

 **Reflective Questions**

1   Review some job advertisements in social work and social care. How are recent labour-market reforms apparent in job titles, conditions, roles and duties?
2   Think of a social issue (e.g. youth crime) and identify the different professions that have a stake in the issue. How might these professions construct the issue differently, develop alternative or competing responses and stake their claim to expertise on this issue?

Social Work and Managerialism

This picture of social work in the labour market is of a profession that is both changing and under threat. And there is no doubt that many social workers feel they have been under threat for the last few decades, given the ongoing neo-liberal restructuring of the welfare state. This began in earnest in the 1980s and 1990s with the push towards small government, increased competition in the welfare 'marketplace' and individual responsibility. It has accelerated in the twenty-first century with the imposition of austerity measures in many western economies which, arguably, 'reflects the determination of those who manage global capitalism that the costs of the [global financial] crisis shall be paid by the mass of ordinary people who played no part in its creation' (Ferguson and Lavalette, 2013: 96). Alongside cuts to public spending, one aim of neoliberal reforms is to ensure that voluntary and for-profit organisations are the main providers of services, while governments set the direction for service development and regulate its delivery. The well-used phrase in the mid-1990s was that governments should be 'steering, not rowing' (Osborne and Gaebler, 1992). For Carey (2015: 2409), 'the expansion of ever more independent providers reconstitutes a myriad of services as "business units" which may concentrate introspectively upon core business interests whilst neglecting wider public service objectives'. Of increasing concern is the emergence of cartel-like monopolies where a small number of large, often private-sector, providers dominate the market through mergers and take-overs of smaller organisations (Carey, 2015). And while consumer-directed care and personalisation strategies are appealing because they facilitate individual service users' control over their own care, they have been critiqued as being influenced by neoliberalism, for example by treating the relationship between service users and providers as a transaction, and as being a cloak for the introduction of cost-cutting (Ferguson and Lavalette, 2013).

Linked to the rise of neo-liberal thinking has been a rise in managerial discourse and practices. This is often presented in the government sector as 'new public management', and more widely and pejoratively as 'managerialism'. Just as politicians and policy makers turned to the principles of the market to inform welfare policy and practice, so too did they come to rely on the current developments in business management as a guide to steering human service organisations. If the setting up of a competitive market was the answer at a macro (policy) level, then surely the answer at a mezzo (organisational) level was the practices employed by those who are most competitive: big business and their corporate leaders. This shift would, it was hoped, herald a departure from what were seen as the failings of large welfare bureaucracies (Fawcett et al., 2010). The ideal organisations – both government and non-government ones – would be those directed by management to be the most efficient and competitive.

Thus, from a managerialist perspective, the ideal organisation is the 'flat' organisation: stripped of its supposedly wasteful and bureaucratic middle management. The organisation would be led by a charismatic and transformational leader, guided by science and its determination of what works best, and driven by teams that evaluate and adapt their work in synch with the environment (market) and its demands. This image of the flat, efficient, competitive organisation draws widely from management and organisational theorising; often relying on what is most popular at the time. The take-up of Total Quality Management (TQM) across the private, public and not-for-profit sectors in the 1990s is a useful example of this.

For social workers, one of the challenges of managerialism and the 'flattening' of organisations is that they are increasingly managed by those who are not social workers and who may have little affinity with the profession and its values. Even where social workers continue to report directly to a senior social worker or practice manager, increasingly these work teams are called on to demonstrate their effectiveness to non-social work managers. Thus, those who are often employed in management positions are those with skills and qualifications in management, and not necessarily those professing a detailed and specialist knowledge of the work tasks. In this sense, management is seen as content-free: any good manager can manage any workplace, regardless of whether it is a social services department or a supermarket. And the experience of the rise of managerialism in social work organisations has been one of constant change, most commonly through the practices of:

- *downsizing*: shrinking the organisation through redundancies, forced retirements or increased casualisation;
- *re-engineering*: re-evaluating the purpose and goals of the organisation and re-inventing the organisation (to varying degrees) in line with new goals, usually so that the organisation is more responsive to the needs in its environment (i.e. more competitive);
- *continuous improvement*: continually engaging the organisation in small-scale change through reliance on performance measuring and making adjustments to improve quality and the responsiveness of the organisation to the marketplace (draws on TQM ideas); and
- *limiting professional autonomy*: regulating the activities of professionals through, for example, performance monitoring, evaluation and financial control. (Lymbery, 2004)

Many social workers have experienced organisational change as being done to them, rather than as a process in which they were key players. This is examined further in Chapter 3.

While managerialism strives for (and employs the language of) rationality, the use of managerialist strategies within organisations can also be understood as a response to wider environmental pressures. For example, the adoption of TQM practices had as much to do with normative pressures from governments and funders as it did with improving efficiency (Suddaby and Viale, 2011). The disconnect between the perceived and actual rationality of manageralism is most evident in the significant organisational restructuring undertaken by government departments and quasi-autonomous government agencies. For example, according to the UK's National Audit Office (2010), there were 90 reorganisations of central government departments and related agencies between May 2005 and June 2009. The cost of 51 of these reorganisations, as surveyed by the Audit Office, was £780 million. However, none of the departments or agencies set up measures to identify what the specific benefits of the changes would be and to see if the benefits outweighed the costs. Thus, despite the stated desire to become more efficient and effective by reorganising, none of the usual tools of the managerialist trade – such as developing a business plan and carrying out a cost–benefit analysis – were employed.

The influence of management thinking and practice on human service organisations remains considerable. While some approaches to management may coalesce with progressive social work and progressive social workers bring many qualities to management (Healy, 2002), the dominant expression of management in human service organisations is managerialist. That is, what is valued by the most powerful stakeholders in human service organisations – government and other funding bodies – is an ostensibly content-free management that actually espouses neo-liberal organisational practices emphasising efficiency and competitiveness in the human service 'marketplace'. These neo-liberal practices involve consumerism, or notions that the customer has a choice and that customer service is paramount. Thus, much of the language within current social work discourse is that of consumerism, and, increasingly, of risk and its management (Gregory and Holloway, 2005). We return in detail to a discussion of risk in social work organisations in Chapter 5.

Social Work Knowledge and Organisational Work

Social work draws broadly on a knowledge base grounded in sociological, political, psychological and philosophical research and scholarship. In particular fields of research, social workers have been leaders, for example in researching children's issues, domestic violence and mental health. Social work has also developed and applied this wider knowledge base to the formation of practice theories. There is also an enormous amount of social work knowledge, theory and research that either directly relates, or can be applied, to organisational practice. Social workers, for example, commonly have sophisticated understandings of communication processes, group and community development, social and family systems, and policy-making processes: all this knowledge can be effectively applied to organisational work.

It is important to note that social work has not engaged with its knowledge base uncritically. We have actively questioned the construction of knowledge through the scientific model and have engaged in debates about the nature of positivism (a particular theory of knowledge underpinning the scientific model), as well as promoting alternative ways of developing and synthesising knowledge for practice. Social work has questioned the sources of knowledge and resisted elevating particular knowledge to doctrinal status. This reflexive and critical capacity makes social work vulnerable in the labour market because we may appear uncertain and lacking in a distinct and closely defended knowledge base. However, we argue that it also provides social work with great strength, as social workers actively seek to engage with the complexity of knowledge and to look honestly and openly at the problems involved in knowledge development and application. This reflexivity surrounding knowledge for social work is no more evident than in the current debates, both in academic and practice contexts, about evidence-based practice and best practice.

Evidence-based Practice

We have already noted the co-opting of science, and its language, within professionalising agendas. The incorporation of evidence-based practice (EBP) within social work in part reflects this trend (McDonald, 2006), in an attempt to position social work as an equal alongside other professions, especially those in health care. Indeed, Carey (2015: 2416) argues that social work has shifted its base from social policy and sociology to health care and nursing, which has resulted in 'disruption, uncertainty and confusion', as well as 'intense pressures to enter and engage with a health and social care discourse that privileges medical and health care-related methods and evidence-based treatment models'. EBP arose in response to concerns that professionals, initially doctors, based their decision making on accepted wisdom and asserted their views based on their authority. EBP, as reflected in Sackett et al.'s (1996) definition of evidence-based medicine, is about using current best evidence to inform decision making to the benefit of patients or clients. To implement EBP, social workers thus need to evaluate existing research and knowledge and use this to inform their decision making. At least two components of this definition are subject to debate. First, what comprises 'current best evidence'? Second, what are the implications of focusing on professionals' decision making?

There is no more hotly contested question in EBP than 'what is evidence?' The word 'evidence' refers to what is plainly visible not just to one person but to many; it implies the existence of an objective reality that is easily discernible. In research terms, evidence is related to positivism: a valuing of research based on scientific principles, probability theory and data that are observable to the senses. It is unsurprising then that many proponents of EBP in health and social care conceive of 'current best evidence' as in line with positivist principles. This is particularly apparent in the promotion by some of a hierarchy of methodologies, with randomised controlled trials and outcome evaluations (which seek to mirror the classic experiment) at the apex. These studies are particularly concerned with determining the accuracy with which the treatment, intervention or programme causes the desired outcome. For example, in evaluating the success of a programme to support bereaved parents (with increased support being the outcome), how confident are we that it was the programme that increased parents' feelings of support and not other variables, such as the influence of friends and family or the use of anti-depressant medication? However, while some (e.g. Macdonald, 1999) promote these designs as a 'gold standard' for social work and social care, others caution against over-generalising their usefulness. For Qureshi (2004), it is the nature of the research question that should determine the appropriate methodology, and there are many methodologies relevant to social work and social policy – including qualitative methods – that are often more appropriate than experimental and quasi-experimental designs. (See Figure 1.1.)

Nonetheless, these designs continue to be promoted within social work. Outcome evaluation studies are particularly favoured by managers and governments as they are seen as providing evidence of the effectiveness of professional interventions and programmes. A particular concern in relation to outcome studies is the risk of either

Figure 1.1 Hierarchy of evidence, based on traditional EBP model

focusing too narrowly on easily measurable outputs (e.g. hours of service) or too broadly on outcomes that are hard to achieve for any intervention (e.g. improved well-being). Despite these risks, outcome evaluation is used to help determine whether the benefits gained from the interventions or programmes are worth the costs (cost–benefit analysis). It can also be used to evaluate the extent to which policy or organisational objectives are achieved. Such an approach rests on the assumption of 'top-down' decision-making processes where knowledge is transferred from a macro (policy) level to a mezzo (organisational) level and through to a micro (practice) level. However, according to Webb (2002), EBP is an attempt by policy makers and managers to control the production of risk and to instil trust in health and welfare delivery. Such attempts are based on the assumption that those who incorporate this approach into their work can directly influence and determine the outcome of decision-making processes. As we discuss further in Chapter 5, it is argued that this is not always possible given the irrational and contingent decision making that is observed in many organisations (Webb, 2001).

Social workers have expressed concerns that positivist, managerialist and top-down approaches to EBP undermine professional autonomy (Webb, 2002) and ignore the perspectives of service users. Beresford and Evans (1999) question the capacity of evidence-based approaches to involve the so-called subjects of research in research processes and to hear the views of consumers on the way services are provided. According to Rose and Gidman (2010: 39), 'people are not passive recipients of evidence – they are stakeholders in the decision-making process'. A further concern is that, when relying on positivist principles, EBP strives towards increasing levels of accuracy in measuring observable phenomena and thus tends to operate at a surface (observable) level. It may miss the deeper and more complex realities underpinning social issues, including the effects of social and cultural stratification according to such dimensions as 'race', gender, sexual identity, age and disability.

Best Practice and Practice Guidelines

Two strategies for knowledge collection and dissemination, related to EBP, are best practice modelling and the production of practice or clinical guidelines. Best practice involves identifying high quality practice interventions and promoting these as the 'best' or most appropriate responses in given situations in a particular field of practice. The notion of what is considered to be best practice is typically drawn from evidence-based practice principles and strategies, such as determining the quality of research methods (including assessment of validity and reliability) employed to test the effectiveness of social work interventions (Schalock et al., 2014). Different bodies – such as funders, regulators and service user groups – use best practice (as well as related concepts of good practice and excellent practice) in an attempt to influence the work of social workers and other professionals (Manela and Moxley, 2002). As with EBP, best practice can be driven by managerialist agendas and can be experienced by social workers as limiting their autonomy. Demonstrating that an organisation conforms to best practice within a particular area or that it has established a best practice model is frequently used as a strategy to gain funds from government and other funding bodies.

Such a strategy may be seen to give a particular for-profit or community organisation the 'edge' when involved in competitive tendering processes, which have become increasingly common since the neo-liberal restructuring of the welfare state.

Determinations of what practices are considered 'best' are based variously on the views of experts in the field, on outcomes from research and, sometimes, on the effectiveness of the marketing of particular practices (Manela and Moxley, 2002). A particular concern is that once best practices have been identified within an organisation, these practices can then become overly standardised. This may result in an inability to identify opportunities for further improvement or adjustment to suit unique circumstances (Manela and Moxley, 2002). The development of computer-based client management systems has also been based, to an extent, on the principles of best practice in different fields (e.g. child protection), and concerns have also been raised that these systems are applied too rigidly and reduce professional autonomy and creativity (Broadhurst et al., 2010). We discuss this issue in more depth in Chapter 4.

A similar concern can also be directed at practice or clinical guidelines. These are statements that assist the practitioner to make appropriate decisions, based on research evidence and expert consensus (Howard and Jensen, 1999). They can be conceptualised as statements to guide the practitioner towards best practice. According to Howard and Jensen, practice guidelines should be developed by an expert panel – which may be multi-disciplinary and may also include service user representation – that weighs up the available evidence and evaluates the costs and benefits of different intervention or treatment approaches. In the United States, concerns have been raised about the way practice guidelines may be used as the basis for determining poor practice in malpractice litigation, although they are also promoted as a tool for protecting practitioners against such action (Howard and Jensen, 1999). However, rigidly applying practice guidelines may lead to defensive practice, as outlined by Harris (1987), and as we discuss further in Chapter 5.

A Reflexive Approach

Concerns about narrow and overly scientific approaches to evidence-based and best practice have been well expressed within social work. Like Qureshi (2004), we choose not to dismiss scientific approaches out of hand or because of a rigid commitment to an alternative epistemology. Social science methods have assisted the development of practice theories in social work and have enabled the exposure of underlying inequalities within society. We also recognise that concepts like EBP and best practice are ones that social workers need to engage with because they are such important features of the health and human services industries, and, if engaged with in a certain way, they can stimulate greater understanding of the complexities of practice and its potentials. Evaluation, too, does not need to be constrained by a focus on narrow outcomes or outputs – it can be used to generate knowledge of changes in community need, to get a greater sense of how the organisation is responding meaningfully to clients and communities, and to provide feedback to workers and managers to facilitate deeper learning and reflection. So, we argue for a critical, reflexive and inclusive approach to knowledge generation and sharing within organisations. Such an approach would incorporate concepts like EBP and best practice but would not be constrained by them. It would draw widely on theory and research emerging from other disciplines, particularly from organisation and management studies, and the broad social sciences. It would also recognise the value of social workers being involved in researching organisational practice and, in particular, in researching service users' experiences and needs.

An essential part of such an approach is the recognition that there are different levels of experience and interaction within human service organisations (this is examined further in Chapter 8). It is important to note that our discussion here focuses on knowledge for organisational work, rather than on social work knowledge generally. In this section, we have adopted the convention of identifying micro, mezzo and macro levels and have focused on different organisational practices (as outlined in Figure 1.2). The micro level of experience within organisations relates to person-to-person relational encounters. Thus, micro organisational practices include the small-scale everyday interactions between the key players within an organisation. How people experience organisations is in part defined by these relational encounters. If conflict occurs, if personalities clash, if there is a feeling of dislike or distrust, then the implications for the organisation and the delivery of its services to particular individuals or communities can be considerable. From our perspective, social workers need detailed knowledge of these micro practices.

Another level of experience that we need to develop an understanding of involves mezzo organisational practices: these relate to the systems and processes the organisation has established to ensure optimal organisational functioning. For many employees, including social workers, mezzo organisational practices often feel imposed on them by managers and they are usually written up as organisational procedures. However, without these mezzo practices organisational work would almost certainly become chaotic. As outlined in Figure 1.2, such practices include the organisation's information management systems, such as its computer and record-keeping systems, as well as its systems for staff supervision, training and recruitment. Social workers need an understanding of how these systems guide and direct the micro organisational practices, and, in turn, how these micro practices might influence the development – including the undermining – of the mezzo practices. For example, if social workers are receiving limited supervision, how does this affect their micro encounters with service users? Additionally, if in their everyday relations some staff prefer to liaise with others and make decisions in informal settings, such as the tea room, in order to avoid including those other staff whom they find difficult, how does this affect the effectiveness of weekly staff meetings?

In turning to macro organisational practices, we identify a need to understand those wider organisational practices, usually initiated by people in senior management positions, which affect the overall direction and work of the organisation. These practices are most clearly seen in formal organisational policy documents, including those released to the public, such as annual reports, strategic plans and mission statements. However, macro organisational practices relate not just to internal organisational policies, but also to the effects of wider social policy and legislation on the organisation and its work.

Social workers need knowledge of how these wider macro practices affect both mezzo and micro practices, and where there may be tensions and inconsistencies.

For example, professional codes of ethics may directly influence the micro practices of social workers employed in an organisation, even though these macro practices may not be recognised at the mezzo level. Additionally, what happens at a micro and mezzo level determines the effectiveness of macro practices. If staff ignore a particular policy initiative, either of the organisation or of government, then in that context the initiative exists only on paper. In the model we outline in Figure 1.2, policy implementation is not conceptualised as a 'top-down' process; rather, we emphasise the interactions between micro, mezzo and macro practices in shaping the ultimate effectiveness of policy. Importantly, policy makers, both at organisational and societal levels, need information back from the mezzo and micro levels on how policies are enacted on the ground and how future policies might be better constructed.

In addition to understanding the interactions between the micro, mezzo and macro levels of organisations, we also acknowledge in Figure 1.2 that organisations operate within wider social and cultural contexts. In order to understand the interactions between different organisational practices, social workers will also need to appreciate them in relation to social and cultural norms, to wider knowledge which includes but is not limited to professional and disciplinary knowledge, and to wider power relations and inequalities. For example, despite the fact that equal opportunity and anti-discrimination policies might exist at macro and mezzo organisational levels, it is not until we locate micro practices within the wider context of power inequalities within society that we can understand the barriers women and black and ethnic minority workers experience within human service organisations. Similarly, in order to understand how ethical principles, such as the right to privacy and confidentiality, might be breached when faced with an alternative principle, such as a right to safety, it is helpful to understand these principles within the context of wider social and cultural norms and values.

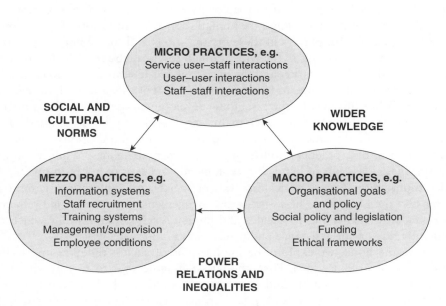

Figure 1.2   A reflexive approach to knowledge in organisations

In developing our understanding of organisational practices, we need to draw on different sources of knowledge. These include: our knowledge of organisational and social work theories; knowledge gained from organisational systems (e.g. information systems); shared experiences and knowledge of the organisation and its members; and our own ongoing critique of our practice. This might involve some of the strategies employed by evidence-based practice, best practice modelling and practice guidelines, but would not be limited to these. It would also come from research on organisational dimensions of social work, including research on the interactions between different levels of experience within organisations.

For us, a key focus for knowledge development should be the everyday organisational practices and their impact on service users and communities. Knowledge generation could also be a reflexive process in that we would be constantly critiquing our involvement and would be striving to learn and improve our practice.

 Reflective Questions

1 What do you think are the strengths and weaknesses of evidence-based practice, best practice and practice guidelines?
2 What are some alternative sources of knowledge which are essential for organisational practice?

Conclusion

In this chapter, we have provided a broad overview of issues for a socially active and engaged social work in contemporary human service organisations. Social workers are one of a number of players in these organisations and they compete with other professions and occupations in the wider human services labour market. The changing nature of this labour market and the impact of neo-liberalism and managerialism have been perceived by some to be threats to social work's status and integrity as a profession. While this may be the case, these developments determine the contemporary organisational contexts in which many social workers practise. Similarly, many social workers (and academics) are grappling with the implications of evidence-based practice, best practice modelling and practice guidelines. While we do not discount these ideas out of hand, we recommend, and seek to adopt in this book, a wider, thorough and more critical analysis of social work's place in organisations. We reassert the place for values, standards, engagement, relationship and reflexivity in dealing with clients and the health and human service organisations which they commonly rely on for assistance and transformation in their lives.

Later in the book, we explore the implications of such a reflexive approach to social work in organisations. First, though, it is important to turn to the theory emerging from organisation and management studies, which variously provide insights into the different levels of organisational experiences, as highlighted earlier. This is the focus of our next chapter.

2 Theorising Organisations

In this chapter we overview

- traditional, critical and postmodern approaches to organisational theory;
- metaphors as a way of understanding theoretical perspectives;
- 'upstream' metaphors that challenge organisational practices and 'downstream' metaphors that reinforce existing practices;
- social work critique of technical and apolitical approaches to organisational theory;
- encouraging a healthy scepticism of theory and relying on multiple theories for holistic learning and understanding.

Introduction

Different theories have been influential in constructing and understanding organisations. During the twentieth century, the theory and practice of organisations have shifted from machine-like authority-laden constructions to nuanced and networked approaches. Nonetheless, the archetypal human service organisation remains the bureaucracy. According to Weber (1971 [1922]), the public service bureaucracy was both the most efficient state apparatus and, somewhat ambiguously, a dehumanising instrument. This reveals the darker undertones of administration, as reflected in the words of Franz Kafka's character Joseph K. in his book *The Trial*: 'behind my arrest and today's interrogation there is great organisation at work' (Kafka, 1984 [1925]: 54). This is perhaps one of the great modern fears of any client: that of being lost in and held hostage by a large uncaring organisation, waiting for your number to be processed. However, while the notion of bureaucracy is still of consequence, the forms of organisations are now multiple. Shifts in the shaping of organisations over the previous century mean that a range of organisational theories and metaphors are necessary (Morgan, 2006).

Metaphors and Schools of Thought

Metaphors are used in this chapter as a learning device for bringing organisational theorising into social work practice, theory and research. Metaphors give some life and reality to each school of organisational theory without going into copious detail, providing, through suitable imagery, an entrée into the realities of an organisation (Morgan, 2006: xxi). They offer windows of understanding that help explore 'the parallels between an object of interest and something that is better known to you' (Hatch, 1997: 51). The largely sociological and cultural theories of organisations can be used alongside the more specific professionally oriented social work theory – ranging from individual psychosocial approaches to theory in the management and leadership literature (e.g. Fisher, 2009; Milner, Myers and O'Byrne, 2015; Payne, 1997). The philosopher Paul Ricoeur (1978: 3) has argued that metaphor is a unit of reference that displaces and extends 'meaning' largely by substitution. Metaphors have been used extensively in imagining the theoretical portrayal of organisations (Morgan, 2006).

Our selection of metaphors and theories is based on our assessment of key priorities in social work and what is current in the field of organisation studies. A wide spectrum is covered to capture the diversity of theory and methods of study in the area. The focus of the discussion is sociological and society-centred, rather than individual-centred or on organisational psychology.

We pay particular attention to the distinction made by Chia (1996) between 'downstream' and 'upstream' thinking in organisational analysis and theory. This can be understood as posing a choice as to whether you, as an astute practitioner, 'go with the flow' of conventional and cumulative theory building or challenge dominant assumptions by utilising more politically subversive and creative components in theorising organisations. This might mean making a choice between drawing on theories that form a necessary part of academic convention and are cast sometimes as discrete, static or fixed knowledge, and using a more 'upstream' approach that is resistant to dominant theories as 'lived' and 'real' in the everyday life of an organisation (Al-Amoudi and Willmott, 2011) (see Figure 2.1).

Front-line workers, professionals, policy designers and managers of organisational change do not rely on technical manuals and textbook learning for reorganising the workplace. We have chosen to focus on metaphors and associated schools of thought in part to move beyond the constrictions of earlier paradigmatic and perspectivist thinking (see Burrell and Morgan, 1979; Egan, 1985; Jones and May, 1992; Morgan, 2006; Netting, Kettner and McMurtry, 1993) that tends to restrict overlaps and distinctions. Rather, we want to emphasise the power of competing explanations and the practical ways in which an organisation can be thought about.

This picture of organisations is a complex one. The various metaphors represent competing definitions of an organisation. And the various perspectives and schools that construct these metaphors suggest different ways of understanding and working within organisations. While these may often be in conflict, they may sometimes

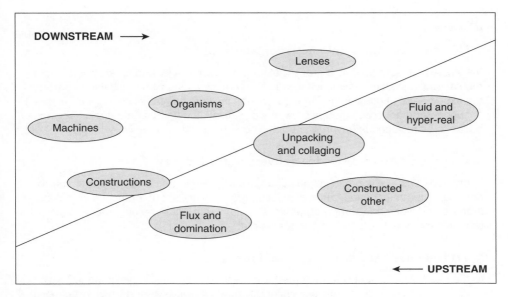

Figure 2.1 Upstream and downstream organisational metaphors

coalesce in promoting a particular agenda. For example, the development of a complaints system for service users might be promoted by machine metaphors – improved customer relations – as well as by flux and domination metaphors – increased user control – although, at a later stage, there may well be conflict over how to respond to the complaints. Organisations are influenced not just by one dominant metaphor but by many – often competing – metaphors. Such an approach offers social work, as a profession, and social workers, as organisational operators, opportunities to work strategically to change the organisation. While we may choose to operate in line with the dominant downstream metaphors – through necessity, habit or strategy – we may not have to do this all the time.

In Practice Example 2.1, we outline the development of a hypothetical non-profit human service organisation, from a small community enterprise to a major service provider. Following a discussion of each of the metaphors in the first part of this chapter, we highlight some reflective questions that relate back to this practice example. Inevitably, the details provided will be limited and you are encouraged to fill in some of the gaps, given your own knowledge of these kinds of organisations.

A restructured human service organisation

Avalon Care is a large non-profit provider of services to people with mental health needs, older people and homeless people. The values and philosophy of the organisation have shifted over time. In a review of the history of the organisation for a recent annual report, a long-standing board member identified four key stages in the organisation's development:

(Continued)

PRACTICE
EXAMPLE 2.1

(Continued)

1. Grass-roots community activism and support

Initially, Avalon saw itself as a grass-roots organisation run by and for survivors of the mental health system. Social action was a core activity and was motivated in part by the exposure of abuses in the large psychiatric institutions of the day. As the number of support and advocacy groups grew, the organisation gained greater legitimacy and began to be included in government planning and consultation activities.

2. Community-based service delivery and advocacy

In the early 1980s, the organisation set up two activity centres for people with schizophrenia. Later that decade, the organisation grew rapidly, set up branches in regional areas and developed a range of services, including in-home respite, meal services, drop-in centres and a friendly visitors' scheme.

3. Professional service delivery and research

In the 1990s, the organisation adopted a professional outlook, developing links with professional associations and university social work, medical and nursing schools. During this period, the organisation continued to grow and it added research as a major area of activity.

4. Corporate community services

Difficulties attracting funding led the Board to appoint a chief executive officer based primarily on management experience and offering a significantly bigger salary package than had been offered to previous coordinators. Under the new CEO's direction, Avalon Care has been successful in gaining further government contracts and today it is a major non-government provider of community-based services to people with mental health needs, and a large supplier of semi-independent accommodation services to older people and homeless people.

    The CEO recently initiated a strategic review. As part of this, consultants have been asked to examine the delivery of social work services. Since the 1980s, social workers have undertaken a range of roles including assessment of client circumstances, individual and family counselling, support group facilitation and community development. However, the CEO is concerned that this is unnecessarily restrictive and that there may be other well-qualified and experienced people who are just as well placed to carry out these roles. Thus, the review will consider developing generic case manager positions, replacing social work positions, and making them available to appropriately qualified and non-qualified experienced staff. These changes to case management practice in the organisation reflect broader trends and changes in social policy and the basis of social advocacy over the last decade in Australia and the UK (Hughes and Wilson, 2016; Wearing, 2016).

Organisations as Machines (Bureaucratic, Managerial and Technocratic Theories)

The machine metaphor describes the organisation as a working machine that has complex parts and mechanical dynamics that are designed for efficiency and productivity.

Strati (2000: 52) refers to the metaphor of the 'psychic prison' for workers in organisations, who, as if they were entering a machine, are imprisoned and alienated through unconscious, cognitive and ideological traps. These metaphors invoke a market perspective or neo-classical economic view where organisations are best understood as comprising individuals competitively pursuing their self-interest in a market economy (Jones and May, 1992). According to this perspective, rational economic 'man' will work hard in order to fit the moral and economic imperatives of 'the good life' that capitalism can provide through the profit-making firm (i.e. the capitalist work ethic). Workers are willing, in this sense, to literally become 'cogs in the wheel' of the machine to share in the moral and financial profitability of the firm and the broader market economy. This view of organisations is today closely allied with the managerialist imperatives of neo-liberal ideology that global and national market economies are the final arbitrators of all policies, and organisational decisions are notably based in efficiency measures and the economic productivity of workers.

One of the more salient and powerful theories of large organisations, that fits within the machine metaphor, is that of bureaucracy as critiqued by Max Weber (1971 [1922]). In the early twentieth century, Weber framed bureaucracy as an ideal type: an analytical construct that synthesises related phenomena. He saw bureaucracy as being characterised by efficient, streamlined administrative structures. These structures were seen as facilitative of modern capitalism and would thus sweep away 'old world' forms of organisation based on traditional and charismatic leadership.

A key principle underpinning bureaucracy, as conceptualised by Weber (1971 [1922]), was rational-legal authority. This form of authority is seen to emerge from clearly defined and procedurally determined rules and regulations that coordinate and control relationships between administrative units within the organisation. There should be a clear division of labour between each role, and a clear indication of the corresponding responsibilities and specialisations. Central to this is a hierarchy of authority or chain of command in which each level is accountable to the one higher up. Even senior management has to follow the rules and regulations. Their authority comes from the office they hold, not from themselves as individuals. Thus, bureaucracy legitimises authority and domination over staff and clients of an organisation, and rationalises world views to the codes, standards and values of the organisation.

It is notable that while Weber's conceptualisation of bureaucracy was as an efficient machine, much of the critique of large bureaucratic organisations focuses on their inefficiencies. As organisations grow bigger, the rules and regulations take on a symbolic significance beyond their functional value. This may result in ritualistic and rigid behaviours and a resistance towards change, even when this is deemed necessary for efficient production. Bureaucrats with detailed knowledge of the rules and regulations are accorded special status, and thus they have a vested interest in things staying as they are. Consequently, the term bureaucracy nowadays is associated with unnecessary documentation or 'red tape', and bureaucrats are widely seen as insensitive to the complexities of human situations.

During the latter part of the twentieth century, bureaucracy's decline in popularity corresponded to a rise in popularity of other forms of organisations, which were more directly controllable by management. Managerial and technocratic approaches tend to use the machine analysis to focus on the operations, 'fine-tuning' and out-comes of the organisation as part of a 'change culture'. In order to maximise their outcomes in quality and cost-efficient services, the organisational sub-units are conceived as 'parts and bits' of the organisation that require fixing. The aim is usu-ally to improve the productivity of the workforce by restructuring the organisation to make it more efficient, effective and economically viable.

In 1911, Frederick W. Taylor published his *Principles of Scientific Management* that would so greatly affect the managerial agendas for industry in the USA and further afield over the next century. Scientific management was seen as a way for managers and owners of industrial production to control labour in order to increase the productivity of profit-based organisations. Thus, this theoretical school developed a narrow focus on the needs and concerns of management in industry. Taylorism involves a mechanistic view of organisations: through time and motion studies and careful observation, specialised tasks could be set for workers to maximise productivity. Managers could better govern the organisation by using their secretive knowledge of goals and process. Many private firms use managers trained initially to think first of productivity and setting goals and, second, of other aspects of work culture, such as the well-being of workers. The theory assumes that the interests of managers and workers are the same and that unions are unnecessary.

Such a view matches the post-Fordist emphasis on the labour market (as discussed in Chapter 1), including the shift to 'flexible specialisation' (especially for service sec-tor and hi-tech industries), low levels of union membership, and consensus building between unions and managers. According to this view, social conflicts are made invis-ible and the politics of wider capitalist society appear not to affect the internal work-ings of organisations. The organisation, as technical and managerial apparatus, is used to achieve 'outcomes' and overrides or denies the divisions of the social context such as those based on 'race', class or gender. These organisations today conform to market principles for their rationality and are commonly and pejoratively known as managerialist in orientation (Clarke and Newman, 1997; Zifcak, 1994). In certain instances in modern times, where government and non-government organisations have become very large, we can talk about the creation of a hyper-bureaucracy with 'speed'-driven managerialism that tries to act quickly but essentially creates greater inertia, anxiety and risk in short-term, hurried and unplanned decision making (Dominelli, 2002; Webb, 2006).

How useful is the machine metaphor in understanding a human service organisa-tion? There are several weaknesses with the approach. First, there is the concern that the metaphor lacks sophistication and does not match organisational realities. This mismatch reifies organisational complexities by making out that they can be repaired or fixed when things go wrong or when workplace cultures are ineffective or inefficient. For social work practitioners and managers, this approach could sig-nificantly obscure or filter the real bases for decision making and sources of power in organisations. The critique of scientific management raises issues of how and whose values, ideologies and discourse (as dominant conversations) around social division and social conflicts hold sway. Critical assessment and evaluation of organi-sational roles, functions and goals may reveal different processes to those described as a machine. After all, a machine merely requires fine-tuning and a 'set of tools' for change to occur or identified problems to be fixed. Or does it? Let us not forget that, in the post-industrial age, 'machines' such as computers can be complex, and thus so too can organisations.

Second, the industrial 'machine' metaphor also fails to understand how organisations capture and are captured by the specific values and ideologies involved in social service and policy implementation. These processes can be illustrated by critical sociological theories that better describe and explain organisational realities and hierarchies. The feminist critique of bureaucracy as hierarchical, patriarchal and male-centred is one such approach (Ferguson, 1984). This is most obviously the case in human service organisations in Britain and Australia, which are predominantly run, managed and organised by men in senior executive positions. However, beyond this, dominant masculinity helps rationalise and construe organisational forms to suit men's interests (see also Brewis, 2001).

Another key concern or criticism of the machine metaphor for organisational analysis is that it does not allow for a content-rich, energy-replenishing and holistic view of the organisation. Other theories and associated metaphors offer such elements, most notably the systems, ecological and functionalist theories of organisations.

 Reflective Questions

1   In the Avalon Care example, the most recent development of this organisation involved a shift towards a corporate structure. This was seen as necessary to sustain service delivery and maximise outcomes for service users. What does a machine metaphor have to offer an analysis of large organisations such as Avalon Care?

2   What are some elements of an organisation that are not explained by managerial and technocratic thinking? For example, what about conflict between workers and managers or managers and professionals, or other power dynamics? What about workers' rights in organisations? How is day-to-day case work affected by the corporatising and managerial frameworks used in such organisations?

Organisations as Living Organisms (Systems and Functionalist Theories)

Systems analysis has served social work well in terms of understanding organisational environments and sketching out the interrelatedness of various action systems involved in changes and continuities in organised behaviour. The systems, ecological and functionalist perspectives on organisations emerged in the 1950s and 1960s as dominant schools in American sociology. The organisation is perceived in these schools as a 'living organism'. They employ a biological model of human behaviour: 'open systems theory ... emphasizes through the basic assumption of entropy, the necessary dependence of any organization on its environment' (Katz and Kahn, 1966: 13). In systems analysis, workers are involved in 'a dynamic and interactive way, exercising influence and expecting in turn to be influenced by other organizational participants' (Jones and May, 1992: 45). Hence, the metaphor of an organisation as a living biological organism is an apt one. A profession, such as social work, can be involved in managing or being part of the rights, roles and relationships of staff in such systems, while still adhering to autonomous professional roles and discretionary activity.

In the ecological perspective, organisations are viewed in ways that are analogous to animal life as observed by naturalists. The focus is on: how organisations and their members survive, thrive or die out; the ability of organisations to adapt; and the (resource and people) service capacity of small to large organisations. The emergence of new hybrid organisations and those most adaptable to environmental change might best be suited to the privatising and contracted basis of provision of human services management and organisations. An additional point to remember is that systems can be open or closed given the transfer of physical and mental energy. A closed system is where energy is contained within boundaries and an open system is where energy crosses permeable boundaries (Payne, 1997).

According to Talcott Parsons, the founder of structural functionalism, there are functional prerequisites for a social system to operate (Cuff and Payne, 1984). The structural functionalist studies of organisations in the 1950s and 1960s were particularly concerned with internal change and dysfunction. Structural functionalism sees the social system as a whole with functional and dysfunctional elements that maintain social order. A healthy organisational system, for example, would ensure that all functional units within it, such as professional teams and management, have defined roles and responsibilities that match their professional expertise. This would produce harmony and equilibrium in the system. In an organisation, dysfunctional activity, if it occurs, requires retraining (re-socialisation) into the healthy functions of the system. By 1959, critics such as C. Wright Mills (1977 [1959]: 43) had demonstrated some of the limitations of functionalism, calling it 'unimaginative' and 'an arid game of concepts'.

Katz and Kahn's (1966) work combined both functional and systems theory and indicated the high tide of functionalist analysis in organisational theory. While not always assuming equilibrium as found in a biological organism, other evolutionary organisational phases are seen to parallel an organism's development from birth to death. This development includes the input of energy to keep the organisational system alive, the possibilities of ill-health or dysfunction if synergy and equilibrium are not replenished, and the very real prospect of the organisation dying without open system feedback and continual evaluation of its functions and purpose. In fact, most contemporary management texts incorporate some systems and functionalist organisational thinking, including principles such as 'people are not machines' and 'people form cultures based on mythologies' in organisations (Macdonald et al., 2005). These texts can include and integrate elements of other schools to supplement their focus on systems or the functional prerequisites of organisations.

By the early 1970s, structural functionalism was seen to have serious shortcomings in understanding organisational complexities and did not retain the same continuity of significance as open systems theory (Hassard, 1995: 50). Functionalist theory has often been criticised for its incremental view of organisational change. It is, however, possible to theorise the movement of energy between sub-systems in equilibrium and stable external environments. Accordingly, organisational change may occur by internal adjustments to reach equilibrium by adapting to external changes to the organisational system and sub-systems: the organisation altering its goals and structure to fit changing circumstances. In this way, certain organisations survive and others die out. Usually, organisations need to plan for change, set goals and then deliberately change their structure to fit new processes or outcomes (Donaldson, 1986: 30–1). Some organisational change will come about by adaptation that is a random process. In Chapter 3, we further explore how social work responds and can contribute to organisational change.

There are ways of conceiving of organisations in systems theory beyond that of the closed system offered by functionalism. Scott (2002: 25–30), for example, gives three system theory definitions of organisations – rational, natural and open – that perhaps overcome some of the problems of a closed system model. Understanding adaptations to change might better explain how change cultures and change management have occurred in the privatisation or contracting out of human service organisations in recent public and social policy programmes. The speed of this change in recent decades can also be linked to hyper-bureaucratisation in modern society.

Similar themes are present in the social work practice literature. Payne (1997), drawing on Pincus and Minahan (1973), also identifies three kinds of systems: informal or natural systems (e.g. neighbours), formal systems (e.g. sporting clubs) and societal systems (e.g. childcare centres). According to this approach, the social worker is able to see where interactions between clients and their environment are causing problems. It is the interaction between client and environment that is problematised, not one or the other. The aim is to help people perform life tasks, alleviate distress and set their own goals. An extension of this systems analysis is the ecological perspective or the life model of social work that 'sees people as constantly adapting in an interchange with many different aspects of their environment' (Payne, 1997: 145). These systems both change the environment and are changed by their environment.

The main criticism of the 'living organism' metaphor and related schools is their undue focus on survival and growth, rather than values, policy and the political dimensions of organisations. Ecological theory tends to reify the internal dynamics of organisations in arguing that they act as a unified whole rather than as multiple forces that can be contradictory or ambivalent in effect. For example, the larger an organisation becomes, such as in the Avalon Care scenario, the more complex and differentiated it becomes. In such a circumstance, it is possible that organisational behaviour becomes more rule-governed as management tries to exert top-down control over the various sub-systems. Ecological theory also neglects how organisations themselves shape the environment and dominate social life.

Systems and structural functionalist accounts are also limited in their application to social work practice because of the lack of analysis of power relations and dominance. This is especially so for explaining change and describing organisational culture. Not only are issues of 'who governs' or rules organisations left unexplored by the theories and their biological metaphor, but also overlooked are 'when and where' governance occurs in the whole system and to what effect. These general criticisms highlight a lack of focus in these schools on the internal micro-cultures and external pressures governing an organisation. Other theories of culture, communication and decision making in organisational theory can offer a more complete understanding of the everyday and communicative effects of organisational cultures, processes and structures.

Reflective Questions

1   How can a service organisation, such as Avalon Care, be understood as a system? What might be some of its sub-systems?
2   What are some of the weaknesses of adopting a systems and functionalist approach to human services?

Organisations as Lenses (Culture, Communication and Decision Theories)

The lens metaphor is used here to mean how we see or view an organisational culture with its 'symbol systems', 'shared meanings', cultures, micro-cultures, countercultures and subcultures. These are all involved in setting the mood for decision making and influencing communication processes and information sharing, among other issues (Jones and May, 1992). The metaphor also connotes the visual part of communication in organisational culture that can '"see" and search, filter, distort and gatekeep information' to be processed by individuals, organisational units and the environment (Strati, 2000: 23). We also include the decision-making perspective under the lens metaphor because this tradition has primarily focused study on observable decisions rather than on covert conflict and decision making (see Clegg, 1989).

From this perspective, we might ask: when is an organisation not seen through a lens of some kind? The main impact of the cultural perspective is a challenge to the machine metaphor's view of an assumed rationality and efficiencies in planned organisations. Instead, cultural approaches look to the subtle patterns, rituals, symbols and norms that make up the culture and subcultures of an organisation. In these, it is possible to find competing voices and values about organisational process and strategy.

The best-known study of formal organisations in social science using an anthropological/ethnography approach was the Hawthorne study of the 1920s and 1930s conducted at the Western Electric Plant in Chicago, USA. This spawned a range of studies that focused on organisations and work, including, in recent years, hi-tech industries and communities. This style of field research examined organisations from 'the inside out' and also established the school known as 'Human Relations'.

Social work itself has moved away from the 'cog in the machine' analysis of organisations to considering how all staff and clients make contributions to the system. Change in organisational culture is required to achieve successful outcomes 'with greater emphasis on trust and participation, managed risk, corporate loyalty, teamwork and good staff care' (Coulshed and Mullender, 2001: 51). Managed change needs to occur under these conditions when the organisational change itself is of such proportion and significance that the whole workforce is affected in some way, for instance in the loss of key elements of the workforce or the need for new skill set development in existing staff.

The cultural approach to organisations has led writers in social work to discuss different forms of culture, depending on the size and type of the organisation, including:

- *power culture*: strong leadership from a small group at the top;
- *role culture*: with a clinging to bureaucratic roles, rules and regulations;
- *task culture*: that emphasises technical know-how and project teams; and
- *person culture*: that matches tasks to people. (Coulshed and Mullender, 2001: 51)

Cultures can intersect across and within organisations. Factors that join with cultural forms include power, staff avoidance and uncertainty, individualism and collectivism, and masculine or feminine dominance in the gendering of workplace culture. Today, management's role is often focused on all parts of the culture 'pulling together', rather than on dividing up loyalties through harsh top-down practices, so common in large-scale managerial change.

Organisations, in particular managers, will often set norms to maintain consensus and a common goal in efforts to stabilise possible dissatisfaction or dissent among staff over various policies and programmes. Formal statements of values and mission are often established in larger organisational environments, such as in the Avalon Care practice example, where conflicting assumptions and meanings over decisions may result in subcultures that compete for decision-making space. This raises questions of 'when, where and who' in terms of decision making, as well as questions around the significance of the decisions for organisational change.

An important concern for social work here is how written policy values may conflict and compete with personal or professional values in an organisation. The reason for social work's close study of these cultures is to develop cultural and social competency for workers and professionals at the individual, group and organisational levels. To this could also be added the need for management and leadership competencies as significant resources for social work to participate in a change culture. In Chapters 3 to 5, there are several examples of how social work can intervene and enable these changes or work with other staff to encourage such change.

In moving away from 'top-down' and imposed management styles, writers on management in social work also suggest that certain styles can be used to overcome resistance to change. Models of the 'learning organisation' and 'competent workplace' views of change are, according to some writers, closest to social work values and ethics, particularly in terms of using reflective organisation techniques that evaluate and feed back issues to management for potential change (e.g. Argyris and

Schön, 1978; Gould and Baldwin, 2004). The current aim of change in many human services is for the structure and culture of organisations to serve the overall strategy often determined from the top. This involves looking inward, using reflective practice techniques but also developing leadership and organisational competence. A critique of this view is developed in Chapter 3.

Though not fully within the 'lens' cultural school, the decision perspectives can be said to derive from both systems and cultural approaches to organisations. This was the key approach taken in mainstream North American political science in such fields as public administration. Critical and Marxist theory provided strong critiques of the approach, based on concerns about whose 'real interests' are reflected in key decisions, and what then are the sources of real power, interests and latent conflict in the organisational system (see Clegg, 1989; Lukes, 1974; Morgan, 2006). Nonetheless, the decision approach still provides a useful understanding of overt and covert behaviour involved in decision making within organisations. In this approach, organisations are framed as decision-making systems. This is a useful approach as part of social work's focus is on understanding micro-process issues and micro-management among staff and for clients of human services. See Chapter 5 for a fuller discussion of decision making in organisational practice.

Open organisations that encourage competition between different groups or views can be said to want change. Organisational thinking also needs to serve the overall mission rather than always be inwardly focused on structure and culture, and this requires energy, effort and good practice from staff and senior management. From the perspective of the living organism and lens metaphors, these strategies might be said to be effective when staff morale and achievements are high and in line with programme objectives. However, as the rest of the book shows, effective organisational practice for social work can involve complex and spontaneous endeavours that move well beyond such a focus.

 Reflective Questions

1   In Avalon Care, how might the cultures of this organisation have shifted with the four different stages of development? What effect might these cultures have had on the care of clients or patients by this organisation?

2   What interpersonal and group skills and processes, such as mediation (see Chapter 4), can lead to clearer communication in organisational cultures and boost morale?

Organisations as Constructions (Interpretive and Interactionist Theories)

Berger and Luckmann (1966) developed a social constructionist view of knowledge and everyday life that re-emphasised some tenets of earlier classical sociology, such as symbolic interactionism. The focus of this is the experience of organised life and how this is integrated into self-understanding as an abstract symbol system: 'language is capable not only of constructing symbols … but also of … presenting them as objectively real elements of everyday life' (1966: 55). The building metaphor of physical 'constructions' defines organisations as a constructed site of personal assumptions and social interactions or as 'accomplished' from inter-subjective experiences (ethnomethodology). For example, such a view would argue for the accomplishment and/or negotiated construction of masculinities in organisations (Telford, 1996).

Interactionist theories arrive from what were originally the interpersonal and quality-of-life studies of the Human Relations School discussed earlier. A behavioural social psychology orientation is evident in that 'what happened in organisations was felt to be understandable only if one looked closely at interaction and interpersonal communication' (Gross and Etzioni, 1985: 44). According to critics, the 'construction' metaphor suffers from the problem that the rules and realities of organisations are 'real'. Thus, no matter how much individuals or groups try to bend these for their own or others' purposes, the organisation imposes constraints that are 'real' and objective, irrespective of subjective experience (Gross and Etzioni, 1985: 62).

Despite the critics, interactionist and constructionist accounts of organisations continue to challenge managerial and scientific views of organisational analysis. Strati (2000: 59) claims that the interpretive paradigm 'views social reality as ontologically precarious' where social order results from intersubjective experiences. According to the philosophy of phenomenology, which underpins the interpretive and interactionist approaches, organisations *do not exist* as concrete or tangible entities but are 'processual phenomena'. This is perhaps the most radical insight of the constructionist metaphor. The intentional actions of individuals and their collective interactions define and socially construct meaning; that is, they are building social meaning in organisations. This ensures that the organisation is made up of or performed by actions from a variety of different points of view. This leads to, say, a dominant culture and micro subcultures where specific meanings for individual and group actors are created.

The main focus of research in the interactionist school is on organisational order as a 'negotiated order' leading to, for example, a workplace culture. In this shared understanding of organisational structures and cultures, the goals and overall strategy are tied to subtle and complex negotiations over order, stability, conflict, change and meaning. Negotiations are conducted on the courses of action to be pursued (Strati, 2000: 94–8). Teamwork, for example, can be seen as a person lodging parts of their self into the selves, memories and imaginations of relevant others. In this sense, teams or units form within organisations where selves lodge together to perform and negotiate activities that support or resist the organisational goals and strategy.

There are several criticisms of interactionist theory that apply directly to organisational analysis. First, it is a process theory of organisations that concerns itself with form and not social content. Thus, the theory can lend itself to mundane empirical concerns rather than content-based issues. Second, its pragmatism can lend itself to a conservative politics unless linked to social structural concerns. Interactionist theory is part of the American liberal sociological tradition that focuses on the micro-social; that is, a negotiated social and organisational order that involves emotions, attitudes, gestures, rituals, intimacy, competition, and so on. We define and see ourselves as others see us. We are objects of the social environment, including organisations. As such, these forms of constructionism are concerned with human agency rather than structure. As we will see, these issues have also, in recent years, become part of the theorising of newer schools, such as postmodern approaches to the emotions and intersubjectivity in organisations (see also Chapter 4 on emotions and Chapter 8 on experience in organisations).

Reflective Questions

1   In the Avalon Care practice example, how might inter-personal conflicts arise between management and professionals if there are significant differences in policy understandings, work conditions and salaries between the two groups?
2   Observe a human service organisation to see what work is done and who does it. How is social meaning created within the organisation? For example, what are some common rituals?

With the next four metaphors and associated schools of thought comes a stronger emphasis on 'upstream thinking' rather than downstream. We see a shift in the conceptualisation and focus of study: from the organisation as an entity to organising as a process. The adoption of elements of these four approaches means that our organisational thinking will become more political and challenging for the social order. We relate Practice Example 2.2 to the discussion via a series of reflective questions.

PRACTICE EXAMPLE 2.2

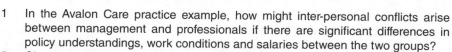

A new social enterprise

InterCreate is an online business initially set up under the auspices of a major disability organisation, InterAct. It was established three years ago with assistance from a government programme promoting the development of social enterprises. A social enterprise is an organisation that is run as a business mainly for social or environmental purposes rather than purely for financial gain. The government sees social enterprises as one of the main vehicles for promoting the community participation of disadvantaged groups, enabling self-reliance and reducing 'dependence' on welfare.

There are two primary aims of InterCreate. The first is to provide an online venue for the sale of creative works produced by people with learning/intellectual disabilities (artists), by themselves, through InterAct's network of community centres, or via other organisations. In developing its 'brand' and position in the marketplace, InterCreate prioritises a particular style: bold colours and the depiction of flowers, animals and children. The second aim is to enable people with learning/intellectual disabilities to become more computer and business literate. All artists are involved in the process of setting up and managing their own online accounts (hosted on the InterCreate website). The site is also linked to Facebook and Twitter to facilitate artists' networking and product promotion.

InterAct has been surprised at the financial profitability of InterCreate, which generated significant revenue last year. Part of this money was distributed to the artists (people with learning/intellectual disabilities), part was used to pay permanent staff and part was invested to grow the business. In the next stage of development, it is planned that InterCreate will become an independent 'community interest company' – this means that new governance arrangements need to be established and that the organisation will now rely on its own income for its survival, rather than receiving any further support from InterAct. Currently, InterCreate is developing appropriate governance arrangements with the aim of facilitating the participation of both its key constituents – people with learning/intellectual disabilities – and the other people needed to ensure the maintenance and profitability of its programmes.

The shift from operating under the auspices of InterAct to setting up as an independent company arose not only from the financial success of the project, but also from the desire of people with learning/intellectual disabilities to take more control of the organisation. When operating under InterAct, InterCreate was staffed by an executive officer and two project workers without learning/intellectual disabilities. The organisation was also supported by a reference group, which did include people with disabilities and some parents and carers. There were complaints from some artists that too much control was exercised by the full-time paid staff over which creative works were allowed to be sold on the site and which were not. The current style branding was felt to be too restrictive. Other artists, as well as the current permanent staff, were concerned that the brand not be diminished (and thus the revenue diminished) through poorly produced or 'inappropriate' products being made available through the site. There were also complaints that not enough of the revenue was being directed back to the artists themselves, although all recognised the need for some of the income generated to be directed to administration costs.

Organisations as Unpacking and Collaging (Postmodern Theories)

The 'unpacking' metaphor connotes taking things out of a box and examining them carefully. This is the case with postmodern theorising of organisations. The 'collaging' metaphor might mean jumbling things up to create the illusion of an overall picture, but one that can be easily disassembled and constantly changed into new understandings (Hatch, 1997: 52). These two metaphors help sum up some of the philosophy of postmodernism in that this philosophy is not concerned with fixed holistic thinking or providing foundational material on which to build. Such postmodern thinking can be applied to organisations. Chia (1996) contends that concepts of organisation – such as the theories presented in this chapter – are used in particular ritualised, unthoughtful and often de-contextualised ways to normalise organisational life: 'theories and knowledge … are better thought of as communal artifacts passed on in highly ritualized settings' (Chia, 1996: 215).

The metaphor of 'unpacking' enables us to think critically about organisational theories. Postmodernists argue that these theories conceal as well as reveal understanding of organisations. Some writers, such as Power (1990), claim that postmodernism stands for 'the death of reason' since reason is itself an invention of secular and rational science from the seventeenth-century enlightenment onwards. Power also contends that postmodernism is an assault via deconstruction analysis on unity. He argues that philosophers such as Lyotard (1984) envisage social organisation as irreducible language games that cannot be essentialised to artificial structures, boundaries and order in anything other than their spontaneous and continually changing sense.

This problematising of structures, order and boundaries makes an analysis that focuses on their continuity and stability seem rigid and uni-dimensional. Postmodern organisational theories emphasise indeterminacy and multiple ever-changing perspectives on organisations. Postmodern theorists would not agree on a single metaphor, such as a 'collage', as having a fixed meaning. However, the metaphor can signify the bringing together of different parts of theory traditions to capture some of the style of postmodernism (Hatch, 1997: 54–5). This enables old and new theories and experiences of organisations to be brought together like an artist might create an object of beauty or wonder, as well as offering some challenges and interpretations of social and organisational reality.

Postmodern approaches to organisations have challenged the basis of modern organisational theory, in particular the theory of the (rational) bureaucracy as an effective instrument of social change and administration in society. Hancock and Tyler (2001: 93) argue for a postmodern meta-theory whose core propositions, when applied to organisational analysis, indicate that the modern organisation is in decline. The idea that organisations have definable structures and rules that govern or universalise all activities towards one common goal does not reflect the complexities and multiple layers of organisations. If the reality mirrors the theory, then human service organisations are becoming more eclectic in purpose, more irrational and unstable, with many moving parts that are alternately visible and invisible to staff and clients.

The postmodern view can be criticised not least for its failure to grasp other microsocial schools, such as ethnomethodology, that also employ notions of organisational 'accomplishment', or interactionist schools that also establish the precariousness of one's being in organisational change and process. Feminist and other critical approaches to social work and organisations are addressed in the next section. However, it is important to highlight the similarities between postmodern approaches and feminism and other critical approaches. Fook (2002: 40), for example, claims that there are distinct similarities between feminism, postmodernism and her own arguments for a critical–reflective approach to practice. In more recent years, the postmodern approach has turned to direct engagement with the everyday realities of practice with clients in organisations. Under the banner of 'social constructionist approaches' in social work, counselling and family therapy authors, such as the constructionist theorist Kenneth Gergen, have had a leading role in developing theory that helps practitioners understand suffering and healing from within a constructionist and postmodern lens. These theories commonly challenge dominant knowledge such as the biomedical model in the health care system. The perspective is one that acknowledges the holistic self-knowledge, and self-understanding involved in 'owning' and defining one's own health, and thereby de-medicalising illness and mental health (Ravi-Priya, 2012).

The postmodern and related approaches also have their origins in the subversion of existing political and organisational order. So, postmodern approaches to organisational theorising are 'oppositional'; they 'stand against' or challenge existing arrangements or order (Crook et al., 1992; Hancock and Tyler, 2001). This leads us onto the next schools and the related metaphors of flux and domination.

Critics of postmodern approaches to organisations and to social work argue that the effect of the approach is to create a conservative political agenda that deals only with marginal issues rather than with the power structures, inequalities or institutional dynamics of modern-day large organisations and of capitalism. In this critique, there is a sense that postmodernism has 'come and gone', and is now incorporated into social and political theory, though the significance of social constructionist approaches in counselling therapy and social work literature is still very apparent and can offer useful counter-knowledge based on subjective experience. This can be drawn on to challenge the dominant frames in organisational service cultures such as the biomedical model, used extensively in health policy and programmes, or the legalistic models used in the criminal justice system. Most writers today include some form of postmodern analysis in discussing organisational study or analysis. However, this has involved the incorporation of postmodernism into the modernist views of organisations, rather than its forming a distinctive research programme. Those who might be regarded as postmodern in approach, such as Power (1990), Hough (1999), Hancock and Tyler (2001) and Chia (2002), all give ground to the modernist school of critical theory. Power (1990), for example, argues that theorists such as Habermas demonstrate a strong and profound understanding of the role of reason in society, how organisations dominate people's lives and how the sources of management and control are exercised. In the next section, we address areas of critical theory particularly relevant to organisational analysis in human services.

 Reflective Questions

1   How does the postmodern metaphor of 'unpacking' help us understand the changing organisational conditions in InterCreate? Imagine, for example, unpacking InterCreate or an organisation you know, and identifying the dominant players within the organisation. Can you also indicate whose voices are silent, for example service users, families, volunteer workers, and so on?
2   How do postmodern frameworks in organisations conceive power and inequality in the workplace and with clients?
3   What are some weaknesses of the postmodern approach?

Organisations as Flux and Domination (Critical Theories)

When an organisation is said to be in a state of 'flux', as a metaphor, it is constantly changing and in the uneasy tension of change. These dynamics depend on the configuration of force and power being exercised within and externally around the organisation. For some, as we have seen with functionalist theories of organisations, stability is more highly valued than change. However, within critical theories flux and domination are assumed on the basis of sources of power and the ensuing relations of domination. This school began, in part, with Weber's views on the administrative order as governed

by the legitimate rule of domination and power. However, a perpetual change metaphor may be a more accurate depiction of social reality in organisations as it can enable
social work to question and challenge 'official versions of the nature of organizations
as well as their own perceived beliefs' (Jones and May, 1992: 71). Critical theories can
include neo-Marxist, political economy and feminist versions that emphasise the relationship between organisations and dominant groups, and the way this shapes organisational processes.

The political economy school understands organisations in the context of the political
and economic relations in society. It also emphasises power relations in the internal
structures and processes of organisations. The structural feminist perspective focuses on
gender relations, the roles and responsibilities within gendered organisations, male
dominance in management, and the subordination of women in organisational structures and hierarchies. These theories, among several others, fit within the metaphors of
flux and domination and can be thought of as modernist in that they contain some sense
of hope that modernity can be transformed and that there is evolutionary progress to a
new social objective and identity. The issues of emancipatory practice and self-reflexivity
are also taken up in postmodern and feminist analysis of practice in social work. So, as
discussed, we see some considerable overlap of critical theory with critical and postmodern approaches to social work practice, and to human service organisations.

While a sophisticated understanding of the concept of reflexivity is evident in qualitative research analysis (Alvesson and Skoldberg, 2012), the translation to practice knowledge is not straightforward or quite as apparent. A multi-layered approach to how
practitioners interpret their world and recorded data on clients are needed to engage
with a deeper understanding of reflexivity as a concept and as requiring the necessary
space within organisations. This idea of reflexivity is emphasised in Chapter 9. The self-
knowledge of practitioners of their own interpretative work, self-scrutiny, values orientations and biases in engaging with clients have yet to be fully developed in organisational
practice frameworks, notably those coming from critical and postmodern theory
(Alvesson and Skoldberg, 2012: 271–8; Wearing and Hughes, 2014).

Critical theorists point to the social problems created by the rise of organisations. A
particularly useful example is feminist theory which linked the personal and the political in social work and elsewhere. Arguably, the critique of gender in work organisations, including the human services, began in the earlier waves of twentieth-century
feminism, especially in the organisational agendas for citizenship set by women for
their suffrage in Britain, Australia and elsewhere (Ferguson, 1984). At the same time,
critical theory and socialist feminism saw the shift in management towards women,
especially in human services, as the rise of femocracy. The concept of the 'femocrat'
acknowledged that some had access to senior executive positions in the public sector
or as part of the business elite (Yeatman, 1990). The question was raised as to whether
these, usually well-educated, women had been incorporated into bureaucracy and the
hierarchy relations of domination as rational-technical authority – arguably a male
constructed view of the world – suggested by Weber (Ferguson, 1984).

Mainstream management literature also started to recognise gender issues during the
1980s. Organisational principles, feminists argued, are structured by masculine thinking
and male power to encourage inequality, hierarchy and impersonality; these are particularly apparent in large bureaucracies (Ferguson, 1984). Male-dominated western society

discourages alternative modes of organising. Feminine styles of organising are claimed to be more caring and nurturing, and the gender bias of formal organisations discourages such styles, valuing rather achievement and competition. These criticisms can be joined with, say, interactionist and critical theories, such as Marxism, to argue that organisational structures can damage the psyche of individuals, creating alienation, conformity and the stunting of self-discovery and development (Scott, 2002: 5–6).

In applying ideas from critical theory, including feminist theories, to social work practice in organisations, some problems may be apparent. Parts of the theory may be taken and dropped into the language of social work without a clear sense of whether they legitimise social relations and the status quo or challenge the social order. Critical, Marxist and feminist (just as other) modes of practice can reduce the heterogeneity of social reality to a narrow and sometimes limited practice that fails to engage with broader macro–micro social processes and change (Rojek et al., 1988).

A second issue is that organisational theory, even of the critical kind, tends to deal with external pressures as secondary or unproblematic when it comes to policy reform processes and the need for change in organisations. There are notable exceptions to this, and some theorists offer a useful synthesis of critical and micro theories of organisations. Cohen (1985: 82–90), for example, addresses issues of social control, notably organisational convenience, as part of the planned response to those who are vulnerable, different or marginalised. Giddens (1990) also looks at issues of professional and disciplinary surveillance in organisations to give a clearer picture of workplace social control. He uses the term 'carceral organisations' to refer to closed systems that incarcerate prisoners or the mentally ill. Such a view connotes the idea that in terms of work or client identities people can feel they are 'trapped' in a closed organisational environment or system where 'speaking up' or stepping 'out of line' can mean that certain punishments are measured out to them. Thus, being shut in or closed off from the outside world is akin to the nature of a prison system or a 'cage'.

Finally, the important insights of deconstruction in breaking down totalising theories into multiple interpretations should not be lost on a critical modernist analysis of organisations. Such an approach can emphasise 'difference' and facilitate a fine, detailed analysis of organisational decisions, conversations and policy. This is something that is explored more in the final metaphor of this chapter. We argue that being able to critically assess and scrutinise organisational process and structure in this way is key to less totalising professional knowledge and theory in social work.

Reflective Questions

1   What perspective does critical theory bring to management and governance practice in InterCreate, and how should things change with the establishment of an independent company?

2   Compare the strengths and weaknesses of critical and postmodern approaches to organisations. What is similar and what is different? How do the two approaches understand the concept of reflexivity and power relations in organisations?

Organisations as Fluid and Hyper-real (Hyper-modernity Theories)

Bauman (2000) has used the metaphor of 'fluidity' to describe the modern world as liquid modernity or in 'continuous change under stress'. We can add to this the view that in 'hyper-real' environments there are 'big issue' decisions that occur at great pace and that are almost solely reflexively governed by experts (Beck, 1992). This hyper-modernity view enables new understandings of central concerns in social work and organisational analysis today, particularly regarding issues of managing risk and 'at-risk' clients, establishing trust between staff and clients, and the role of professions in defining such risk (see Chapter 3). In the social work and social policy literature, authors such as Kemshall (2000, 2002) and Dean (2000) have focused on risk discourse in social welfare organisations and programmes. The layering in of 'risk discourse' via policy implementation is a newly intensified part of human service delivery. See Chapter 5 for a fuller discussion of risk in organisational practice.

The critical policy and practice literature in social work today has taken issue with how social problems are defined and by whom. How social needs and risks are seen to arise from these definitions is also a key concern. For example, as highlighted in Chapter 1, Jamrozik and Nocella (1998: 73) discuss the issues of how human service and health professions are centrally involved in defining social problems and setting policy agendas on the then identified problems, and, in such cases, are also involved in pathologising such problems. This important issue of social problem identification also raises concerns around how expertise, specialised knowledge and professionals are understood in the organisational perspective we have called 'hyper-modernism'.

The hyper-modern view of the organisation comes largely from some of the common ideas of theoretical sociologists such as Anthony Giddens, Ulrich Beck and Zygmunt Bauman, among others. While these theorists do not necessarily agree, there is some distinctly familiar background in their post-Marxist and critical theory concerns. None of their theorising matches the canon of poststructuralist and postmodern writing discussed previously. In counterpoint to and against the theoretical relevance of Post Modernity (PM), Giddens (1990) has argued for a kind of Radical Modernity phase, rather than, say, a postmodern society, in which the distinct feature is an intensified and reflexive global politics of self and risks that engages with the consequences of modernity. These consequences can be extremely high risk for national populations, contributing to events such as war, ecological disasters, economic depressions and the excesses of totalitarian regimes and fundamentalist movements.

Linked to these ideas is the argument that organisations, especially industrial firms, are postmodernising in particular ways that no longer fit the Fordist assumptions of mass production and consumption. These organisations are now seen to reflect a newer, hyper-modern phase of capitalism (see Crook et al., 1992; Hancock and Tyler, 2001). As mentioned, this may, in fact, be closer to what some argue to be the post-Fordist shift in work relations towards 'flexible specialisation', including specialised knowledge and skill, as the new basis of professionalism/professional practice in the workplace.

Beck (1992) also develops a theory of reflexive modernisation that focuses on the reflexive turn in the modern period to confront the reality of the social risks around us. Today, experts use the knowledge of social science and science and their social technologies to help engineer a sense of heightened or 'hyper' reality, especially over what is risky and dangerous in society. Examples include mobile phones causing brain cancer as a health risk, the risk of 'strangers' for children walking home from school, and the risk of 'unsafe' playgrounds. This encourages an anxious or uncertain view of the everyday world around us and promotes an increased reflexive monitoring and surveillance of professionals by their service organisations (e.g. schools, health and care services, workplaces).

In following this argument, new organisational and inter-organisational realities in human services and for social work reflect these hyper-modern concerns with risk, anxiety and uncertainty. The anxieties of dealing with high-risk or at-risk clients in health, community care and criminal justice areas mean that organisations and professionals need to respond to the hyper-real situations of risk in new and complex ways. Risk discourse infiltrates the management of services at the client, internal organisational and inter-organisational levels. A key aspect of this infiltration into service cultures is to emphasise 'organised irresponsibility' (Beck, 1992) or a lack of organisational accountability by shedding the most difficult or high-risk cases (see Beck, 1992; Wearing, 2001). Dean (2000) and McDonald, Marston and Buckley (2003) indicate that new moral economies have developed around risk. These create judgemental, harsh and stereotypical categories of clients that help to ration resources in the neo-liberal climate of residual welfare to only those deemed deserving.

In sum, the metaphors of 'fluidity' and 'hyper-reality' in human service organisations indicate how rapidly time and space compression in late modernity can change, warp and speed up or slow down (hence losing control of) the structure and internal and external relationship networks of organisations. In these organisations, surveillance and discipline, via reflexive monitoring of clients and supervision of staff, become intricately intertwined with the thinking and techniques of management in organisations. Professionals contribute, albeit autonomously, to these new mechanisms of social control by also classifying and conceiving clients in particular local, national and global ways (Wearing, 1998). We have further emphasised the importance of a new social work and welfare practice using Bauman's ideas on fluidity within and across organisations (Wearing and Hughes, 2014). Commonly, it is the better off who can move and remain fluid in their lifestyles, compared to those who are fixed in time and space by the stereotypical categories of the other such as 'the homeless', the single parent, 'old people', the person with 'a disability', 'the unemployed', 'the poor' and non-White and Aboriginal peoples (see also the next section on constructed others). All these populations or subsections within them have been tagged as being 'at risk' or 'high risk' populations, often in association with negative cultural representation, and have been fixed by these tags within social service administrations and increasingly through criminalisation by the criminal justice systems (Wearing, 1998). Organisations are only now coming to terms with the intensification of risk discourse and risk profiles. An interesting development in social work is that risk cases can be associated with the prediction and possible prevention of 'dangerous' professional behaviour on behalf of or towards clients by social workers (Burke, 1999: 116). We return to such issues in various chapter discussions on the ethics and accountability of social work as a profession, and how new understandings of risk are challenging these criteria for ethical conduct.

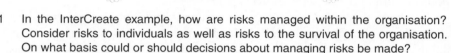

Reflective Questions

1   In the InterCreate example, how are risks managed within the organisation? Consider risks to individuals as well as risks to the survival of the organisation. On what basis could or should decisions about managing risks be made?

2   What risky situations does social work find itself in when dealing with potentially difficult or violent clients? What threat of harm or danger does social work place service users in through intervention in their lives?

Organisations and the 'Constructed Other' (Anti-racist, Postcolonial and Aboriginal Theories)

To be a 'constructed other' or part of a community of 'constructed others' is to be marginalised, different, not able to speak in the language of 'us' or 'I', and to be excluded from speaking or even listening: 'Individual struggle to change consciousness must be fundamentally linked to collective effort to transform those structures that reinforce and perpetuate white supremacy' (hooks, 1996: 195). The comments of the eminent black feminist bell hooks challenge the silencing of oppressed voices in organisational theory and discourse. Anti-colonial theory, or what is increasingly known in the literature as postcolonialism, is one of the most challenging and important frameworks for social work's understanding of human service organisations. This approach is concerned with the oppressions of imperialism, colonialism and the inferiorising of the other on the basis of 'race'. There are several connections here with anti-racist, anti-oppressive and anti-discriminatory approaches to social work practice (see Dominelli, 1997, 2002; Payne, 1997; Thompson, 1993). Furthermore, the critical organisational literature now includes some postcolonial theorising in deconstructing those western rationalities used to construct others, especially women in postcolonial feminisms (Scholz, 2010; Westwood, 2001).

The 'constructed other' metaphor can highlight the organisational construction and classification of 'difference' in the texture of organisational structures and processes, effectively the colonisation of the other (Roy, 2010). Westwood (2001), for example, uses a postcolonial critique to show how the comparative management literature appropriates and 're-presents' the other. He describes this 'appropriation of the other' as part of western rationality's essentialising, exoticising and creating identities that have 'a lack' or a 'deficit', which are then grouped together to make up the constructed racial, religious or indigenous other. Much of the social work literature could be accused of silencing black and other minority voices or of being silent on 'race', and there is some evidence for this (Dominelli, 2002).

One example used by Westwood is Gatley et al.'s (1996) management typology of cultures: from 'the pioneering action oriented cultures of the West, to cool rational cultures of the North. We then travel South to the traditional, family oriented cultures and then move on towards the reflective, idealist cultures in the East' (quoted in Westwood, 2001: 258). Westwood's point is that these characterisations of cultures and peoples are crude reductions that appropriate the localised spaces and interactions of non-white cultures and indigenous communities.

Nonetheless, these people are not passive and there are many forms of interaction between the colonised and the coloniser in their local cultures, and as mediated by organisations that move beyond direct oppression or 'inferiorisation' (see Bhabha, 1994). The postcolonial critique has itself been criticised for being one-sided about western rationality and not looking more deeply within western societies for different expressions of and oppositions to rationality (Robotham, 2000: 94). It is equally true that political systems, such as those in Australia and Britain, have both encouraged and discouraged political struggles for the equality, identity and citizenship of ethnic minorities and indigenous groups. On balance, however, the history is one of using welfare organisations and other societal agents, such as the police, to commit acts of genocide, oppression and exploitation. For example, both direct oppression and social service programmes based on racist policies have been institutionalised in social welfare systems. This was most evident in the shift during the twentieth century from colonial to postcolonial rule, with consequences for Aboriginal communities in Australia, and for African and African-Caribbean communities in Britain (see Bennett, 1999).

Applying this critique to human service organisations, we begin to understand how racism, prejudice and discrimination construct others as inferior and different – clients and staff – in management structures, workplace cultures or programme delivery (e.g. Baldry et al., 2006; Begum, 2006; Frenkel and Shenhav, 2006). This requires an awareness of how cultures and change in organisations can be challenged on the local and global dimensions of their prejudice and racism, among other colonising and oppressive organisational processes and strategies. The philosopher Homi Bhabha suggests that in postcolonial politics categories of 'others' – women, natives, the colonised, indentured and the slave – are 'becoming the people without a history' (Bhabha, 1994: 196–7). What this can suggest is that even organisational history itself is largely a white imperialist story that silences and excludes the voices of those who are written about or written out in various ways (see Reynolds, 1999). The human service worker needs to become aware of how the history of struggles and conflict over 'race' deeply embed certain white supremacist attitudes and discourses in society and therefore also in organisational forms. This itself has been illustrated in the debates over the 'stolen generation' and in frontier wars between black and white in Australia (Bennett, 1999; Reynolds, 1999).

Also, according to postcolonial theory, cultural identities are not immutable in the face of the older structural divisions of class, gender, 'race', nationality and location, but are now in disarray or fragmented. This has important implications for the politics of practice in organisations for clients and staff, as well as in the individual, group and community work dimensions of social work. Gilroy (1997: 304) uses the term 'diasporas' to understand identity as trans-national: 'diasporas are the result of "scattering" of people whether as the result of war, oppression, poverty, enslavement or the search for better economic and social opportunities'. Other writers refer to the hybridisation of identity under conditions of globalisation (Held and McGrew, 2000), postmodernism or postcolonialism (Bhabha, 1994). As the hyper-real and fluid metaphors suggest, however, this does not mean political engagement is detached from abstract systems that are global or national. Morgan's (2006) classic revised text indicates the role multinational companies and the global economy play in organisational change. The most notable outcome of neo-liberal reform is an increased focus on worker productivity and resource efficiency, which may include 'downsizing' or forced worker redundancy, particularly in periods of economic decline (see Berman, 1998).

The metaphor of the 'constructed other' in welfare or human service organisations has a history of oppositional discussions in social work practice literature around anti-discrimination and anti-racism. Lena Dominelli (1997, 1998, 2002) has been outspoken in her concerns that practitioners and educators alike take on a non-racist and counter-white view of social work (see also Chapter 7). There has also been some Australian social work writing on human service organisations from non-white perspectives, such as Jones and May's (1992) Aboriginal view on organisations and Weeks and Quinn's (2000) collection, which contains significant contributions by Aboriginal authors. As one Aboriginal social work author argues, there is a need to be highly sensitive to the cultural ways and insights of Aboriginal peoples and communities. She suggests that those who wish to work with Aboriginal people need 'to be well versed in Aboriginal culture, and respected and acknowledged by the Aboriginal community in which they live and work' (Bessarab, 2000: 84). Bessarab also says it is important to become acquainted with key Aboriginal and non-Aboriginal people who can link to appropriate others (see also Zubrzycki and Bennett, 2006).

The postcolonial approach to organisational theory suggests a double-edged strategy in challenging the logic of pure marketeering and global economics in the oppression of indigenous and minority ethnic communities (Held and McGrew, 2000; Hoogvelt, 1997). This can effectively create a politics of organisation and reorganisation from the margins that resists the cultural spaces and construction of racialised essentialism in human service encounters. From within social work approaches such as anti-oppressive practice, it is suggested that there are particular dispositions, value orientations and skills that social workers can develop to enable more 'bottom-up' positions on social work's professional role that listen to and include vulnerable and disadvantaged clients (Strier and Binyamin, 2010). Both hosts and colonisers, among other social actors, can participate in reconstructing human service organisations and social welfare spaces as the Third Space in civil society (Briskman, 2003; Frenkel and Shenhav, 2006; Roy, 2010; Wearing and Wearing, 2006).

Reflective Questions

1   What do you think are some of the tensions in the way people with learning disabilities are worked with in InterCreate? How might people with learning disabilities be treated as 'the other' in this situation and what might be some strategies for addressing this?
2   Given a stated commitment to social justice, what responsibilities does the social work profession have to challenge racist thinking? See also Chapters 7 and 9.

Conclusion

Metaphors have been used in this chapter to encapsulate and group many organisational constructs together to stand in for a theoretical approach or world view. Constructs such as needs, inputs, goals, energy, culture and structure are ways of making sense of the complex processes, form and content of organisations. The 'machine' metaphor, for example, relies on human interpretation to see how the organisation operates or what 'parts' of the organisation may not be working so well. Several key writers in the organisational literature have re-emphasised the importance of metaphors for our thinking about organisations. Morgan (2006), for example, has updated his range of metaphors since his book was first published 20 years ago to include categories such as 'flux and transformation', in order to help describe the social flow and dynamic collective change that can occur in organisations and in organisational cultures.

Each of the organisational metaphors overviewed in this chapter is recognisable in organisations that employ social workers. In many organisations, quite a few of the metaphors may be apparent in parallel. For example, in a government social services department it may be that the dominant metaphor is that of the organisation as a machine, such as a bureaucratic or rule-driven machine, or an ostensibly more efficient machine operating along managerialist and scientific principles. While such metaphors and ways of thinking may dominate in human service organisations, other metaphors may also be apparent, even though they may not carry the authority of the organisation's leadership. In social work and multi-disciplinary teams within the organisation, their work arrangements and relationships may be conceptualised as a living organism: an organic system adapting to its environment and creating the relationships and leadership necessary in order to survive and sustain itself.

Within social work organisations, including social services departments, metaphors which challenge the dominant conceptualisations in the organisation may also be recognised: upstream metaphors that question and critique the organisational power relations. Groups of social workers or other employees may form on the basis of marginalised social circumstances or identities – such as women workers or black or ethnic minority workers – and engage in strategies that seek to transform organisational practices. This can involve strategies that include challenging everyday inequalities that intersect in 'race', gender and class (Bill and Zabrana, 2009), and providing socially inclusive practice based on the human rights of vulnerable and marginalised citizens such as older people, women and children, young people, the homeless and the mentally ill, among other oppressed social categories (Wearing, 2011).

From our perspective, social workers are not just of the organisation – they have wider responsibilities – and they can influence strategically the organisations in which they operate. At the same time, we acknowledge that social workers are not always in control of their own destinies and are frequently influenced by organisational power plays and unplanned-for organisational dynamics. The tensions between the different organisational metaphors figure as we note social workers' various commitments: to the organisation and its management, to service users, to the profession and to themselves as individuals and members of society. Social workers can learn the art of studying organisations and change processes on the ground and the positive or detrimental effects caused by such change. In the next chapter, we examine organisational change and some of its intended and unintended consequences in depth.

3 Organisational Change

In this chapter we overview

- the impact of organisational environment;
- a planned approach to organisational change;
- strategic planning and operational or programme planning;
- change management approaches;
- emotions, experience and resistance to change;
- learning for organisational change.

Introduction

Some social workers complain of being overwhelmed by organisational change. There is a sense of exhaustion from being bombarded by a series of government and organisational policy initiatives and strategic plans. Some fear that we may be constantly 'reinventing the wheel'. These concerns suggest a negative and reactive orientation to organisational change, which stands in contrast to social work's often stated commitment to achieving change for the people and communities with which we work. Concerns for social justice and for social change have long been espoused as core social work values (Bisman, 2004; O'Brien, 2011), even though in practice we may often have fallen short of the ideal. Social workers have presented themselves as change agents. So why, if we are always going on about the need for change, do we often seem so negative about organisational change? What role can social work play in the organisational change and innovative strategies necessary to achieve such change?

From our perspective, some of the answers lie in the nature of recent organisational changes, the way these change processes have occurred and the extent to which social workers have been involved in planning, legitimating and evaluating these changes. The organisational change that social workers have felt most acutely has been managerialist change, and thus has often been experienced as a top-down process that is done to them, rather than as a process in which they have been able to fully participate. The need for social workers to promote organisational change, in line with the profession's values, lies undiminished and is arguably strengthened by these developments. In order to promote change in the lives of the people and communities we work with, social workers must be committed to participating in, and at times leading, organisational change.

The Environment of Organisational Change

Organisation–Environment Relations

In an Australian study of 258 community-based disability services, some important pressures that resulted in organisational change included:

- changing government policy and priorities;
- increased time spent on managerial and financial functions;
- increased competition in gaining resources;
- escalating expectations for increased efficiency;
- one-off events, such as the introduction of a goods and services tax (GST, or VAT in the UK);
- increasing pressure to be innovative;
- seeking funds from a proliferation of government programmes;
- increased regulatory activities by government;
- increased time spent defining outputs;
- increased time spent on clarifying organisational goals. (Spall and Zetlin, 2004: 290)

Many of these pressures, which are similar to those found in community or voluntary sector organisations in other western economies, reflect the demands of the wider environment in which these organisations operate. In the main, these pressures represent the changing priorities within dominant social discourses and ideologies, such as neo-liberal economic restructuring and managerialist organisational reform. While it is possible to critique organisations that bow to such pressures, it is nonetheless important to recognise that many human service organisations may undergo such changes simply in order to survive in the form they believe best meets their organisation's purpose.

So, to understand the reasons for organisational change and the experiences of such change, it is necessary to develop an analysis of organisational environments. Social workers have long had an understanding of the relevance and impact of a wider environment on people and practice, and thus these critical skills can be brought to bear in analysing organisational environments and the changes that occur in them. For Mulroy (2004), macro-level environmental factors – which include such societal/policy forces as globalisation, immigration, poverty and the market economy – impact on local communities and the organisations within these communities. However, she also argues that organisations and communities can find solutions that help break down the oppressive barriers within wider society. Organisational change, therefore, can be seen to occur in the context of interaction with a wider environment, not just as a reaction to the changes within that environment, but also as a proactive strategy to change the environment and its destructive effects.

In terms of analysing the nature of organisational environments, a common strategy within the social work and human services literature (Garrow and Hasenfeld, 2010), and in the management literature (Bourgeois, 1980), has been to differentiate the organisation's immediate task environment – including regulatory bodies, competing agencies, funding bodies, pressure groups and professional organisations – from a wider general environment, which has less of a direct impact on organisational life. This general environment comprises political, societal, legal, technological and economic dimensions and would include, among other factors, government policies and legislation, political and constitutional arrangements, societal attitudes and values, and knowledge and technological developments (Jones and May, 1992).

A range of theoretical ideas have emerged to explore the relationship between organisations and their environments, and these are usefully overviewed by Schmid (2004). Broadly, these ideas reflect some of the dominant perspectives and metaphors in organisational theory, as discussed in Chapter 2. Ecological and institutional theories appear particularly relevant to human service organisations trying to adapt to environmental change.

Ecological theories (reflecting our living organism metaphor) incorporate accounts of the birth and death of organisations and see these as arising from the capacity of organisations to occupy a particular ecological niche. Those organisations that survive are ones that contain particular characteristics that the environment requires (Schmid, 2004). Thus, by anticipating and predicting changes in the environment, organisations can develop new niches and behaviours. In this sense, changes within organisational environments offer opportunities – not just challenges – for organisational growth and development. For example, one of the community-sector disability organisations mentioned earlier could have foreseen, given the trends in government policy, the emergence of the social entrepreneurship approach to delivering human services and taken steps to develop such an approach. If developed at the right time and place, this organisation could become a leader in the field.

Institutional theories of organisation–environment relations suggest that successful organisations are those that are able to reflect the work practices adopted within their institutional environment (Suddaby and Viale, 2011). As discussed in Chapter 1, this has often involved accommodating managerialist practices, such as Total Quality Management (Suddaby and Viale, 2011). It may also involve adopting the mantle of science and rationalism in work practices or, at least, in the language used to describe work practices. For example, community disability organisations – such as those included in the study by Spall and Zetlin (2004) – may find it helpful to incorporate the practices and language of evidence-based practice, best practice, risk management and efficiency if they are to gain credibility, and, crucially, to secure ongoing funding from government. Thus, the more such organisations incorporate or are seen to incorporate institutional rules and procedures – and their symbols, myths and rituals – the greater their chance of survival (Schmid, 2004); although, in doing so, these organisations run the risk of losing their identity, values and connection with communities (Schmid, 2004).

The Impact of Environmental Change

The nature of environmental change would inevitably affect the nature of the – potentially adaptive – organisational change. Suarez and Oliva (2005), in the management literature, propose four dimensions of environmental change:

- *frequency*: the number of disturbances within the environment over a particular period in time;
- *amplitude*: the magnitude of the shift from the initial conditions as a result of the disturbance;
- *speed*: how quickly the disturbance takes place; and
- *scope*: the range of environmental dimensions – such as social, legal, technological dimensions – that are produced as a result of simultaneous disturbances.

According to Suarez and Oliva (2005), these dimensions co-occur in different ways to produce different types of environmental change. They classify *regular change* as occurring where change across all four dimensions is of low intensity and gradual – for example, the development of the theoretical literature on management and organisations.

Changes that are frequent and quick (high frequency and speed, but low amplitude and scope) are said to produce *hyper-turbulence*. The rapid production of government memoranda or guidance in relation to particular policies and practices – such as the setting of eligibility criteria for services – could produce hyper-turbulence.

Specific shock occurs when the change marks a major shift with past patterns (high amplitude) and where the speed of change is rapid, but where the frequency and scope of the change is low. For example, the deregulation or privatisation of particular industries might be seen as producing specific shock. These changes are generally uncommon and narrow in scope (Suarez and Oliva, 2005).

Where amplitude is high – that is, there is considerable deviation from past conditions – but other dimensions are low, the change is said to be *disruptive*. These changes are relatively infrequent and develop gradually, although they can produce enormous challenges for organisations. An example of such changes would be the development of information communication technology in human service organisations.

Suarez and Oliva (2005) characterise the most extreme change – *avalanche* – as low in frequency but high across the other dimensions. That is, the change is profound, rapid and affects a wide range of environmental dimensions. A good example would be the onset of a major economic crisis. In Practice Example 3.1, a real situation, HIV/AIDS organisations were faced with a dramatic change in their immediate environment.

PRACTICE EXAMPLE 3.1

The impact of environmental change on HIV/AIDS organisations

An example of environmental change which has affected voluntary or community sector organisations is the development since the late 1990s of HIV/AIDS treatments. In countries such as Britain, Australia and the USA, HIV/AIDS organisations grew from grass-roots initiatives within gay and lesbian communities in response to the AIDS epidemic among gay men in the 1980s (Hampton et al., 2016; Lewis and Crook, 2001).

Two such organisations are the Terrence Higgins Trust (THT) in the UK and the Bobby Goldsmith Foundation (BGF) in Australia. Both of these organisations emerged from the work of friends of men who died of AIDS in the early 1980s. Throughout the 1980s and most of the 1990s, the people who contracted HIV in these countries remained predominately gay men, and thus these community organisations reflected gay male culture in both their organisational membership and their safe-sex and health-promotion campaigns.

In 1996, researchers identified a way of stopping the virus from reproducing by using newly developed protease inhibitor drugs in combination with other drugs. With the use of these new 'drug cocktails', HIV became a manageable chronic illness for the majority of the traditional constituents of community HIV/AIDS organisations. However, the additional costs borne by governments in providing the new treatments have been partly recompensed by withdrawing funding from these organisations. This is despite the rate of HIV infection remaining steady and even increasing among some communities, and the need to provide support services to people living with HIV over a longer period than was originally envisaged (Lewis and Crook, 2001).

While not all organisations survived in their original form, both THT and the Sydney-based BGF continue to this day, as have other community-based organisations that were under threat in France (Weller, 2003) and the USA (Lewis and Crook, 2001). In 1999 and 2000, THT merged with a number of smaller HIV/AIDS organisations, including London Lighthouse, which was a significant provider of hospice care to people with AIDS. BGF has shifted from solely providing direct financial support to providing a personalised case management service which helps ensure clients receive the services and support – including financial assistance – to which they are entitled from other agencies, including government departments. While THT and BGF retain their focus on HIV/AIDS, other organisations, including ACON (formerly the AIDS Council of NSW), have decided to broaden their mission to include health promotion to gay, lesbian, bisexual and transgender communities, which includes strategies to address such issues as suicide, substance misuse and domestic violence.

Applying Suarez and Oliva's (2005) framework, we would argue that the changes in the environment of HIV/AIDS community organisations represented a specific shock. They involved a rapid and major shift from the past situation, although the frequency and amplitude of the change can be characterised as low. That is, the environmental change – the development of the new treatments – occurred only once and its effects were limited to a specific group of organisations. Nonetheless, the environmental change was so significant that the very survival of the community-based HIV/AIDS organisations was thrown into doubt (Lewis and Crook, 2001).

For human service organisations, the nature of external change, such as that suggested by Suarez and Oliva (2005), demands different internal change responses. Moxley and Manela (2000) conceive the different types of change response as:

- revitalisation;
- renaissance; and
- recovery.

For some organisations, changes in their environment require making small incremental modifications that are easily accommodated by reforming existing structures and procedures. Moxley and Manela classify this type of organisational change as *revitalisation*: it involves improving the organisation's performance and some of its systems, but overall does not involve any substantial restructuring of the organisation or its mission.

Renaissance change, however, does require a fundamental reconfiguration of the organisation in response to its changing environment. For Moxley and Manela (2000), this type of change is needed when there is a sense that the organisation has lost its way and that members of the organisation at different levels no longer have a sense of what it stands for and hopes to achieve: 'The agency, as it has been conceived and constituted, is dying' (2000: 319). This type of change requires a reinvigorated sense of the organisation's mission and goals and a restructuring of systems to meet these goals.

Recovery is required when the changes in the environment are so fundamental – such as avalanche change – that the organisation's survival is under direct threat. In response to such change, the organisation must, if it wishes to survive, reinvent itself with new values, new internal power relations, new understandings of social need and new strategies for meeting such need (Moxley and Manela, 2000). Adaptation to the new environment will not be immediate and there are likely to be ongoing struggles and conflict as the organisation adjusts.

Planning for Change

Lewin's Approach to Change

An understanding of planned organisational change invariably begins with Lewin's model (Bartunek and Woodman, 2015), although it should also make use of the literature on strategic planning and management, and on operational or programme planning. The planned approach reflects a rational and linear conceptualisation of change and is usually seen as 'top down' in that managers lead the change effort, albeit by harnessing the cooperation and motivation of employees. Planned organisational change – often characterised as organisational development – is typically contrasted with a change management approach, which tends to view change as emerging dynamically from within organisational systems, rather than as something that can be controlled or directed by managers. From our perspective, both approaches have something to offer to an understanding of organisational change and no doubt social workers will encounter different organisational activities that are reflective of both planned and change management approaches. The focus of this section is on planned change, while change management is considered later.

The application of Kurt Lewin's work to organisation studies equates organisational behaviour with group behaviour. For Lewin (1947), planned change can occur by understanding group dynamics within a wider environment and by taking action to shift the group's norms and practices. Lewin's approach to planned change is based on four related components: field theory, group dynamics, action research, and the three-step model of change. Field theory attempts to map the environment or field in which group behaviour occurs. Different forces within the field are said to determine group and individual behaviour, and thus changes within the field may result in changes in group dynamics. Lewin saw the field as being involved in an ongoing state of adaptation which he termed 'quasi-stationary equilibrium' (Burnes, 2004). If change is to occur then the focus should be on the group rather than the individual, as individual behaviour is bound by the rules and norms of group dynamics. Action research is needed to facilitate change: this involves the group collaboratively engaging in research, taking action, evaluating that action and then engaging in further action. For change to occur, Lewin (1947) advocated a three-step model:

1. *unfreezing*: disrupting the equilibrium that maintains current group behaviour. This may produce conflict within the group;
2. *moving*: engaging in action research methods to help the group learn new behaviours; and
3. *refreezing*: stabilising the group in a new equilibrium.

Force field analysis (FFA) is a technique used to evaluate organisational change situations and, in particular, those operating forces which are resistant to change and those that act to facilitate change (Patti, 1983). Initially developed by Lewin (1951), the underlying principle is the idea that a problem or an issue is held in equilibrium by these restraining and driving forces. A force field diagram is often used to assist the analysis. This involves identifying the change issue at the top of the diagram, and then listing the driving forces pushing on one side and the restraining forces pushing on the other. This can then help identify ways in which the restraining forces may be reduced and the driving forces increased.

Lewin's approach, in particular his three-step model, initially proved extremely popular and has been widely applied and developed (Bartunek and Woodman, 2015). One of the enduring benefits of this approach is that it helps focus attention on a particular change process at a particular point in time. While Lewin recognises that the environment of the change initiative is in constant adaptive motion – a point that is not often acknowledged by his critics (Burnes, 2004) – the three-step change strategy seeks to introduce a temporary rational and linear process to disrupt and reconfigure pre-existing group/organisational dynamics.

The rational and linear process has been expanded on by other writers and is characterised by Martin (1992) as the sequential model of change. While broadly critical of this model, Martin recognises that there is value in the way it helps remind people involved in initiating change of some of the tasks and requirements involved in change processes. Martin (1992: 322) outlines the common stages of a sequential model:

1. recognition of the problem or discrepancy in service provision by management or practitioners;
2. preparation for change through investigation of the problem, building readiness within the organisation for change ('unfreezing');
3. search for and assessment of possible solutions or innovations, selection of and building support for the best of these;
4. implementation of change, possibly after a pilot project and a consequent refinement of innovation;
5. consolidation and stabilisation of change ('refreezing'); and
6. ongoing monitoring and evaluation.

An example of a sequential model in practice is provided by Medley and Akan (2008). They document a change process in which a non-profit job assistance agency went through the processes of unfreezing, moving and refreezing in response to a declining client base. The first stage involved a survey of community perceptions of the agency, which highlighted a lack of awareness among certain groups, including men, low-income families and young people. This led to changes to the way in which employment programmes were run and how the agency engaged with local businesses, as well as to more innovative strategies to facilitate other forms of wealth generation among clients, such as home ownership. The refreezing stage involved developing a revised mission statement to reflect the broader remit of the agency.

From the 1980s – with the rise of change management approaches – an increasingly common critique of sequential models was that they are simplistic and linear. Kanter et al. (1992: 10) refer to Lewin's approach as 'organization as an ice cube' and argue that organisations are never frozen or refrozen, and if change were to occur in a stage-like fashion then these stages would overlap and intersect. However, it is argued that when the four components of Lewin's approach are analysed together, a more complex understanding of planned change emerges which recognises that change is a constant process, albeit one where the rate of change varies depending on the environment (Burnes, 2004). It is also important to acknowledge that Lewin's focus was on group behaviour and that he did not necessarily intend his work to be applied to organisational change or complex organisational systems (Bartunek and Woodman, 2015). Although Lewin's approach may have fallen out of favour with some theorists, it remains influential in management and organisational practice.

Strategic Planning

In addition to the approaches conceptualised by Lewin and others, an understanding of a planned approach to change within organisations is assisted by the literature on strategic planning and operational or programme planning. As their names suggest, strategic planning generally relates to the overall direction of the organisation, while operational or programme planning is about the day-to-day running of the organisation. If an organisation employs both approaches, then operational or programme plans should be the means by which the strategic plan is put in place.

Strategic planning involves the development of a mission, key objectives, plans for action and policies that best position an organisation to respond to the changes in its environment that are expected to arise in the foreseeable future. It is based on the assumption that a carefully planned and deliberate strategy can help organisations achieve concrete measureable results (Medley and Akan, 2008). Strategic plans will usually need to link long-range planning goals with mid-range operational plans (Glaister and Falshaw, 1999). For van Breda (2000), the value lies partly in the processes of producing the plan, not just in the final document itself. It 'forces people to stop and think about what they are doing. It helps one think about the future and about what needs to be done to achieve that future' (van Breda, 2000: 3). He argues that the plan incorporates:

- a macro strategy that is in line with the overall purpose of the organisation;
- a reading of the external and internal environment of the organisation;
- an identification of the key stakeholders in the organisation;
- an explication of the purpose, vision and mission of the organisation;
- achievable end results or outcomes;
- criteria for determining excellence within the organisation; and
- an outline of how the organisation will enable employee motivation, capacity and opportunities.

The strategic planning field has developed particular techniques to assist an analysis of the environment and to feed into the planned strategy. Possibly the best-known and most widely used of these techniques is the SWOT analysis which involves identifying the internal strengths (S) and weaknesses (W) of the organisation, as well as the opportunities (O) and threats (T) that can be found externally within its environment (Andrews, 1971). SWOT analysis attempts to facilitate a better fit between the external situation an organisation is facing and its own internal qualities. It is often conducted as a brainstorming exercise in a group or workshop format (see the example in Figure 3.1). A common critique is that the action required from the analysis is not always clear or followed through (Hill and Westbrook, 1997).

Another common technique is the PEST analysis which focuses on the political–economic–social–technological features of the organisation's environment (as discussed

STRENGTHS (internal)	OPPORTUNITIES (external)
For example: Strong public image Valued relationship with clients	For example: Increasing need for services IT developments
WEAKNESSES (internal)	THREATS (external)
For example: High staff turnover Unclear chain of command	For example: Legislative changes More competitors

Figure 3.1 Example of SWOT analysis

earlier in this chapter in relation to the general environment). Other commonly used strategic planning tools include:

- spreadsheet 'what if' analysis;
- analysis of key or critical success factors;
- financial analysis of competitors;
- core capabilities analysis;
- economic forecasting models; and
- stakeholder analysis. (Glaister and Falshaw, 1999)

Each of these techniques reflects a managerialist orientation and is invariably implemented in top-down ways. Despite this, there is recognition within strategic planning of the impact of change processes on organisational members, particularly employees, and effort is made to overcome resistance to the plan. Considerable effort is also devoted to ensuring that the plan is legitimated by those in powerful positions, such as funding bodies.

Legitimacy might also be seen to arise from the commitment to the plan from other stakeholders, such as service users. This suggests that while strategic planning is often conceptualised and implemented as a top-down process, there are ways of enabling people in less powerful positions to influence the plan. Thus, from our perspective, strategic planning processes provide unique opportunities for social workers to have their voices heard and to influence the organisation. They may also provide opportunities for engaging service users and communities – depending on how wide the definition of stakeholder is – in a change process.

Operational or Programme Planning

Operational or programme planning focuses on the setting and realisation of organisational goals in the everyday life of the organisation. Where a strategic plan exists, these goals should directly relate to that plan. Like strategic planning, operational or programme planning generally follows a rational and linear process, although the development of ongoing programme evaluation and monitoring systems within organisations suggests a potentially circular approach. For Schalock et al. (2014: 114), 'planning is based on self-assessment, builds on a shared vision that is values-based and action oriented, and results in the alignment of the organization's resources to personal outcomes and organizational outputs'.

According to Patti (1983: 69), a programme plan establishes the desired outcomes to be achieved within a time frame and the means and resources by which these outcomes will be realised. Patti further elaborates five important reasons for developing a programme plan:

1. It provides a framework within which key decisions can be made, such as how to secure funding, what staff are required and what technologies are to be utilised.
2. It specifies objectives and standards that can be monitored and evaluated to determine the success of the programme.

3. It supplies information about the operational issues so that management boards, funders and other legitimating bodies can have confidence in the programme and its likely outcomes.
4. It provides a basis for communities, other organisations and potential service users to determine if the new programme will serve their interests.
5. It serves to generate staff enthusiasm and commitment to the programme, providing energy and optimism.

Below, we outline the typical stages involved in the development and implementation of programme plans. We include the implementation and evaluation stages as these are the automatic follow-ons from the planning activity:

1. *Assessing needs*: what are the needs of the individuals, groups and communities at whom the programme will be targeted? Assessment activities include interviewing key informants, surveying communities, conducting focus groups with stakeholders and using local information and statistics, such as those collected by government statistics offices.
2. *Setting goals and objectives*: based on the needs identified, what goals should the programme aim for and, as a result, what objectives should be specified? Objectives, according to Patti (1983: 78), are statements that 'express in specific, observable, preferably measurable terms, those changes (outcomes) the program seeks to produce within some designated time period'.
3. *Developing action strategies*: how is the programme going to deliver its objectives? This includes detailing each activity that needs to be carried out, identifying what happens when, and clarifying roles and responsibilities for each activity.
4. *Identifying, accessing and allocating resources*: how will the programme be resourced? This relates not just to the direct costs, such as staffing and equipment, but also to indirect costs, such as accommodation, electricity and insurance. Will funds be diverted from existing programmes or sought from funding bodies, or will service users have to pay for the programme? Invariably, there is some degree of conflict over how funds are allocated to different goals and programmes within an organisation.
5. *Implementation of the programme*: following through with the plan, carrying out the various activities and trying to meet the objectives is the next step. For those involved in programme implementation, there are inevitably a number of issues that arise, including leadership, supervision of staff, management of resources, teamwork, decision making and information management.
6. *Evaluation of the programme*: how do we know the programme achieved its objectives? Was it experienced positively by those receiving the programme or service? Was it delivered in a way that met accepted quality standards? Different evaluation processes and methods will reflect different priorities and commitments. For example, outcome analysis and cost–benefit analysis may be driven by managerial demands, while process analysis – establishing the quality of delivery of the programme – may be more a concern of professionals and service users. Invariably, a range of evaluation strategies will be needed to ensure the effective monitoring of programme implementation.

Increasingly, evaluation is seen as something that is not just done after a programme has been implemented but as an activity that is integrated throughout and is factored into programme planning. For example, as Patti (1983) suggests, programme objectives should be framed in a way that lends itself to evaluation.

 Reflective Questions

1   Identify some form of organisational change that has occurred in an organisation with which you are familiar. How well planned was the change process? Were there unforeseen outcomes?

2   What might be some limitations with just having operational plans without a broader strategic plan?

Change Management and Learning for Organisational Change

In Chapter 2, we overviewed theories of hyper-modernity in contemporary society (as encapsulated in the fluid and hyper-real metaphors), a phenomenon which is said to be characterised by constant, rapid and reflexive change. Bauman (2000) argues that this modernity is liquid: that it is more about processes than conditions and that its hallmarks are risk and uncertainty. Thus, from this perspective, hyper-turbulence – as we characterised it earlier in this chapter – is seen as a constant feature within the environment of human service organisations.

The literature on organisational change increasingly reflects this orientation and often presents the chaotic world in which organisations operate as the rationale for the need for change (Oswick et al., 2005). The argument is that this change should not just occur once or twice, but that it should be an ongoing feature of the organisation's day-to-day life. In essence, the organisation must embrace a culture of continuous change in order to survive.

By, Oswick and Burnes (2014) thus acknowledge the rise of the idea and discourse of 'change management' within the organisations and management studies literature, and the corresponding decline in popularity – at least among theorists and academics if not practitioners – of the 'organisational development' discourse associated with planned approaches to change. Two important ideas within the change management literature are emergent change and the learning organisation. We overview these now and return later in this section to a discussion we began in Chapter 1 on reflexive learning within organisations.

The ideas related to change management and emergent change developed largely as a critique of the planned approach as encapsulated in the sequential models and Lewin's three-step model. The proponents of change management argue that it is simply not possible to plan for organisational change because the environment is too complex and is changing too rapidly (Osborne and Brown, 2005). We have already noted Kanter et al.'s (1992) opposition to Lewin's three-stage model. Kanter (1983) and others (Peters and Waterman, 1982) promote a bottom-up approach to organisational change which has been framed as 'culture-excellence'. This approach would encourage organisational cultures that enable innovation and cooperative change throughout the organisation (Burnes, 2005).

Others have pointed to the processual nature of change: that it is dynamic and complex and that 'the context, politics and substance of change overlap and inter-weave over time (past, present and future) as individuals and groups make and give sense to processes of organisational change' (Dawson, 2014: 65). Rather, change is seen as emergent: it *emerges* in an unplanned way from within organisa-tions in response to environmental changes. According to Beeson and Davis (2000: 182), 'change processes in complex non-linear systems produce new behaviour – behaviour which is not built-in, prespecified or predictable'. Although there is little managers or others can do to try to rigidly control this type of change, they may be able to facilitate it by stimulating a culture of learning within the organisation. Thus, the focus for organisations and managers is managing or facilitating organi-sational change.

The Learning Organisation

The idea of the learning organisation is promoted as a way of facilitating emergent change (Osborne and Brown, 2005). According to Tsang (1997), it is important to note the distinction between the concepts of organisational learning and the learning organisation. The former is descriptive and relates to academic studies of both indi-vidual and collective learning within organisational settings. The latter is a more prescriptive concept that seeks to inform the work of practitioners and managers. It is intended to promote positive behavioural change within organisations. Organisa-tional learning is the means by which an organisation can become a learning organi-sation, although this may be an ideal that is never fully achieved (Finger and Brand, 1999; Marsh and Doel, 2004). Nonetheless, there is growing evidence that the application of learning organisation ideas to human service organisations is impact-ing positively on performance (across different criteria), as well as on key indicators of staff morale such as organisational commitment and retention (Maynard, 2010). The use of evaluation tools and reviews of social work practice for organisational learning is also discussed in Chapter 7.

The learning organisation was popularised through the success of Peter Senge's (1990) book *The Fifth Discipline*. According to Senge, and drawing on systems theory, organisational learning should not just be about survival but it should also be generative. Thus, a learning organisation is one 'where people continually expand their capacity to create the results they truly desire, where new and expansive pat-terns of thinking are nurtured ... and where people are continually learning how to learn together' (Senge, 1990: 3). For Osborne and Brown (2005), the aim of the learning organisation is to create a culture of ongoing learning within the organisa-tion. Kerka (1995) identifies some common characteristics of learning organisations. Invariably, they are seen to:

- provide continuous learning opportunities;
- use learning to reach their goals;
- link individual performance with organisational performance;
- foster inquiry and dialogue, making it safe for people to share openly and take risks;
- embrace creative tension as a source of energy and renewal; and
- be continuously aware of and interact with their environment.

The literature on the learning organisation intersects with a wider literature on experiential learning (Kolb, 1984) and the reflective practitioner (Schön, 1983). Particularly useful is Argyris and Schön's identification of two types of learning. Single-loop learning involves identifying error and making corrections in order to better achieve existing objectives. Double-loop learning involves a more fundamental adjustment: it 'occurs when error is detected and corrected in ways that involve the modification of an organization's underlying norms, policies and objectives' (Argyris and Schön, 1978: 3). This second type of learning is a much more reflexive and critical engagement with knowledge and has the potential to transform the organisation.

To facilitate a learning organisation, Shaw (2004) emphasises the importance of human service organisations building evaluation processes into their everyday practices. Evaluation might involve surveying clients about their satisfaction with the service, determining whether or not a programme's objectives are being met, and carrying out interviews with workers to see if best practice models are being implemented. Skills in research are needed for this kind of activity and the agency may need to invest in staff training in this area. The aim would be to evaluate not just specific programmes, but also the whole organisation, as well as to encourage collaborative learning and working (Wearing, 2016).

Evaluation and Reflexive Learning for Organisational Change

Thus, agency-based evaluation strategies provide the key to effective, participatory change processes within organisations (Moxley and Manela, 2000). Critically, they can generate knowledge to assist organisational change in the face of different types and levels of environmental change. According to Moxley and Manela (2000), ongoing evaluation processes can act as an 'early warning system', as well as providing insight into how change should take place, and as a basis for determining if the changes implemented are effective.

In Chapter 1, we argued for a critical, reflexive and inclusive approach to generating knowledge for social work as it is practised within organisational settings. We emphasised the need to better understand interactions between the levels of experience within organisations – micro, mezzo and macro levels. We also identified the potential impact of wider social and cultural norms, power relations and inequalities, and wider knowledge of these levels and their interactions. Different sources of knowledge for organisational practice were identified as important: formal disciplinary knowledge, knowledge emerging from the organisation's information systems (e.g. information on service use), and personal action and reflection strategies.

Organisational learning to assist organisational change is also facilitated by participatory evaluation strategies that enable action and reflection at a group and an organisational level. Responses to organisational change require 'close to action' knowledge development and reflection. This comprises organisational planning and evaluation strategies that are tied to everyday organisational practices and that stimulate a culture of critical thinking, reflection, creativity and innovation within human service organisations.

Appreciative inquiry (AI) is one approach to change management that incorporates participatory and reflexive learning. In social work, it has much in common with strengths perspectives as its focus is on identifying the capacities and resources available to individuals and organisations, rather than on their problems and deficits (Bellinger and Elliott, 2011). According to Cooperrider and Whitney (2005: 1), 'AI offers a positive, strengths-based approach to organizational development and change management'. The AI process involves a four-stage cyclical process, referred to as the 4-D Cycle. This involves:

- Discovery: exploring what is best about the organisation, what gives it vitality;
- Dream: imagining what could be, incorporating new perspectives, generating stories about what the organisation could and should become;
- Design: sharing ideas for the future, finding common ground, developing a shared vision;
- Destiny: bringing in new participants and committing to action and innovation. (Ludema, Cooperrider and Barrett, 2001)

In an example of a change process in residential aged care, Miller et al. (2015) outline the way AI was used to move a facility from a traditional 'care for' model to one in which the residents are more in control of the decisions that impact on their life and are more integrated into the wider community. The discovery stage involved meetings, surveys and focus groups with different stakeholders, including family members and staff. To help the residents move towards the centre of decision making, a local advocacy group was brought in to facilitate residents' participation in the change process. This included creative workshops to enable people to express their views. The dream stage involved workshops that drew on feedback about how residents were becoming more in control of everyday tasks and activities, and enabled stakeholders to imagine a new vision for the facility. The design stage involved generating, through structured exercises, creative ideas for improvement. A series of areas for improvement were identified (e.g. ensuring care planning is more person-centred), mini-project groups were formed and a project plan was developed (destiny stage). Training was brought in to facilitate the achievement of the goals. The 4-D Cycle process was then repeated a year later to review the change process and its impact.

For us, there is something different in the focus of the organisational development literature, with its emphasis on top-down planned change, and the change management literature, with its attempts to stimulate a culture of learning that supports continuous change. As Oswick et al. (2005) argue, the shift in organisational change discourses from organisational development to change management reflects a movement away from seeing organisational change as a response to a problem, towards a more positive conceptualisation. Similarly, Butcher and Atkinson (2001) argue that the emergent approach to change provides a more positive understanding of the role of informal systems within the organisation. Rather than seeing these as a problem to overcome, informal systems from a change management position provide the basis for creative local initiatives. The informal relationships between employees within the organisation are the powerhouse for change.

While recognising that external demands – particularly managerialist demands – are likely to continue to be imposed on organisations and thus not all organisational change can be seen to emerge from informal organisational systems, we also emphasise the value in shifting the discussion of organisational change from a problem orientation towards a more positive approach. As we discuss later in this chapter, organisational change may provide unique opportunities for human service organisations to better respond to the needs of service users and communities and for social work employees to gain a better fit between their professional ideals and organisational realities.

Emotion, Experience and Resistance to Change

Emotion is a neglected concept within the literature on organisational change, particularly that advocating rational and planned approaches (Carr, 2001). Where the literature does examine emotional issues, these are generally framed in terms of managers understanding and overcoming resistance among their employees. According to Butcher and Atkinson (2001), the language of this work is of the imposition of the rational on the irrational. Overcoming resistance to change represents, for some, the triumph of rationality over emotion, while for others emotions are open to manipulation to ensure motivation for the change among employees.

After considering some ideas around resistance to change, we highlight the contribution of psychodynamic and grief/loss approaches to an understanding of emotion and the experience of organisational change. We also examine stress and coping as emotional and psychological issues involved in organisational change and an extension of Merton's (1957) adaptation typology. (Work stress is also examined further in Chapter 8.)

Overcoming Resistance to Change

The literature on overcoming resistance to change can be sourced back to Lewin (1947) who focused on resistance to change within the field – that is, within the environmental systems in which change takes place. Recently, the focus has been on the psychological processes that individuals experience when faced with change situations. Invariably, the approach to overcoming resistance to organisational change reflects the orientation of the change strategy itself.

If the change strategy is managerialist and implemented in top-down ways, then the focus is often on ensuring employee compliance with management's ideas.

According to Dent and Goldberg (1999), the literature on overcoming resistance to change reflects this orientation. Common strategies from this position include:

- education;
- participation;
- facilitation;
- negotiation;
- manipulation;
- coercion;
- discussion;
- financial benefits; and
- political support.

However, like Kotter (1995), they argue against an assumption that employees are innately resistant to organisational change; rather, their resistance is usually seen to arise from such factors as 'loss of status, loss of pay or loss of comfort' (Dent and Goldberg, 1999: 26). Furthermore, sometimes the problems encountered in change processes lie not so much with employees but with managers. Some barriers to coping with organisational change identified by employees in the financial sector include:

- poor communication – e.g. not being kept informed or receiving contradictory messages;
- problems with the change process – e.g. it's occurring too slowly or too fast, managers seem to have unrealistic expectations, or the change is not properly sequenced;
- ineffective relationships – e.g. managers seem remote, or behave autocratically;
- lack of consultation – e.g. employees' ideas are ignored;
- change leaders being seen as lacking skills and experience and thus lacking credibility; and
- lack of motivation among senior management – e.g. managers fail to participate in all aspects of the change programme. (Woodward and Hendry, 2004)

If, however, the change strategy is less top-down or more reflective of a change management approach, then, invariably, the strategies used to overcome resistance are likely to be different. A comparison of two articles on organisational culture and organisational change points to this difference. Reflecting a managerialist orientation, Higgins and McAllaster (2004) argue that managers need to pay attention to the cultural artefacts that help define the organisation and distinguish it from others. If the organisation is to successfully gain the commitment of employees to a change strategy, then these artefacts – including key values and norms, myths and sagas, common language, and symbols, rituals and ceremonies – will also need to change.

In contrast, Jaskyte and Dressler (2005) focus on organisational innovation and produce findings from a study of older persons' organisations in the USA, suggesting that strong adherence to a shared culture may actually act against innovation. Heterogeneity within the organisation was identified as better facilitating innovative organisational change. The authors conclude that to facilitate innovation, organisations must enable employees to 'express their creativity, be allowed to take risks, experiment, and take advantage of opportunities' (Jaskyte and Dressler, 2005: 36). This suggests that from a change management position, resistance may be considered a positive force for change within the organisation – or at least for organisational learning and longer-term innovative change. Resistance could provide an impetus for conflict and debate and result in employees and managers becoming involved in a more meaningful engagement than might otherwise have been the case had managers simply devised crafty ways of gaining employees' commitment.

Thus, the culture shift required in human service organisations is one which enables the organisation to become more open, responsive to its community and better able to learn from its mistakes. This is the antithesis of the traditional bureaucracy where individuals hide behind their job role and take refuge in the hierarchy. It also runs counter to the overly managerial organisation where the CEO acts as a 'puppeteer', and where difference is accommodated only to the extent that it improves competitiveness and efficiency. Staff and managers need to be empowered to be more creative, critical and self-aware in their organisational practice. Given the current managerialist climate, this approach is rarely seen in practice.

 Reflective Questions

1   What do you think are some of the main reasons why employees might resist organisational change?
2   Consider an organisational change situation (regardless of how minor) that you have been involved in. How did you feel about the change at the time it was proposed and at the time of implementation? What would have helped you feel more positive about the change?

Psychological Responses

An understanding of the emotional and experiential qualities of organisational change – and not just those relating to resistance to change – is also facilitated by the psychological literature, including that on psychodynamics, grief and loss, and stress and coping.

Underpinning a psychodynamic approach to organisation studies is the idea, derived from Freud's work, that the seemingly rational behaviour apparent within organisations is actually an expression of unconscious issues, concerns and forces (Kersten, 2001). A psychodynamic analysis of organisations involves 'bringing to the surface an awareness of hidden and repressed motivations, feelings and dynamics' (Kersten, 2001: 454). Thus, people's emotional responses to organisational change will be affected by both conscious and unconscious factors. For Ruch (2012), a psychodynamic analysis of management (and concomitantly managerialist organisational change) can help make visible defensive behaviours, fragmented experiences and marginalised aspects of work.

According to Antonacopoulou and Gabriel (2001), we need to develop a sophisticated understanding of the diverse experiences and meanings associated with organisational change. For example, resistance to change may be seen as a strategy to cope with anticipated loss and as 'an attempt to recover meaning or to preserve what was valuable in the past' (Antonacopoulou and Gabriel, 2001: 446). French (2001) applies the concept of 'negative capability' to organisational change. Negative capability, originally conceptualised by the poet Keats and later developed within psychoanalysis by Bion (1978), relates to a person's capacity to live with uncertainty, ambiguity and paradox, and not to react in a defensive way when faced with an ongoing change situation. When negative capability fails and an individual can no longer manage to contain the ambiguity, they may respond with avoidance, denial or other forms of resistance. Alternatively, they may rush headlong into action or try simplistically to break down complex problems into manageable bits (French, 2001).

Emotional responses to organisational change have also been characterised in terms of grief and loss (Elrod and Tippett, 2002; McAlearney et al., 2015; Zell, 2003). Perlman and Takacs (1990) drew similarities from the stages of coping with death and dying conceptualised by Kubler-Ross (1969) – denial, anger, bargaining, depression and acceptance – with sequential models of organisational change. They identified 10 phases relating to the emotional experience of the change:

1. equilibrium;
2. denial;
3. anger;
4. bargaining;
5. chaos;
6. depression;
7. resignation;
8. openness;
9. readiness; and
10. re-emergence.

For Elrod and Tippett (2002), a study of models of change – both in relation to individual and organisational change – reveals a common pattern: in general, a movement from a normal situation through a disruption and then on to a re-defined normality. In passing through a stage of disruption in terms of organisational change, it is reasonable to expect that the quality of work will be reduced. Elrod and Tippett describe this disruption as the 'death valley' of organisational change and acknowledge the support and motivation which employees need as they take their day-by-day steps through the change process. More recent applications of grief and loss theory have highlighted the continuing bonds – through ongoing inner and symbolic representations – that employees may have with the way things were (Bell and Taylor, 2011).

A stress and coping approach is also useful in understanding how people adjust psychologically to organisational change. According to Terry and Jimmieson (2003: 92), organisational change 'can be viewed as a critical life event, which has the potential to evoke stress reactions and other negative consequences'. They argue that the most common psychological reaction to organisational change is uncertainty, often produced through changes in role, as well as through perceived threats to job security, career paths, financial well-being, power, prestige and the sense of a work community. They present a stress and coping model based on Lazarus and Folkman's (1984) cognitive-phenomenological model, an evaluation of the organisational change literature, and their own research on organisational change. While some particular elements have yet to be evidenced in research findings, the overall model provides a sense, from a psychological perspective, of why and how some people experience organisational change positively and others negatively.

In Terry and Jimmieson's (2003) model, the characteristics of change events and individuals' coping resources have an indirect impact on the adjustment of employees to organisational change. Key event characteristics include the degree of employee participation in decision making, the provision of clear information about the change process, and employees' perceptions of the quality of the leadership during the change period. They emphasise the source of the information about the change and suggest that employees who rely on informal sources are vulnerable to rumour and inaccurate speculation, which will impact negatively on their experience of the change process. Individuals' coping resources include self-esteem and support from other people, such as colleagues.

Another key factor impacting on the experience of organisational change is the speed, frequency and timing of the change events. In a qualitative New Zealand study, Smollan et al. (2010) identified the timing (i.e. point in the year) as not particularly significant, except when major change occurred immediately prior to Christmas, which elicited strongly negative emotions. Sudden, frequent and rapid change was also reported to lead to unpleasant emotional responses. Crucially, the degree of control people felt they had over the change process – including the speed, frequency and timing of the change – was most often linked to positive emotions (Smollan et al., 2010). Inevitably, though, it may be difficult to draw conclusions that a change process led to one dominant emotion and that this emotion can be characterised as 'positive' or 'negative'. According to Klarner et al. (2011), what is needed is a more detailed analysis of the phases of organisational change and the way in which emotions shift over these periods.

In Practice Example 3.2, a social worker is seeking to change her organisation in order to make it more responsive to community needs.

PRACTICE
EXAMPLE 3.2

A social worker initiating organisational change

Ngaire is a social worker recently employed by YPC (Young People Connections), an inner-city not-for-profit organisation that arose from a local church-sponsored youth group about 12 years ago. While YPC is independent of the youth group, many of those involved as volunteers have been youth group members and a number of those on YPC's board are from the local church. In addition to Ngaire, YPC is also staffed by a manager, chaplain, housing project worker, receptionist and about 20 volunteers.

Over the period of the organisation's existence, the demographic make-up of the local population has changed considerably: from a largely white Anglo population to a more ethnically diverse community, with an increasing number of refugees settling in the area.

The original purpose of YPC was to provide support services and material resources to young homeless people who had made contact with the church and youth group. For many years, the youth group had tried to reach out to local disadvantaged young people but found that they couldn't manage this without paid staff. YPC served this function well for a long time, developing a range of programmes, such as peer mentoring, life coaching, life skills workshops, and assistance finding accommodation. However, in the last few years, referral rates and total client contacts have dropped about 30 per cent and the organisation may be at risk of losing its contract for the accommodation assistance service because it is having difficulty meeting its required targets. On starting work at YPC, Ngaire quickly discovered that people from ethnically diverse backgrounds and refugees were significantly under-represented in the organisation's client group, despite considerable need among these local residents. When she approached other local agencies to provide feedback on their perceptions of YPC, it was reported that young people were wary of the organisation's affiliation with a religious group, and that they would be reluctant to talk with the staff there about some key issues such as drug and alcohol use, sexual relationships and family conflict.

During a recent supervision meeting with her manager, Ngaire raised her concerns about YPC's direction and suggested that the organisation develop some kind of strategy to address the issues. However, the manager expressed the view that the organisation should not lose touch with its core constituency, nor alienate the volunteers and board members which he described as the 'backbone' of the organisation. Nonetheless, he acknowledged that if the organisation is to survive then change is needed. After a number of meetings within the staff team and with the board, it was agreed that the organisation would undertake a six-month 'knowledge-building exercise', involving a series of research activities (such as focus groups, interviews with key stakeholders and follow-up interviews with former clients). It was agreed that this would also involve people from diverse ethnic backgrounds and people who had never had contact with the agency before. Following this 'knowledge-building exercise', it is planned to hold a community forum to present the results and discuss ways forward. Ngaire was appointed as project manager for the overall change initiative.

Reflective Questions

1   What do you think will be some of the key challenges for Ngaire in pursuing this organisational change initiative? What strategies could she put in place to overcome these challenges?

2   Consider some of the changes that the organisation could implement as a result of the 'knowledge-building exercise' and the community forum. What could be done to ensure that workers and the organisation overall are receiving better feedback on the quality and effectiveness of its work into the future?

Integrity and the Experience of Organisational Change

Our final reflection on emotion and the experience of organisational change focuses on the concept of integrity or being true to oneself (Jones, 2000). Banks (2010) identifies three versions of professional integrity: morally good or right conduct; standing up for or being committed to something; and having the capacity to engage in critical self-reflection to promote responsibility taking. Each of these understandings of integrity can be challenged in times of organisational change, particularly if this change is experienced as a top-down process.

However, Jones highlights the potential of organisational change to actually enable a better fit between workers' espoused values and the realities of organisational practice. He draws his observations from a series of change management workshops with 80 human services staff in the UK. Three main responses to organisational change were identified:

- *Engagement*: workers identify the possibility for putting into effect important values or for new convergences between values and practices. There is a sense of hope and a commitment to learning and innovation. Examples included being involved in new working parties and contributing to the development of protocols and service standards.
- *Overt compliance/private resistance*: workers go along with the change process but only to the minimum degree possible, while continuing to do what they used to do (and which is now considered redundant by management). 'In constructing integrity, then, there is an embattled view of fighting against the worst excesses of the incoming system and of not being drawn into collusion with it' (Jones, 2000: 369). An example included continuing to provide counselling or support when the job had basically been reclassified as administrative. In this response, hope is balanced with despair.
- *Withdrawal*: involves withdrawing from active participation in the workplace while still officially being an employee. It might be apparent through long periods of absence, possibly as sick leave, or the symptoms of burnout. Withdrawal – either physically or emotionally – is the only means by which the person can maintain their integrity. Despair is the predominant feeling and where there is hope it is found outside of the workplace.

Jones (2000) noted the absence of what was hoped to be a fourth strand of responses: a collective form of resistance or rebellion. In Jones's analysis, we discover that employees' – and particularly social workers' – response to organisational change may not just be a knee-jerk instinctive resistance, but a response that speaks of the nature of the change being implemented. Where the change promotes integrity in the workplace, staff may be motivated and fully engaged in the change process; however, it is understandable that where integrity is threatened, the responses are likely to be less positive.

Conclusion

Social work has undergone enormous change in recent years. The emergence of the post-industrial labour market and the rise of neo-liberal and managerial orthodoxy in human service organisations have challenged the identity and coherence of social work as a professional occupation. These changes have not just been experienced by those writing about or researching social work, but, importantly, they have also been directly experienced by social workers 'on the ground' as employees in human service organisations.

However, while much of the social work literature on organisational change focuses on the negative effects of managerialism, it is also important to recognise the benefits that can come from other forms of organisational change. As Jones (2000) suggests, no doubt there have been many organisational changes that have produced positive outcomes for the people we work with and that have enabled social workers to gain a closer fit between their ideals and values and the realities of their day-to-day practice within human service organisations. For us, social workers need to actively engage in change strategies initiated within organisations in order to promote social work values and wider social change. Additionally, as we examine further in Chapter 6, there is also considerable potential for social workers to exercise formal and informal leadership roles within organisations by promoting change strategies. Central to leadership, and facilitating organisational change, are effective communication and the ability to work collaboratively with others. This is the focus of our next chapter.

4 Communicating and Collaborating

In this chapter we overview

- responding to emotions in the workplace;
- conflict management;
- communicating via information and communication technology;
- inter-agency collaboration;
- inter-disciplinary teamwork.

Introduction

It would be nice to say that most of social workers' days involve communicating directly with clients. The reality, however, is that much of our time is actually devoted to communicating within and across organisations, for instance negotiating with colleagues, completing paperwork and participating in team meetings. However, rather than being distractions from our real work, these sorts of activities are central to working effectively with service users and communities. For example, without an ability to manage conflict in our relationships with colleagues, then access to resources for clients may be blocked. If we are not able to use computer-based client records effectively and with an awareness of their impact on our practice, we may not be responding to the complexity and depth of clients' needs.

We have argued already that social workers, in order to be effective, need to be competent, strategic and ethical organisational operators. We also recognise that the active and reflexive involvement of social workers in the organisations in which they work will encourage such effectiveness. Implicit in this is a recognition that social workers need to be effective communicators within their own organisations and with people in other organisations. The verbal and non-verbal skills required in organisational practice are similar to those needed in other areas of social work practice, as detailed by Egan (2014) and O'Connor et al. (2006, 2008). Our initial focus is on three particular areas of communication for organisational work: responding to emotions in organisations, conflict management, and communicating using information and communication technology. We then examine the communication and other strategies needed to work effectively within teams and when working collaboratively with other agencies. First, we turn to emotional issues.

Responding to Emotions in Organisations

Effective organisational communication requires attention to the emotional life of the organisation and a capacity to acknowledge and, where appropriate, respond to our own emotional experiences and those of others, including managers, colleagues and service users. According to Trevithick (2014), awareness of emotions and feelings is central to social workers' 'use of self' in their relationships with clients and in other aspects of their work, such as their relationships with managers and colleagues. Throughout the book, we have noted the dominance of rational approaches to understanding organisations, such as when engaging in organisational change, planning and decision making. A concern is that while a rational approach may, for many, remain an ideal in organisational life, the everyday lived experience of people within organisations often fails to live up to this ideal. Kersten (2001: 452) says that many of us work in pathological organisations 'where conflict, contradictions, and recurring problematic behaviors are the norm, rather than the exception'. One of the major problems, according to Carr (2001), is that all the talk about rationality either avoids or problematises emotion – often framed as irrationality:

> In our everyday experience in work organisations we have become all too familiar with the idea that 'rationality' – along with its close cousin, 'efficiency' – is the sensible 'good guy' that is to be used as the touchstone by managers. In the shadows it seems there 'lurks' a perceived alternative or dichotomous 'bad guy' called 'emotion' or 'emotionality'. (2001: 421)

Yet, the idea that emotions cannot be part of organisational life, and the political context in which it plays out, is illusory. In both managerialism and neoliberalism, emotions and emotional language are employed to frame certain individuals, experiences and situations as worthy or problematic. For example, in Britain, austerity rhetoric stresses the guilt and shame associated with supposed profligate welfare spending, as well as the shame of being 'welfare dependent' (Clayton, Donovan and Merchant, 2015). Managerialism also seems captured by the anxiety of not knowing how to control the complexity of everyday social work practice, or at least is an attempt to manage this anxiety (Ruch, 2012).

The illusion of rationality is also critiqued by Hoggett and Miller (2000) in their discussion of the emotional life of community organisations. They argue that the dominance of rational models of social change in community development not only underemphasises the complexity of social systems and capacity for human agency, it also ignores the emotion and passion necessary for individual and collective action. This highlights a useful point: that emotions may not just be framed as negative experiences or as having negative impacts on organisations, but may also be understood as a positive aspect of organisational life and be necessary for carrying out the organisation's work. For example, in brainstorming organisational change initiatives, social workers may want to display their own enthusiasm and excitement about the potential of working creatively together and about the sorts of changes that could occur. Having a deeper insight into the feelings and emotional worlds of colleagues and clients can mean that more appropriate communication and responses to problems in the workplace can be undertaken. Again, interpersonal skills that involve empathy and respect for others can be a highly valued asset for positive organisational action, change and growth.

Sources of Emotions

We identify three sources of emotions that impact on organisational life, based on Hoggett and Miller's (2000) conceptualisation of emotions in community life. First, at a personal or micro level, people have emotional needs, which they seek to have recognised and fulfilled. These include needs for companionship, belonging, appreciation, affection and respect. These needs are present and sometimes fulfilled in our workplace. Those of us who may at times have been out of work may appreciate particularly the role of work organisations in meeting these sorts of emotional needs. What happens then when these needs are not met in the workplace, or if they are undermined and challenged by organisational experiences?

Second, just as there is collective thinking at a societal or macro level (e.g. via discourses) so too are there collective emotions (Hoggett and Miller, 2000). For example, racism or homophobia can be considered to be as much a societal collection of expressed feelings (e.g. hatred and fear) as they are a collection of ideas or beliefs. These collective emotions are present in organisational life, just as they are in other contexts. They will inevitably impact on how people – such as those from ethnic minority backgrounds or gay and lesbian people – experience the organisation.

Third, it is also possible to recognise that people in particular groups (at a mezzo level) have common emotional experiences. Each group – in this case, each organisation and probably each team within the organisation – can be seen to express particular emotions and, according to Hoggett and Miller (2000), to express a dominant emotional culture. For example, apathy may appear to permeate the social networks within an organisation or team, rather than be simply an individually expressed emotion. A new member of the organisation may easily find themselves taking on the dominant emotion expressed within the group.

Thus, our emotional experience of an organisation could be seen to emerge from the unique interaction between each individual's emotional needs and experiences, the societal collective emotions transmitted within the organisation, and the emotional culture expressed by our particular organisation or team. This experience is also influenced by non-work aspects, such as family life.

Areas of Emotional Complexity

All work has emotional qualities, particularly where that work involves contact with other people. However, arguably social work and other human services work involve a more frequent and intensive emotional labour than other jobs (Thompson, 2015). Dwyer (2007: 49) says:

> I know what it is to wake in the night feeling pangs of worry about a service user, or some other aspect of my practice as a social worker. Even though I have done my best, will the relatives of that person criticise and condemn me for supporting the service user to take risks? Will my employers support me if things go wrong? Will the person whom I did not section commit suicide? Along with many approved [mental health] social workers, I have felt exhausted after doing a distressing mental health act assessment resulting in a section [involuntary admission to hospital] late on a Friday night, and have then been unable to stop running the circumstances through my mind until Sunday tea-time.

Emotional labour refers to the managing of other people's emotions and controlling of our own emotions as an inherent part of the service provided (Hochschild, 1983). Social workers are required to hear other people expressing painful emotions, such as anger and despair. We are also required to draw on our own feelings and express our own emotions as if they were a tool. Empathy involves being aware of our own emotional response to other people's emotions. Taking on and enacting leadership roles within organisations also involves emotional labour, particularly with respect to the need to influence the emotional climate of the organisation and positively value the work and identity of employees (Iszatt-White, 2009).

Later in this chapter, we examine issues involved in collaboration and teamwork. For teams, all of the issues and conflicts arising from group membership are likely to be critical in the emotional experience of the members. Additionally, tensions around multi- and inter-disciplinary work – such as anxieties regarding status and role – are likely to affect emotional experiences. One of the closest emotional relationships a social worker can have in the workplace is with a supervisor, and when it works well it can be supportive, empowering and challenging. Sometimes, though, supervision can produce strong negative emotions; this may arise in the normal course of good supervision (e.g. when receiving feedback that is difficult to take on board), but it is more likely where conflict or other difficulties emerge in the relationship.

Understandably, where social workers experience negative pressures on their role and identity, then complex emotions are likely. In the current climate, this is most likely to emerge from threats to status and autonomy arising from increased managerialism and competition with other professions in the labour market. According to Jones (2000), social workers often find it difficult to match their ideals of social work with their organisational realities. In these dilemmas, they struggle to maintain a sense of integrity – or being true to oneself and one's profession – while accommodating management and organisational demands. The key tension is between the emotions of hope and despair.

Organisational change, as we discussed in Chapter 3, is likely to elicit strong emotions among employees, social workers included. We considered some factors that might lead to a positive response to organisational change and thus it is possible to recognise that people may not always respond negatively to change situations. Indeed, change may be a source of excitement and motivation. However, change situations are likely, at least initially, to be accompanied by some degree of anxiety. This may not mean that people are innately oriented to resist change (Dent and Goldberg, 1999), rather that people struggle to deal with the emotional experience of change, particularly in relation to a loss of how things were. Indeed, as noted in Chapter 3, it is quite common within the organisations literature to find references to grief and loss theory – such as Kubler-Ross's (1969) stages of grief – when describing the emotional experience of organisational change (Elrod and Tippett, 2002).

Of all the emotions that are experienced within the workplace it is fear that is probably the most detrimental to both individual well-being and organisational functioning. Fear can arise from a sense of insecurity, possibly as a result of organisational change, as well as from direct threats, such as bullying or harassment. It is identified as one of the major causes of organisational silence – the times when employees don't speak up when they know they should, undermining their organisational and social responsibilities (Kish-Gephart et al., 2009). Overcoming fear to give voice to concerns requires enormous courage and emotional resilience (Smith, 2007).

Social workers' capacity to deal with the complexities, including the emotional complexities, of our work has important ramifications for the quality of organisational practice, and ultimately for the quality of service delivered to clients. As discussed in Chapter 3, social workers may need to develop a degree of negative capability; that is, a capacity to live with uncertainty, ambiguity and paradox (French, 2001). This is a challenge as there are inevitably times in social work practice when we are confronted by complex situations where there are competing ethical principles and where there may be no perfect decision that will make all parties happy. Similarly, as noted, social workers may experience hostility, harassment or other threats in the workplace, leading to fear. If workers are unable to cope emotionally with such difficulties, then they may respond by avoidance, denial or other forms of resistance.

Thus, practitioners need a degree of emotional intelligence in order to manage their own emotions and respond effectively to those of others (Morrison, 2007). Broadly, emotional intelligence refers to the ability to monitor emotions and to use this information to guide action. Goleman (1996, cited in Morrison, 2007: 246) says that emotional intelligence is 'being able to motivate oneself and persist in the face of frustrations; to control impulse and delay gratification; to regulate one's moods and keep distress from swamping the ability to think; to empathize and to hope'. Morrison argues for the need for practitioners to develop *intra*personal intelligence – self-awareness and self-management of emotions – as well as *inter*personal intelligence – awareness of others' emotions and relationship management. Emotional intelligence also involves an awareness of how emotion impacts on – and sometimes can help clarify – thinking and decision making (Ingram, 2013). To avoid the traps of street-level bureaucracy and defensive social work (as discussed in Chapter 5), social workers need to recognise their own emotional experiences and, similarly, be able to recognise and respond to the emotional experiences of others within the organisation. In Practice Example 4.1, a team is faced with complex emotions when a staff member acts unprofessionally.

Acknowledging and responding to powerful emotions

John has worked as a social worker in a youth offending team for about 12 years. He is a well-liked member of the team, although some team members have expressed concerns that John has difficulty establishing appropriate boundaries between himself and his clients. On a number of occasions, he has been formally cautioned by his supervisor for inviting young people to his home and arranging activities with them on the weekend while he is off duty. This contravenes the organisation's policy on appropriate conduct with young people.

The issue came to a head when a complaint was lodged by a parent to the duty social worker. She complained that she didn't know where her 15-year-old son (Graham) was, although he had had an appointment with John earlier that day (even though it was John's day off). After tracking John down, the duty social worker discovered that Graham had been playing computer games at his house. The duty social worker took the issue up with the manager, who gave a final warning to John the following day.

This situation generated strong feelings between Graham's parents, John, the duty social worker and the manager. While there was no suggestion that there had been any abuse, the parents felt that John's behaviour was unprofessional and that their son was potentially at risk. The duty social worker was also upset with John because she had to deal with the parents' initial anxieties and with their anger once they discovered what had happened.

In dealing with the strong feelings relating to this situation, the manager organised a series of meetings with Graham's parents and with John and the duty social worker. A key part of these meetings involved encouraging people to identify and name the emotions they were experiencing and to clarify the impact the situation had on them. The situation was partly resolved when John recognised the impact his behaviour had had on the other people involved and when he agreed to work closely with his supervisor on boundary issues. Through this supervision process, John developed a greater awareness of his emotional responsibilities in relation to clients and other staff. Members of the team also decided to seek out training on conflict management.

Responding to Conflict in Organisations

One form of communication which inevitably involves emotional investment is interpersonal conflict, and social workers are routinely required to respond to conflict situations within organisations. We need to be able to understand, respond to and even, sometimes, engage in conflict. While the latter might be surprising, sometimes engaging in a degree of conflict is necessary to ensure effective organisational functioning (e.g. that poor or unethical performance is not left unchallenged). And sometimes it is important in pursuing an issue of justice or equity, such as when a group of clients or staff are marginalised because of particular personal characteristics or a community affiliation (e.g. coming from a non-Anglo cultural background).

Conflict often signifies the need for change (Parker, 2015), but of course conflict can have damaging outcomes for individuals and for the organisation as a whole and needs to be engaged with carefully.

Three broad components of conflict can be identified: interests, emotions and values (Condliffe, 2012). When responding to conflict situations, it is important to respond first to the emotional dimensions of the conflict and then to the competing values and interests (Condliffe, 2012). The value of responding to the emotional aspects was highlighted in Practice Example 4.1. Acceptable levels of disagreement and response strategies are culturally defined and often highly gendered; for example, in western cultures physical violence as a means of resolving conflict has traditionally been seen as more culturally acceptable for men than women. Conflict situations can be seen as involving a number of stages:

1. *articulation*: saying there is a conflict and what the nature of that conflict is;
2. *mobilisation*: seeking out others or other information to support your point of view;
3. *personalisation*: targeting a particular person and expressing emotions towards them, e.g. anger, disappointment, frustration. Personalisation may involve some attempt to discredit the person, which may end up escalating the conflict;
4. *redefinition*: rethinking the options, including possible strategies for resolution; and
5. *resolution and institutionalisation*: resolving the conflict (e.g. one party accepts defeat or compromise is made) and restructuring the relationship to accept this and prepare the way for managing future conflict. (O'Connor et al., 2006, 2008)

How people handle conflict situations can vary. The most common styles identified from research include:

- *integrating*: a collaborative style that seeks to maximise advantages for both parties;
- *compromising*: both parties give some ground to resolve the issue;
- *obliging*: one person denies their own interests by acceding to the other's position;
- *avoiding*: one party withdraws from the conflict and consequently the other party's position prevails; and
- *forcing*: one party forces their interests to be accepted, at the expense of the other party's interests. (Meyer, 2004)

The integrating style is usually demonstrated through research to be the most effective in terms of reducing disruption to the workplace and maximising performance, whereas forcing styles tend to be associated with workplace accidents, absenteeism and generally increasing the intensity of conflict situations (Meyer, 2004).

Integrating styles are thus promoted as a basis for successful conflict resolution and are integral to common resolution strategies: negotiation, mediation, arbitration and reconciliation. These conflict resolution strategies are usually discussed as methods of alternative dispute resolution (ADR) in that they are considered alternatives to legal remedies. While this terminology implies their usefulness in such arenas as community justice, relationship breakdown and industrial relations, they can also be identified as strategies occurring within and between human service organisations.

Negotiation

Negotiation is a non-assisted form of conflict resolution; that is, it does not involve third-party intervention. Lens (2004) identifies a range of situations where social workers are likely to be involved in negotiation. These include case advocacy: where workers negotiate with managers or other organisations to further the interests of a particular service user. It is also a common strategy used in service brokering (where workers negotiate with a range of services to set up a package of care) and in class or cause advocacy (where workers negotiate with law and policy makers to further the interests of a group or 'class' of people around a particular issue). Lens also identifies negotiation as a technique used within a problem-solving approach to practice, and, in particular, argues that the modelling of appropriate negotiation skills by workers can assist clients in expanding their own problem-solving capacity.

A particular approach to negotiation that is widely used within the legal and business sectors is principled negotiation (Fisher et al., 1991). Lens (2004) applies this approach to social work. It is based on four principles:

1. *separate the person from the problem*: this requires negotiators to hold back from blaming the person and to create a positive working relationship. It is important to 'acknowledge an adversary's humanness and that emotions can become entangled with the problem, creating misunderstandings and hurt feelings that can impede its resolution' (Lens, 2004: 508);
2. *focus on interests not positions*: this involves the negotiator stepping back from an entrenched position and looking to see if both parties have some interests that coincide;
3. *invent options for mutual gain*: the negotiator should try to brainstorm different solutions with the other party's interests in mind and introduce these ideas into discussions if no other mutually agreed solution emerges; and
4. *use objective criteria*: this requires negotiators introducing credible knowledge and procedural fairness into the negotiation process so that decisions are based not so much on a battle of wills as an evaluation of what might be best in the given circumstances.

The use of objective criteria is particularly important where the negotiator perceives him- or herself to be in a less powerful position (Lens, 2004). The application of criteria can express an authority that counteracts the pre-existing authority of the other party. While power differences can be challenging, inevitably if the other party does not hold power – that is, the power to change the situation – then there would be little point in negotiating with them in the first place. In summary, the value of negotiation can be that, if done well and in a principled way, it 'pays equal attention to relationships and substance and provides a framework for working out disagreements where both parties can feel they have won' (Lens, 2004: 506–7).

Mediation

Mediation is an assisted approach to conflict resolution in that it involves a third person, albeit without the power to make a decision in favour of either of the two disputant parties. Mediation aims to assist people to find their own solutions to their difficulties (Mantle and Critchley, 2004). The main activities involve getting people to articulate their concerns, suggest solutions, discuss areas for compromise and try to reach an agreement (Severson and Bankston, 1995). The benefits of mediation can include favourable agreement, satisfaction, improved relationships, procedural justice and improved problem solving (Wall et al., 2001).

Severson (1998) argues that mediation is well suited to social work: the 'win–win' orientation of mediation sits easily with social work values such as respecting the dignity and worth of every person, the importance of maintaining relationships, and pursuing social justice. In social work discourse, mediation appears as an everyday part of generic social work practice (e.g. as something that is regularly needed to manage organisational relationships), as an activity undertaken by other professionals (e.g. lawyers) and as a central part of social work in specific practice areas, such as in assisting families and children in separation and divorce proceedings, and in work bringing victims and offenders together to seek restorative justice (Mantle and Critchley, 2004). According to Severson and Bankston (1995), social work also has much to offer mediation (e.g. its relationship, problem-solving and communication skills), although there is sometimes a danger that social workers may slip into a counselling role with one or both parties, thus undermining the mediation process.

Arbitration

Arbitration is another form of assisted conflict resolution and involves a third party who has the authority to make a decision in favour of either of the two disputant parties. Unlike negotiation and mediation, arbitration is rarely discussed in the social work literature as an intra-organisational strategy. Most of the literature on arbitration relates to it as a method of resolving industrial disputes (e.g. to avoid strikes) and its framing as a mechanism within various pieces of legislation or as a resolution strategy recommended by the courts (e.g. to resolve neighbourhood disputes). Nonetheless, it is likely that informal arbitration processes do occur within human service organisations, most probably with a manager or supervisor acting as the arbitrator of conflicts between employees.

Typically, arbitration procedures reflect legal or quasi-legal processes. For example, in industrial relations arbitration involves a third party holding a hearing for disputants to state their positions, call witnesses and provide evidence for their positions (Ross and Conlon, 2000). After considering the evidence, the third party produces a binding decision. The benefit of arbitration compared to negotiation and mediation is that it usually produces a settlement (Ross and Conlon, 2000).

Ross and Conlon (2000) also highlight the ways arbitration can be used in conjunction with mediation. For example, if mediation is unsuccessful then arbitration may be presented as the next step in the conflict resolution process. Knowing that arbitration is the next step and thus knowing that the final decision will be taken out of their hands may provide the necessary motivation for disputant parties to resolve the conflict on their own terms.

Reconciliation

The need for reconciliation emerges from the experience of conflict and the desire to rebuild relationships. In a social work context, reconciliation is often discussed in relation to restorative justice where offenders are confronted by the impact of their actions on victims, are called on to make amends and thus are enabled to take greater personal and social responsibility for their behaviour. However, reconciliation can be considered a valued strategy in any conflict situation, especially where there is a need to maintain positive relationships, such as in a workplace. Key to reconciliation is apology and forgiveness (Gaertner, 2011), which reflect an emotional as well as a cognitive commitment to restoring the relationship. This is understandable in situations where there is a clear transgressor and victim. However, even in relatively mutual conflict situations, it is possible to apologise for and forgive, on both sides, misunderstandings, hurtful emotional responses and communication failings. Thus, reconciliation involves redressing specific wrongs that have occurred and it is important that the nuances of the transgressions are listened to and acknowledged (Gaertner, 2011). For Ren and Gray (2009), reconciliation may also require the demonstration of concern by the transgressor, and some form of restitution or compensation. How this takes place is culturally defined, not just in relation to societal culture but also workplace or organisational culture, and may be enacted through ritual (Ren and Gray, 2009).

An understanding of reconciliation has been influenced by the practices of conflict transformation arising in the field of peace and conflict studies. Here, there is a recognition that conflict is not just necessary but important in pursuing issues of social justice (Parlevliet, 2009). Conflict should be actively engaged in to pursue positive social (and also potentially organisational) change. However, this approach is not so much about resolving small disputes (although this may be important), as it is about facilitating deeper change whereby a new vision, that is jointly shared, can emerge from the conflict. Throughout this process – which may be quite lengthy – there needs to be a lot of effort put into maintaining positive relationships with all parties so that the conflict can be managed and people can be involved in its resolution. In this context, reconciliation plays a key role in healing and forging ahead with the new understanding and vision.

Reflective Questions

1   Consider a conflict situation you have been involved in or the situation outlined in Practice Example 4.1. What would have been the plusses and minuses of the different conflict resolution strategies?
2   What skills do you think social workers have that can help manage conflict in human service organisations?
3   If relationships have been damaged, what would be the potential for reconciliation and how should this be pursued?

Communicating via Information and Communication Technology

As with most parts of society, the social work profession and human service organisations are being transformed by the expansion of information and communication technology. Communication with clients is increasingly employing email, Skype and text messaging (Mishna et al., 2012), while social work interventions are making use of web-based programs and smartphone apps (Reamer, 2015). For each successive cohort of graduating students, online communication will be the norm rather than the exception. In a study of 1088 Australian health and allied health (including social work) students, 52% of first-year and 50% of final-year students said that online media was their preferred primary source of information, while Facebook was used by 93% of first-year students and 91% of final-year students (Usher et al., 2014). For human service organisations, client information systems are becoming more complex and are arguably shaping the nature of social work roles (Gillingham, 2016). Further, while the expansion of social media presents opportunities for collaboration and participation, there are also key risks for organisations in relation to privacy and misinformation.

Email communication is ubiquitous for both informal and formal communication in and between human service organisations. As many would be aware, there are some key limitations with email communication. Group communication via email (which is asynchronous) appears less effective in producing collaborative written documents (such as reports) than face-to-face meetings or synchronous computer-mediated communication (e.g. via Skype) (Barile and Durso, 2002). The circulation of multiple drafts of documents around an organisation via email makes changes difficult to track, resulting in a lack of confidence in which version of the document is the most up-to-date or authoritative. Sometimes the authors of the material are hard to identify and the document may end up in the hands of an unintended reader (e.g. one outside the organisation) (IText Working Group et al., 2001). Saving to the cloud (online, rather than on an individual computer) provides one possible solution, although there remain questions about the security of documents saved to the cloud (Ko and Choo, 2015).

In many organisations, especially statutory agencies, the use of online client information systems is expanding rapidly. Although these systems may not require extensive writing, what is written or selected (often from pull-down menus) has considerable significance. Great care is required to ensure that what is entered or selected is not only correct, but also that the ramifications of what is entered or selected are carefully considered. While this technology certainly has the potential to enhance practice – for example, by helping practitioners to access information quickly and enabling them to follow procedures easily – it has been critiqued as limiting professional autonomy and increasing managerial control (Broadhurst et al., 2010). According to Garrett (2005: 541), in relation to child welfare systems, there is a danger that information and communication technology

> could be viewed as providing swift and easy 'solutions'. That is to say, a greater reliance on databases and other e-technologies risks promoting the

idea that complex social problems relating to children and families requiring child welfare services can be quickly solved.

As discussed in the next chapter, this technology is increasingly being used to manage risk. However, concerns have been raised that the way in which it is being employed does not sufficiently account for the diversity and complexity of specific service user situations. There is also a concern that technology 'all too easily erases the agency of the service user' (Broadhurst et al., 2010: 1059). These issues have been documented in public inquiries in child protection in both Australia and the UK (Gillingham, 2016).

Nonetheless, the expansion of such technologies is inevitable within social work and social workers will need to become skilled in their use, as well as aware of their limitations. The need for practitioners to use data management systems effectively is highlighted by Carrilio (2008), who argues that the data that can be generated is essential in the context of an evidence-based and competitive service environment, where funding is often dependent on demonstrated effectiveness to achieve outcomes. Key barriers for social workers engaging with the systems include not feeling comfortable with computers, negative attitudes towards evaluating practice, lack of support to help people use the systems, and lack of understanding of the purpose and utility of the data being collected (Carrilio, 2008; Naccarato, 2010). Clearly in some cases, the problems lie with the design of the technology rather than with the users. The work of IT developers on client information systems has typically relied on input from managers rather than practitioners (Baker et al., 2014; Gillingham, 2016). Gillingham (2016) outlines the potential for participatory design by involving the end users – social work practitioners – in developing this technology. The potential here is the development of information systems that reflect and support the complexity of practice – for example, by greater acknowledgement of variability and by building in opportunities for reflexivity (Baker et al., 2014).

For many organisations, it is the proliferation of social media which is resulting in some key challenges, as well as opportunities. Most organisations have some kind of social media presence – such as on Facebook, Twitter or Instagram – and wrestle with how to manage their public image in this domain. This technology has the potential to facilitate innovative ways of making and maintaining contact with clients and communities, as well as innovations in how to carry out and fund work. For example, crowdfunding and crowdsourcing via social media – where money and resources are accessed from a wide range of individuals online – can assist organisations to maintain programmes (e.g. advocacy campaigns) independent of traditional funders and their agendas. How staff make use of social media also poses potential risks to clients and to the organisation, such as through breaches to privacy (Hughes, 2016) and professional boundaries (Reamer, 2015). For organisations and employees, a critical resource is a social media policy, which sets out the principles underpinning the appropriate use of social media in the organisation, who is responsible for social media content, and how this will be maintained over time. This is usually framed by a legal context relating to such things as privacy, copyright, harassment and bullying, discrimination, defamation and spam. Key things to consider include the tone of language (professional, friendly), the accuracy of information and the appropriateness of advice and opinion giving. According to Kimball and Kim (2013), senior managers should develop such policy in collaboration with social media users across the organisation, as well as with IT specialists, human resources staff and legal personnel.

Learning to work effectively with new information and communication technologies is no doubt an ongoing challenge. Yet, clearly there are some obvious benefits from engaging with such technology. For example, the continuing development of assistive technologies, such as speech recognition and smartphone learning apps, has much to offer people (including staff) with communication and learning needs (Latif et al., 2015), while written electronic conferences (e.g. via chat rooms) are often identified as a preferred mode of communication for people who are not able to communicate with others in their first language (Fitze, 2006). There are also numerous challenges. For Gillingham (2016), it is about engaging end users in technology design, monitoring and evaluating the impact of the technology on practice, recognising that sometimes it is better not to use everything the technology is capable of, and remembering that the technology does not replace social work skills. Further, challenging the inadequacies of ICT may involve challenging and unpicking the inadequacies of managerialism, which may be intertwined with the promotion of the technology in a particular organisation (Gillingham, 2016).

Collaboration and Teamwork

In Chapter 1, we noted that the ongoing competition between professional and other occupations in the human services labour market is a key tension in collaboration, partnership and teamwork. This is not to suggest that such arrangements are to be avoided. Partnership and collaboration are argued to be aligned with social work values, particularly those around social justice and anti-oppressive practice (Taylor et al., 2006). However, they can also be reflective of a managerialist agenda to set joint goals for multiple agencies. For example, strategies for enabling 'joined-up thinking' and 'joined-up working', now common across Europe, particularly in child and family services, have been critiqued as mainly concerned with the reorganisation of services rather than with improving responsiveness to unique family situations (Roets et al., 2016). In health and social care, the fields of practice where working collaboratively is often highlighted, include:

- hospital and community health care;
- mental health care;
- youth offending;
- aged care;
- hospice care;
- general medical practice;
- childcare and child protection;
- schools; and
- disability and rehabilitation services.

Before looking at some of the benefits and challenges of working together, it is necessary to acknowledge, as others have done (Taylor et al., 2006), the confusion surrounding the terminology. More often than not, a range of terms are used loosely, including partnership (common in the UK), collaboration (common in the USA), teamwork, participation, involvement, cooperation, coalition building and joint working. For our purposes, we use the terms *collaboration* and *partnership* synonymously to refer to two or more organisations working together to improve practice and service delivery (Payne, 2000; Scott, 2005). *Teamwork* is framed as the interpersonal processes involved in a group of people regularly working closely together (Payne, 2000). This usually occurs within a single organisation, although in some inter-agency work – particularly where there has been a long-standing relationship between the organisations – the members of the different organisations can be seen to be operating as a team.

Inter-agency Collaboration

The imperative for members of different organisations to collaborate is frequently stated and widely accepted as a good thing: 'To argue the importance of partnerships is like arguing for "mother love and apple pie". The notion of partnership working has an inherently positive moral feel to it and it has become almost heretical to question its integrity' (McLaughlin, 2004: 103). The benefits of organisations working collaboratively are reported to include:

- sharing knowledge and expertise;
- improving referral processes;
- facilitating holistic care;
- improved continuity of care; and
- enhancing creativity and problem solving. (Burnett and Appleton, 2004; Darlington et al., 2004)

In an Australian study of 300 cases where child protection and adult mental health intersected, a positive collaborative experience was reported in 57.5 per cent of cases, with improved client outcomes identified in 12 per cent of cases (Darlington et al., 2004). While these are important findings, overall there remains inconsistent evidence, across different sectors in different countries, of the extent to which collaboration and partnership strategies produce tangible outcomes, particularly for service users and carers (e.g. Kharicha et al., 2004; McWilliam et al., 2003). The same is the case in collaborative interprofessional education. In a systematic review of interprofessional education programmes, positive outcomes for patients and the health care process were identified in seven studies, while mixed outcomes were evident in four and no outcomes in another four (Reeves et al., 2013).

In building successful coalitions – broad networks of organisations working together towards a common goal – Mizrahi and Rosenthal (2001) identify the importance of four key components: conditions, commitment, contributions and competence. These components can also be seen to apply to other strategies for improving joint working, whether they are within or between organisations.

First, the *conditions* need to facilitate working together. Organisations need to be flexible enough to accommodate the creativity and change that can emerge from people and organisations working more closely together. For inter-agency work, the timing often needs to be right and there needs to be wider political will.

Second, people and organisations involved in working together need to be *committed* to this 'for the long haul', for the benefits that come from mutual engagement and not just to maximise their own position. For social workers, linking core values – such as social justice and empowerment – to partnership strategies can help engender such commitment.

Third, *contributions* are needed from people and organisations in order for the strategies to be maintained for long enough to be effective. Contributions include both tangible and intangible resources (such as expertise), values and ideologies that will influence and motivate others, and power so that the new groupings of staff or organisations can operate with some autonomy (Mizrahi and Rosenthal, 2001).

Fourth, *competence*: people need to have the capacity to work effectively together by building and maintaining relationships in the face of differences in values, knowledge and skills. Effective leadership in this context is about facilitating safe and participatory environments (Mizrahi and Rosenthal, 2001).

Given that collaboration and partnership are often ascribed generic positive traits, it can sometimes be difficult to uncover some of the challenges of working across agencies. In a study of the relationships between police and social workers in responding to domestic violence in Israel, Buchbinder and Eisikovits (2008: 4) identify the main barriers to inter-agency collaboration as being: '(1) struggle over who owns the solution and avoiding responsibility and the power to intervene; (2) boundary preservation work; (3) estrangement from the other organization; and (4) collaboration maintained at the interpersonal rather than the institutional level'.

These concerns resonate with Scott's (2005) identification of important areas where challenges or tensions might arise in inter-agency collaboration. We re-emphasise these levels in Chapter 8. Scott sees these as occurring at different levels:

- *Intrapersonal level*: individuals' own emotional issues or past experiences working across organisations might impede their ability to work across agencies.
- *Interpersonal level*: interpersonal conflicts or rivalries between staff across the organisations might affect the opportunity for collaboration.
- *Interprofessional level*: collaboration may be impacted by conflicts between different professional groups within each agency – such as different values, status, world views.
- *Intraorganisational level*: dysfunctions within one organisation might mean that it is unable to form an effective partnership with the other organisation.
- *Interorganisational level*: tensions exist between the organisations in terms of past histories of working together, incompatible goals, different values or world views.

Imagine, for example, a small domestic violence agency deciding to work collaboratively with a local public relations company to develop a campaign to prevent violence against women. While there may be many common goals, it may well be that each agency is operating from a different value or world view perspective – for example, the domestic violence agency from a feminist egalitarian perspective and the PR agency from a corporate business perspective. These tensions may (or may not of course) be apparent at inter-professional levels and inter-organisational levels. It may also be that the domestic violence agency has gone through a rapid turnover in staff recently, impacting on intra-organisational capacity, and thus does not have sufficient resources (e.g. staff expertise and time) to invest in collaborative relationships.

Teamwork

As discussed, teamwork refers to the activities of groups of people working closely together on a regular basis. While it is a dominant way of working in human service organisations, most of us are probably well aware of the downsides of teamwork, or of what happens when teams are not functioning well. In addition to single discipline teams (where the team comprises members of the same discipline or professional background), it is also common to identify multi-disciplinary, inter-disciplinary and trans-disciplinary teams.

A *multi-disciplinary team* involves different professions working together by performing different roles in line with their own discipline. For example, in health care settings, members of multi-disciplinary teams (such as doctors, nurses, social workers, physiotherapists, occupational therapists) each have their own role and tasks to pursue that together contribute to optimal patient care and key organisational requirements, such as speedy and effective hospital discharges.

In turn, an *inter-disciplinary team* involves members of different professions working closely together, taking on board each other's perspectives and adapting their own roles and work accordingly. It is 'the process by which professionals reflect on and develop ways of practicing that provides an integrated and cohesive answer to the needs of the client/family/population' (D'Amour and Oandasan, 2005: 9). Emphasis is placed on the synergies of working closely together and influencing each other: it is 'an active, ongoing, productive process' (Parker-Oliver, Bronstein and Kurzejeski, 2005: 279). Hospice teams, for example, are shown to involve high levels of inter-disciplinary work, which draw on a long history of working together in the hospice movement. Important features of this work include a sense of interdependency and sharing common goals (Parker-Oliver et al., 2005).

Finally, a *trans-disciplinary* team involves working across and beyond disciplinary and professional boundaries. In fact, these boundaries are at least partly dissolved and a new, wholly integrated, way of working is created (Thylefors, Persson and Hellstrom, 2005). So a trans-disciplinary team might involve team members performing roles and tasks usually ascribed to a different profession or enacting newly developed roles and tasks. In a Swedish study examining perceived efficiency and team climate across 59 teams comprising 337 individuals, trans-disciplinary teams were identified not only as more efficient, but also as comprising greater team spirit, openness and trust (Thylefors et al., 2005). While this suggests that striving to become a trans-disciplinary team will facilitate an equitable and empowering work environment, it is nonetheless the case that the intra- and inter-organisational environment will determine what type of team is likely to evolve.

We can all probably think of some factors that contribute to a successful team. It usually involves a sense of positive interdependence – feeling connected to and reliant on the other people in the group. There is often a high degree of accountability to other team members, and regular working together on common tasks. Effective teams are also identified as having:

- a clear and common purpose;
- a sense of belonging;
- synergy;
- cooperation and mutual support;
- clear roles and responsibilities;
- sound procedures;
- appropriate leadership;
- regular reviews;
- opportunities for individual development;
- good group relations;
- effective external relations; and
- opportunities for working creatively. (Payne, 2000: 52–3)

Of course, teamwork can be challenging. As in other types of relationships where conflict may emerge, power is a key concern in teamwork (Parker, 2015). According to Longoria (2005), the language and ideology of partnership may obscure underlying power issues and inequalities in relationships. In multi-disciplinary teams, there is a sense that, despite the potential for egalitarian ways of working, they continue to 'reflect, reproduce and perpetuate the traditional divisions of labour, status systems and systems of authority' (Irvine et al., 2002: 204). For example, in a US study of 591 medical, nursing and social work students undergoing 'geriatrics interdisciplinary team training', about 52 per cent of the medical students saw medical practitioners as the natural leaders in teams, while only 14 per cent of nursing and social work students agreed with this (Leipzig et al., 2002). Across other items – for instance, 'medical practitioners should have the final say in decision making' – it was clear that medical students saw the physician as being the most important member of the team.

A lack of understanding about different professional roles and constraints is often identified as a barrier to productive relationships between social workers and members of other professions. For example, medical practitioners are often reported to have little understanding of social work's advocacy role (Mizrahi and Abramson, 2000). Thus, attempts within a hospital to advocate on behalf of a patient may be perceived as being obstructive rather than as being patient- or client-focused. In a UK study of social services staff joint working with general practitioners, a lack of understanding of each other's roles was seen as a key problem (Kharicha et al., 2005). A social worker in this study reported the following:

I find doctors don't sometimes seem to understand that we have to do an assessment from a different perspective than they do and they seem to, quite often, have made up their minds of how things are supposed to go and then, it almost feels like they're instructing us, 'this client needs a residential home – and you arrange it'. (Cited in Kharicha et al., 2005: 401)

Language and communication issues are reported to affect the ways in which professionals work with each other. Not only does each profession have its own jargon, but increasingly the professions are using the same terms with different assumed meanings based on their own disciplinary knowledge (Irvine et al., 2002). Thus, what a psychiatrist might mean by terms such as social exclusion, participation and empowerment might differ considerably from what is meant by a social worker or a police officer. This often reflects a different world view or understanding of social issues.

Similarly, there may be variations in how particular values are weighed up in relation to competing values. For example, differences over balancing confidentiality and information sharing were identified in Robinson and Cottrell's (2005) study of five UK teams in the fields of youth crime, child mental health, special needs childcare, neuro-rehabilitation and child development assessment. Social services staff complained that they had difficulties accessing health databases because of privacy restrictions, while the same was not true in reverse. Community or voluntary agencies can also experience difficulties accessing key client information because of the confidentiality procedures of statutory agencies (Secker and Hill, 2001). While other professionals no doubt have a responsibility to better understand social work roles, skills and values, it is also the case that social workers could be better at articulating what they do and how it contributes to client and organisational objectives. An important first step is affirming the professional identities and resources that each member of the team brings to the work at hand (Parker, 2015).

As Practice Example 4.2 demonstrates, it is also essential for team members to be aware of the role and values of other professional/occupational groups that they engage with to support clients or service users.

Working with interpreters in the context of multi-disciplinary teamwork

Mai is a Japanese interpreter working on a contract basis for a private interpreting agency. She specialises in health interpreting and is frequently called on by the local health authority in a major metropolitan city. When called to attend a meeting between the oncology team and a patient's family on the 9th floor of the metropolitan hospital, she was aware it would be a difficult session as that floor is known to provide services to the most seriously ill patients. She was told by the agency that the patient is Shinya Sugimoto, a 54-year-old man diagnosed with lung cancer.

When she arrived, she was asked to wait in the reception area, where she soon discovered that the patient's family – some of whom were crying – was also waiting. They immediately asked her if she was there for Mr Sugimoto and, when she indicated she was, they bombarded her with complaints about the way in which they and Mr Sugimoto had been treated. They said that the last time they were at the hospital a

(Continued)

PRACTICE
EXAMPLE 4.2

(Continued)

doctor told them and Mr Sugimoto (via a different agency interpreter) that he had only six months to live. They claimed that the doctor was very abrupt and did not explain much about the cancer, alternative forms of treatment or avenues for support. The social worker, Jack, had been supposed to attend this previous meeting, but had been called away at the last minute. Mr Sugimoto's wife, Yoko, asked Mai to take their concerns to the team.

Just as Mai was trying to explain that that was not her role as an interpreter, she was asked by a nurse to meet with the multi-disciplinary team in an interview room. When she entered, Jack introduced her to the team members and expressed concerns that members of Mr Sugimoto's family appeared to be upset. They asked Mai for advice on the best and most culturally sensitive way to proceed with the meeting – noting that the purpose of the meeting was to provide post-diagnosis follow-up information. Again, Mai indicated that it was not her role, as an interpreter, to provide advice on how the team should manage the meeting, nor to provide information on culturally appropriate behaviour. Her role, she explained, was to clearly and accurately interpret the dialogue between the relevant parties. She should act as an independent person and should not be used as a 'go-between' between the different parties. When she returned to the agency after a difficult meeting between the team and the family, she recommended that the agency manager work with the hospital to develop a protocol for working with interpreters and to provide training if necessary.

 Reflective Questions

1   What strategies do you think the multi-disciplinary team, including Jack, should have put in place to better manage this situation?
2   What do you need to be aware of when working with interpreters in multi-disciplinary settings?

Service Users, Carers and Parents in Collaboration and Teamwork

As Practice Example 4.2 demonstrates, inter-disciplinary teamwork and inter-agency collaboration do not occur in isolation. Like the organisations that host them, they are embedded in wider social systems and networks. In the practice example, effective teamwork and patient care required an ability to collaborate with an interpreter – but this, itself, was dependent on understanding the role of interpreters in health contexts and the boundaries of this role. In this case, it was clear that the health team needed to engage in training to enable better use of interpreters in the future. However, it is also the case that interpreters may need assistance in understanding and negotiating the requirements of working in a health setting, including requirements related to privacy (Berthold and Fischman, 2014). Payne advocates an open approach to teamwork that understands intra-organisational teams 'within wider multiprofessional, service user and community networks' (2000: 3), which may extend to include other professional systems such as interpreting services. This approach is useful in that it recognises that professionals are not only accountable for effectively maintaining relationships with the people they work with every day in the office, but also that they are accountable for maintaining connections with a range of networks and communities.

Thus, central to understanding teamwork and collaboration in the context of these networks and communities is the role service users, as well as carers and parents, can play in the organising and delivery of health and social care. Recent policy initiatives, particularly in the UK, have exhorted social workers and other professionals to work in partnership with service users in order to improve the quality and responsiveness of services. The focus of professionals working in partnership with parents and carers is not so much on their own needs, but on working together to better meet the needs of their children or adult care-receivers.

However, how service user participation and involvement occurs in practice is variable and runs the risk of being tokenistic if not properly resourced. There are also questions about the appropriateness and capacity of some to be involved in organisational and other forms of decision making in some areas of practice, such as child protection. Empowerment is a frequently stated aim in social work and also increasingly in health care partnerships. However, how empowerment is put into practice often falls short of the progressive transformation espoused in the literature, because professionals resist stepping down from their expert roles (McWilliam et al., 2003). As others have done, we express concerns that the rhetoric around empowerment and partnership may not be matched by the realities of everyday organisational practice.

Recognising the limitations of engaging in 'partner relationships' with service users, carers and parents should not, however, undermine the importance of service user needs being at the centre of collaboration, partnership and teamwork strategies. McWilliam et al. (2003) advocate a flexible client-centred approach to partnership that supports the client as the central partner in his or her care. They argue that the engagement of a service user and a professional should involve a negotiated process of:

- building trust and understanding: this emerges as the client shares their circumstances and expectations;
- connecting as a partner in care: professionals encourage and support comfortable expression of concerns, e.g. via active listening;
- experiencing a sense of caring in the relationship;
- facilitating a deeper mutual knowledge which draws on a greater awareness of clients' own resources, strengths and potential; and
- mutually creating ways of working together to achieve goals.

The aim of the partnership approach is to stimulate increasing levels of client control over their own care. Thus, professionals should be able to work together in a way that respects clients' own leadership roles in relation to their own care. This requires considerable organisational support, including training in communication, teamwork and relationship building (McWilliam et al., 2003).

Communities of Practice

Networked relationships may occur not just in formal organised ways, but also informally, even organically. Communities of practice are described as the naturally formed relationships that occur between people who 'share a concern, a set of problems, or a passion about a topic, and who deepen their knowledge and expertise in this area by interacting on an ongoing basis' (Wenger, McDermott and Snyder, 2002: 4). Drawing on associated concepts such as reflective practice (Schön, 1983) and the learning organisation (Senge, 1990), advocates of communities of practice recognise that knowledge is not just held individually but also collectively and that it is dynamic and constantly evolving. Communities of practice can occur in a range of contexts and not just in formal organisations. For example, a group of young parents who meet regularly together may come to form such a community as they share parenting experiences and further develop their knowledge. The experience of shared learning comes to define the community and promotes spiralling expertise and capacity. This is an invaluable resource for organisations, which, in the twenty-first century, are claimed to need to become more flexible and learning-centred in the 'global knowledge economy' (Wenger et al., 2002).

Despite the original conceptualisation of communities of practice occurring organically, increasingly there have been attempts in the management literature to identify strategies for facilitating communities of practice within organisations. Within social work, they have been seen as a way of facilitating a learning organisation (Gray, Parker and Immins, 2008). Fostering communities of practice is advocated as one particular approach to organisational working to improve organisational outcomes and capacities, as well as people's experience of work and professional development (Wenger et al., 2002). Managers may be able to cultivate such communities by, for example, linking pockets of expertise with isolated workers and identifying organisational problems that cut across team boundaries (Wenger et al., 2002). For organisations, including human service ones, the aim would be to harness the power of these naturally occurring networks and cultivate them to help meet the knowledge requirements of the organisation. But, 'the organic nature of communities of practice challenges us to design these elements with a light hand, with an appreciation that the idea is to create liveliness, not manufacture a predetermined outcome' (Wenger et al., 2002: 64). It is quite possible though that communities of practice be perceived within the organisation as subversive in that they rely on small group processes to achieve goals, rather than on the organisation's institutionalised processes (Gray et al., 2008).

One of the arenas where communities of practice are taking off – and where a lot of the academic literature on them is centred – is the internet, particularly in the use of social media (such as Facebook, discussion boards, blogs, Twitter, etc.) (Gunawardena et al., 2009). This type of media provides a platform for online communities of practice to grow from the bottom up and in ways that might be – well, actually already are – challenging to the traditional authority of the professions and human service agencies. For example, the development of online health discussion forums potentially challenges the authority of the medical profession. However, while potentially challenging for social workers and the agencies we work in, the benefits in terms of community development, citizen participation and linking local and global issues are considerable.

There is little doubt that working effectively with others – whether it be through communities of practice, inter-disciplinary teamwork or inter-agency collaboration – is a core social work practice. Nonetheless, there will be times when a social worker shouldn't be a 'team player', particularly when the norms and practices of the team run contrary to social work values or to organisational standards. Later in the book, we address the notions of accountability and responsibility as they impact on social workers' everyday lives. As mentioned earlier in this chapter, this may require breaking through fear to voice genuine and heartfelt concerns.

 Reflective Questions

1   Consider an organisation of which you have experience. How might a 'community of practice' be formed around a key issue (e.g. improving practice standards) within the organisation?
2   What might be some internal pressures within a team as an organisation strives to work in partnership with other organisations?

Conclusion

How we communicate within and across human service organisations can be as reflective of our ethical commitments as social workers as our communication with clients and community members. While the emotional life of the organisation may be rarely scrutinised, we argue that social workers should become attuned to this dimension in order to be effective organisational operators. This is particularly important when responding to conflict situations. Similarly, how we communicate through the use of computers may often go unexamined. In this chapter, we have suggested that social workers need to be skilled in different technologies and be aware of how these technologies influence practice. Effective communication, networking and relationship building are also essential to working effectively with others within and across organisations. In the next chapter, we advance some issues raised in this discussion: the negotiation of risk in organisational life, as well as the strategies and complexities of decision making.

5 Decision Making and Risk

In this chapter we overview

- approaches to decision making in organisational contexts;
- bounded rationality in decision making;
- professional autonomy and discretion;
- context of risk for organisational decision making;
- risk management and strategies for improving risk decisions.

Introduction

For many of us in organisations, our everyday experience of decision making is messy, unpredictable and chaotic. It is infused by power plays, operating through both formal and informal organisational hierarchies. Decisions are made on the back steps where the smokers gather. Decisions are made in cars driving to appointments. They are made when people are stressed and when they are feeling anxious about how others perceive them. They are made by people feeling so overwhelmed that they can't think through all the possible ramifications. Decisions are made when there is a lack of information about the nature of the problem. Sometimes the most important decisions are the ones that are not made: the ones that are avoided because it's just too difficult to face up to the real problems in the organisation. Thus, it is possible to see decision making as a human, active and contingent process. Not all decisions are handed down to social workers from 'on high' and as faits accomplis. Many are experienced by social workers as being negotiated along the way, with real and sometimes unintended consequences; although, in this chapter, we acknowledge the expectation that decision making – especially that relating to important organisational strategies and critical client situations – is informed by rational thought and evidence.

The tension between the idealised rational approach to decision making and the chaotic lived experience is particularly acute when organisations are faced with assessing and responding to risk situations. Organisational decisions that result in clients or members of the public being exposed to harm are of particular concern. Managers and workers may well be concerned to minimise the harm experienced by those people, but they may also be concerned to minimise their own or their organisation's exposure to harm, such as litigation or media scrutiny. Thus, organisations and governments expend considerable energy, drawing on scientific techniques, in trying to control and minimise such risks. Yet, the extent to which all risks can be minimised is doubtful and some of the more invasive risk management strategies are critiqued as being overly controlling and paternalistic.

Decisions are also about making active, collegial (with input from clients) and reasonable choices between options based on available resources. Good decision making will 'clear a space' and cut across unwarranted indecision to achieve optimal outcomes for clients and the programme objectives of the organisation. In this sense, social workers have to exercise good judgement about possible risks, ethical integrity for self and others, and a reasoned approach to the potential social and personal consequences of such decisions. Risk minimisation and adversity to risk taking will narrow the positive and imaginative ways in which social workers can individually and collectively participate in decision-making processes.

Decision Making

Decisions are occurring all the time in human service organisations. Some of these are big – for example, decisions to restructure the agency – and some are small and clearly insignificant – such as people's decisions about how to spend their lunch hour. Decisions are also made throughout the organisation. While some people in senior positions might have more influence, others can also express their agency through their own decision-making processes. It is not hard to imagine that some front-line workers might make their own decisions to sabotage a new policy directive if they don't agree with management's decision to implement the policy. In social work, some of the most important decisions made relate to 'wicked problems'. These are situations where the problem itself is difficult to define and where the strategies for resolving the problem are unclear (Head and Alford, 2015). An example might be homelessness, where the 'lack of a home' might reflect deeper and more complex problems such as substance use, mental health issues, employment issues, family conflict and so on, and where 'providing accommodation' may not be, on its own, an effective response to the complex interplay between these issues.

In terms of organisational decision making, what we are usually talking about are those decisions that relate to or impact on the functioning and development of the organisation – decisions on things like: staffing, policy and service planning, distribution of resources, information management, allocation of work tasks, allocation of resources (including staff time) to individual clients, and research activities. Just as important, however, is an awareness of the organisational context for making (good) decisions. This relates to the structures, processes and systems in place that assist effective decision making – such as information management systems, the processes used to support communication in teams, and supervision arrangements. Inevitably, organisational culture will have a big impact on this. For example, if there is a culture within an agency that professionals don't share information about clients between each other (e.g. due to concerns about confidentiality or fears of negative scrutiny), then this might have a big impact on decisions that are made in relation to a client when a particular staff member is away. The organisational context for effective client-related decision making has been a particular focus in child protection practice, where key failures within the organisation (e.g. lack of training and supervision for new staff) have led to decisions that have resulted in harm to children (De Bortoli and Dolan, 2015).

For the purpose of our discussion, we define decision making as the process of selecting one option from a series of alternatives. At a personal level, it involves a cognitive process, but it is a process that occurs within contexts – interpersonal, cultural, social – and it is important to understand decision making with these in mind. Inevitably, decision making in social work organisations involves the exercise of power and authority (Miller, Hickson and Wilson, 1996: 43). In particular, it is an expression of autonomy (e.g. professional autonomy) and control (e.g. managerialist control). Thus, power in decision making emerges from leaders, managers and professionals, as well as from clients and carers who make decisions regarding their own lives which impact significantly on organisational processes.

While the legitimacy of employees' decision making comes mainly from their role within the organisation and their professional status, the legitimacy of client and carer decision making comes from their lived experience and expert status in relation to their own situations. For social workers, decisions are made within the context of relationships and their knowledge of how to establish and build good personal networks within organisations. These networks are further discussed in terms of levels of organisational interaction and relationships in Chapter 8.

Rational Decision Making

Understanding the ways in which decisions are made is important for social workers, particularly if they are to exercise their own leadership capacity. The dominant approach to decision making in the human services is rational decision making. This way of thinking about decision making reflects modernist and scientific approaches to organisations and management. It is particularly influenced by neo-classical economics, which assume that people act in a rational, logical and linear way, choosing options that bring the highest number of returns with the lowest costs. This focus on choice and maximising outcomes reflects neo-liberal ideology. Thus, welfare state restructuring and managerialism reinforce this approach to decision making. Rational decision making also draws on positivist approaches to knowledge development, which is reflected in its use of science as a means of evaluating and selecting different courses of action in any one decision event.

In the conventional rational model of decision making, the decision-making process should involve a number of stages, including defining the problem, generating

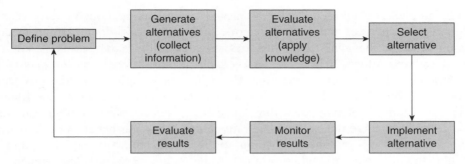

Figure 5.1 Rational decision processes

and selecting alternatives based on available information, implementing the decision, and then monitoring and evaluating the results (Hatch and Cunliffe, 2013). The process can be conceptualised as circular, or spiral, as new problems are defined based on evaluations of the results of previous decisions made (Figure 5.1).

In today's terms, this rational approach to decision making is similar to that proposed by proponents of evidence-based practice. As we discussed in Chapter 1, common definitions of evidence-based social work and social care focus on the selection and application of research knowledge in decision-making processes (Sheldon, 1998: 16). For practitioners, this could involve a search on electronic databases of academic journals for research findings that directly inform practice questions, and then evaluating the information to see if it applies to the specific client (Gibbs and Gambrill, 2002). Alternatively, it might mean drawing on reviews of evidence in particular areas provided by organisations such as the Social Care Institute for Excellence in the UK. Those who are influenced by positivist ideas may particularly value alternatives that have been found to be successful through experimental or quasi-experimental designs, such as outcome evaluations.

Decision theory has been developed on the basis of the rational approach and can be used to direct the analytical processes involved in making decisions. In social work, the use of decision theory has been examined by Munro (2008), who applies it to child welfare practice. Specifically, it involves a process of identifying the options available, the possible consequences of each option, the likelihood of each consequence occurring and the desirability of each consequence. Scores are allocated to each of these dimensions of the decision – including a probability score for the likelihood of each consequence – so that each consequence is given an expected utility value. This then guides the choice of which option is the best to select – for instance, the one that is most likely to produce a good outcome.

Bounded Decision Making

Another way of thinking about decision making that we noted at the beginning of this chapter is based on a critique of the rational model and centres on Simon's (1957) argument that the reality of decision-making behaviour is considerably different from this idealised model. This is especially the case in relation to 'wicked problems', where routinised and hierarchical decision-making models fail to accommodate the range of intersecting factors, including 'institutional arrangements, group behavior, ideologies, issue histories, research findings, media biases, and so on' (Head and Alford, 2015: 718). Simon explains that rational decision making is constrained by a lack of information, the degree of complexity of the problems faced, individuals' limited capacity to process information, the short time frames which decisions are often made within, and conflict between different organisational goals. Simon refers to this as 'bounded rationality'. While this behaviour is intended to be rational – it is reasoned and could not be considered irrational – it is limited by human and organisational constraints (Miller et al., 1996: 45). The strength of this model is that it strives to explain the lived experience of decision making and acknowledges that the ideal – the rational decision – is often not achieved in reality.

In discussing Simon's work, Hatch and Cunliffe (2013) identify two main implications. First, uncertainty arises when there is insufficient information on which to make a decision or when there are questions about the quality or reliability of the information. Second, it is often the case that there is conflict within an organisation over different organisational goals, and which should be prioritised and thus resourced. Hatch and Cunliffe (2013) argue that where such conflict exists, decision making is likely to be ambiguous because decision makers will evaluate the alternatives differently depending on which goals they favour.

The idea that decision making can be rational and straightforward is further challenged by arguments that organisational decisions emerge from different interest groups within the organisation, each vying with the other for power and status. A classic study of a French tobacco company concluded that ostensibly powerless workers exercised considerable influence within the organisation because they had expert knowledge (Crozier, 1964). In particular, those people within organisations who are able to manage the uncertainties that the organisation experiences occupy unique positions of power (Miller et al., 1996: 46). In human service organisations, conflict often appears as a reflection of deeper tensions regarding professional status and turf wars (Shapiro, 2000).

Under these circumstances, not only is decision making influenced by political processes, but the very construction of the decision itself and its possible alternatives is shaped by dominant forces within the organisation. For example, the alignment of the medical profession and management in hospital systems helps construct what decisions are able to be made by the multi-disciplinary teams and the possible courses of action. This dominance might also explain how decisions are made in favour of certain interests in the organisation and how particular conflicts or ambiguities are resolved, at least on the surface.

Other alternatives to the rational model have been framed to reflect the reality of decision-making processes. According to Hatch and Cunliffe (2013), these process models can be seen to be relevant depending on the extent to which there is uncertainty or ambiguity in the situation. They identify *trial and error processes* as more common where there is general agreement over which goals the organisation should pursue, but great uncertainty over how to pursue these goals. That is, there is insufficient information, or the information that is available is so confusing that it is difficult to be confident about how to proceed. The common response in this situation is to work things out by trial and error: making small incremental decisions. This is inevitably an ongoing learning process.

Coalitional processes appear, according to Hatch and Cunliffe (2013), to be common where there is a reasonable degree of certainty over how best to proceed – that is, information is available and uncontentious – but there is conflict over which goals or problems should be pursued. Goal setting is invariably a political process, particularly when one goal is prioritised above another through the allocation of resources (Patti, 1983). In this situation, decision makers will often engage in political processes by developing coalitions with people with similar views or with those who can be convinced, as well as sometimes by silencing or discrediting those with alternative views. In these circumstances, the priority of gaining agreement over the goal can occasionally override the imperative to apply information honestly and openly. For example, the information could be manipulated or some information could be omitted to ensure agreement is gained.

'Garbage can' decision-making processes are most common when there is both a lack of certainty over information and how best to proceed, and conflict or disagreement over which problems or goals should be addressed (Hatch and Cunliffe, 2013). The idea is that in some circumstances decision making is largely unpredictable and chaotic. This is common where the environment or technology is poorly understood and where key actors (e.g. senior managers) are continually moving in and out of the decision-making process (e.g. by changing jobs). In terms of the metaphor, information, problems, solutions, participants and opportunities for making decisions are all thrown together in the garbage can. Occasionally, they are retrieved in the right way to produce a good decision, but, invariably, poor decisions are more common.

Munro (2008) identifies some other approaches to decision making which also arise from an imperfect decision-making context. These include:

- *satisficing*: working out what is good enough and not looking any further for options when this is achieved;
- *pattern recognition*: establishing whether the current situation matches past experiences that have been successfully resolved;
- *one-reason decision making*: identifying one major factor that forces a decision (e.g. in an emergency); and
- *short-sighted decision making*: resolving the immediate difficulty, but not considering long-term consequences.

In spite of concerns about the inevitability of uncertainty, ambiguity and power plays in decision-making processes, some continue to argue for the need to strive for a rational and logical approach to decision making. Gibbs and Gambrill (2002) claim that it is because there is such uncertainty in decision making that we need to rely on evidence-based practice (EBP) as a way forward. For Munro (2008), what is needed is an evaluation of the strengths and weaknesses of the rational or analytical approaches and the more intuitive approaches in relation to particular decision-making points. It seems reasonable that rational approaches (such as decision theory) can be applied in a careful and considered way, with recognition given to the contextual and intuitive factors that also impact on the decision-making process. Decision aides that parallel cognitive processes, such as structured professional judgement, can be used to help guide decision making in a way that recognises both the rational and intuitive dimensions of good decisions (De Bortoli and Dolan, 2015).

 Reflective Questions

1   Think of an organisation in which you are involved. From your perspective, what are some examples of good decisions and bad decisions that have been taken in that setting? What do you think impacted on how effective the decisions were?
2   What are some of the features of the organisation's structure, culture and processes that facilitate different approaches to decision making? What are some of the factors that interfere with decision making? What do you think could be improved?

Client Involvement in Decision Making

Thus far, we have implied that decision makers in social work organisations are the professionals and managers. In fact, there may be a range of people who are involved in or are affected by decision-making processes in social work organisations. These stakeholders include clients, carers and parents, employees (including management, administrative, professional and non-professional staff), volunteers, funding bodies and auspicing organisations. More broadly, the government and the general public may have a stake in decision making, for example due to the use of public resources in service delivery.

These groups engage with each other in different sorts of ways. Some may be collaborating in a cooperative and mutual way to achieve the best decision possible. Some may be engaged in a battle of wills and may thus be prepared to put everything on the line (including their job) unless their alternative is accepted. Others may be working quite separately, sometimes in a way that supports the decision making of others, and sometimes in a way that undermines such decision making.

How have clients or service users been enabled to be involved in organisational decision making, both at personal and policy levels? There have been two important and competing discourses on service user participation. First, a discourse of consumerism emerged from the neo-liberal restructuring of the welfare state as experienced in Anglo-American economies. Consumers' influence on organisations is exercised through their purchasing power and through consultation exercises designed to gain consumer feedback. Second, a social justice or empowerment discourse constructs service user involvement as more than a consultation exercise. Participation in organisations (and their decision making) cannot be separated from a consideration of clients' participation in society more widely. Thus, tokenistic participation strategies are rejected in favour of user-controlled services that better reflect their citizenship and self-determination. These discourses continue to co-exist and inform the participatory decision-making processes of social work organisations in both public and community sectors. In some circumstances, the implications of the two discourses merge. For example, personalisation and consumer-directed care programmes, whereby people with disabilities and older people are provided with money so that they can purchase their own care, reflect the priorities of (limited) user-controlled services and purchasing power.

Inevitably, there are questions about the meaningful involvement of clients in organisational decision making where resources, training and support are not provided. For Croft and Beresford (1990), unless a culture of participation exists people may become easily discouraged. While individuals' mental, cognitive or intellectual capacity to communicate and make decisions may certainly affect participation, so too does the organisation's capacity to enable participation. Where professionals are talking in jargon or where clients or carers are not provided with training or not reimbursed for out-of-pocket expenses, then meaningful participation can be limited and tokenistic. Chenoweth and Clements (2011) conducted a survey of 200 service providers relating to the participation of adults with intellectual disabilities in the planning and delivery of services. They concluded that service providers continue to find it difficult to construct a culture that values service user participation, with some impeded by a lack of resources and others by a belief that facilitating service user participation takes time away from operational tasks.

Determining the level of appropriate service user involvement is necessary to establish the groundwork for meaningful participation. Participation in organisational life and decision making is commonly conceptualised across a continuum, ranging from no involvement to total control. A study by Mackay (2002, cited in Ager, Dow and Gee, 2005) of the participation of mental health survivors in mental health services provided an adapted version of Arnstein's (1969) ladder of participation. Arnstein's ladder was originally developed in relation to social planning and has been widely used to evaluate citizen participation in social policy and service delivery. Mackay's adaptation supplies definitions that are more accessible for service users (Ager et al., 2005). The steps of the ladder include (from the highest level of participation to the lowest):

- controlled decisions and actions;
- delegated function;
- shared action;
- influence on action;
- attending working groups;
- consulted;
- informed;
- not involved. (Mackay, 2002, cited in Ager et al., 2005: 474)

While there is a recent focus on client participation in decision making, especially in the UK, inevitably there are limits to the extent to which such participation is desirable (although the boundaries around 'desirability' will always be contestable). For example, in child or adult protection, where a person is exposed to violence, abuse or neglect, then the state charges certain professionals with the authority to intervene, sometimes against the immediate wishes of those involved. Healy (1998) argues that it is important for social workers not to get so caught up in the culture of participation that they forget that they sometimes need to act with authority. She claims that it is essential that we do not deny or obscure the authority we have to affect clients' lives and that as much as possible we explain our role and are transparent and accountable for our actions. (See also Chapter 7.)

In Practice Example 5.1, a social worker needs to establish a participatory process for making the important decision of how to allocate funds following a natural disaster to help in the recovery and regeneration of Down Bay's sense of community.

Setting up participatory decision-making processes after a natural disaster

Chloe is a social worker currently employed as a community development officer in the social planning office of Down Bay Council. Down Bay is a rural town, with a high unemployment rate, located on the estuary of a major river. Down Bay's major industry is fishing, although in recent years more effort has been put into tourism because the area's fish stocks have become severely depleted. There are nearby turtle breeding areas and also large numbers of dolphins in the area which have been identified as possible tourist attractions.

Down Bay was recently devastated by the largest flood in the area's history. About 40 per cent of the town's dwellings were inundated with water and six people died as a result of becoming trapped in their cars while driving through flood waters. The flood also had a significant impact on fish stocks, especially with the flowing downstream of sand and chemicals from nearby industrial premises. Erosion of beaches has also reduced the breeding areas for turtles.

In the immediate aftermath of the flood, the Council established a 'community regeneration fund' to assist with rebuilding. Following an appeal by a popular breakfast television programme, the fund attracted donations from all over the country. Under enormous pressure from the media and the local Member of Parliament, the Council took the decision to distribute about 70 per cent of the funds within the first month after the floods to people who had lost their homes or whose relatives had died.

The Council was then faced with the decision of how to spend the remainder of the money. Chloe was tasked with running a community meeting to discuss the different purposes the money could be used for. About 50 people attended the meeting. During the meeting, it became clear that there was a lot of anger that so much of the money had already been distributed, and that not enough care had been taken to ensure that the amount allocated to each household was commensurate with need. There was also debate about how much money should have been allocated to people who had flood insurance and those who 'had not bothered' to take insurance out. Local community leaders also voiced concerns that more money should have been directed to flood prevention strategies, while industry leaders felt that money should be directed towards rebuilding fish stocks, or alternatively to building the tourism industry.

In debriefing with the rest of the social planning team, Chloe reflected on what had gone wrong, and considered the different options available for the distribution of the remaining funds. Team members suggested setting up a community consultation committee, involving key stakeholders from the community, environmental and industry sectors. It was recognised, however, that the Council would remain the ultimate decision maker as it was legally responsible for the collection and disposal of the funds.

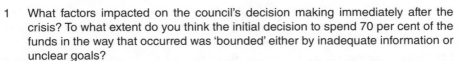

Reflective Questions

1   What factors impacted on the council's decision making immediately after the crisis? To what extent do you think the initial decision to spend 70 per cent of the funds in the way that occurred was 'bounded' either by inadequate information or unclear goals?

2   What do you think of the decision to set up a community consultation committee? How could Chloe ensure that this committee fairly represented the diversity of needs across the community, including those most affected by the floods as well as other disadvantaged groups such as the unemployed? What else would be needed to help the council reach a good decision regarding the distribution of the remaining funds?

Professional Autonomy and Discretion

The extent to which social workers are able to work autonomously and to exercise discretion in their everyday decision making is much debated (Ellis, 2011; Evans and Harris, 2004). For some, bureaucratic and managerialist practices constrain professional practice through the requirement that workers adhere to detailed rules and procedures. The critique of managerialism within social work (discussed in Chapter 1) has emphasised this point. For others, the complexity of front-line social work is such that rules and procedures will never account for all variations of human experience, and consequently social workers are seen to act with autonomy and discretion in many areas. For example, in relation to care managers determining older people's financial status as part of an assessment for long-term care, Bradley (2003) reports variable practices in checking the accuracy of the financial details given to them. Additionally, the more complex and detailed the rules and procedures, the greater the potential for confusion and inconsistencies in how they are implemented.

According to Evans and Harris (2004), there are gradations of power in the relationships between managers and professionals in human service organisations, and rarely does the professional have either total or no discretion in decision making. In a study of social work practitioners and managers working with adults, Evans (2013) identified that while there was unanimity in compliance with the law, the degree to which practitioners felt compelled to obey organisational rules varied considerably. Typically, the rationale for breaking or bending the rules was acting on behalf of the interests of clients. Similarly, Greenslade, McAuliffe and Chenoweth (2015) reported, in their study of social workers in statutory settings, that front-line practitioners routinely engaged in covert activism within their workplace – including noncompliance, rule bending and over servicing – in order to put their professional values into effect.

One way of summarising the tension between professional autonomy and restrictive organisational practices is the 'technicality–indeterminacy ratio' conceived by Jamous and Peloile (1970) and widely applied to social work contexts (Robinson, 2003; Sheppard, 1995). Technicality refers to the detailed knowledge and skill required to implement organisational rules and procedures. Highly technical jobs tend towards routinised and regulated work patterns. In contrast, indeterminacy refers to the complex and ambiguous situations that confront professionals and that require specialist knowledge and the ability to act with autonomy. Jamous and Peloile posit that as the degree of technicality increases in a particular job so the degree of indeterminacy decreases, as does the degree of status that the professional enjoys.

From our perspective, social workers need to strike a balance between technicality and indeterminacy in carrying out their roles. Social workers need to be skilled in the technical aspects of organisational practice, but they also need to be able to reflect and act on their wider professional and societal commitments. At times, these commitments may be used to challenge the organisation, or used as a basis for working strategically to change the organisation.

In striving for the right balance between technicality and indeterminacy, social workers are frequently warned of the dangers of being 'street-level bureaucrats' (Evans and Harris, 2004). Lipsky (1980), in his seminal work, highlighted the extent of the pressures faced by front-line public sector workers, including a lack of resources to meet the needs of clients and unclear and sometimes contradictory policy goals. When facing complex and ambiguous situations with few resources and limited guidance – as might be the case when confronted with 'wicked problems' (Head and Alford, 2015) – some workers resort to making up their own, often arbitrary, rules in order to manage the complexity of the work. The discretion that these workers consequently exercise may lead to 'favoritism, stereotyping, and routinizing' (Lipsky, 1980: xii). Thus, unofficial discretion could produce inconsistencies and bias in the treatment of service users, leading some to get a better deal than others (Bradley, 2003). Kirton et al. (2011) provide a useful example of the variations in the way in which access to childcare files is provided to post-care adults. A lack of policy clarity, debates over the 'ownership' of the information, and the degree of prioritisation of the work within a particular work environment meant that different practices were occurring in different locations.

An important area where front-line workers' everyday decisions can affect service users' experiences is in the rationing of services and resources. Goods or services provided through public resources invariably need to be rationed because demand commonly exceeds supply. According to Lipsky (1980), rationing can occur through a variety of means, including:

- *Monetary costs*: if users are required to pay (or part pay) for services or if they incur other financial costs (e.g. losing wages because appointments can only be made during working hours) then requests for services may reduce.
- *Time costs*: clients are often expected to wait for a service, whether this occurs over weeks or months, or whether it involves queuing for an interview or waiting in a reception area. Depending on the urgency, importance and availability of other resources, clients may determine that the costs of waiting are not worth the benefits. Bureaucrats may reward clients by expediting a service or punish them by delaying it.
- *Information provision*: supplying or withholding information about available goods or services determines who might request them. Bureaucrats may provide

favoured clients with particular information that enables them to negotiate 'the system' better. Sometimes an excess of information or confusing jargon may act as a barrier.

- *Psychological costs*: organisational and worker practices may demonstrate a lack of respect for clients and may undermine their sense of self and autonomy. Such practices include excessive waiting, degrading inquiries into sensitive issues (e.g. financial status, sexual health) and assumptions of dishonesty. Understandably, some of those who bear such costs may withdraw contact with the organisation.

While routinisation of practice attempts to introduce fairness, regularity and accountability to manage the demands of clients on front-line workers, this is often experienced by clients as 'red tape' and as reducing the quality of service.

Evans and Harris (2004: 889) point to another of Lipsky's (1980) arguments as a cause for concern in social work: that faced with the complexity of practice, street-level bureaucrats may deny 'their own discretion in order to protect themselves from having to take difficult decisions and being subjected to blame'. Defensive social work, as conceptualised by Harris (1987), involves practices designed to protect the social worker from blame, especially in the form of malpractice litigation or media scrutiny. In addition to avoiding decision making, negative defensive strategies – those which may act against the interests of service users – may include withholding information, following procedures too rigidly and responding to vulnerable clients in an overly protective manner to avoid the potential risk to safety. As Evans and Harris (2004) argue, the potential for defensive social work has increased considerably in recent years, in line with government and organisational concerns about their exposure to various risks, including litigation.

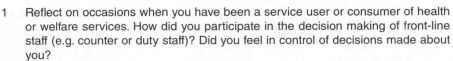

Reflective Questions

1   Reflect on occasions when you have been a service user or consumer of health or welfare services. How did you participate in the decision making of front-line staff (e.g. counter or duty staff)? Did you feel in control of decisions made about you?
2   Imagine working in a busy social services office. If under pressure, how easy would it be for you to engage in defensive practices? What sorts of support would you need to try to prevent this from occurring?

Risk and Organisational Practice

As discussed in Chapter 2, notions of risk so pervade health and social care that residualist welfare states, such as the UK and Australia, have arguably moved from being needs-led to risk-led (Kemshall, 2002). This reflects neoliberal ideas through the promotion of being an active and responsible member of society as a means of redressing supposed welfare dependency. Where social policy might once have been concerned about meeting the needs of vulnerable members of society, or at least minimising exposure to social risks (such as unemployment), its focus today is on promoting individual risk management as a form of social responsibility. Thus, we are encouraged to engage in prudent action, such as taking out various forms of insurance, to minimise our personal exposure to risk and lessen demands on social resources. Where we pose particular risks to ourselves, others or society, the focus is on controlling and preventing harmful behaviour through active social programmes, such as assertive outreach. The emphasis is on managing individual risk rather than on looking at the risks a society might pose for individuals. This is the case even though inquiries into the failures of welfare systems – such as in the protection of children – have repeatedly demonstrated that society, governments and social work organisations pose considerable risks to individuals.

Social workers are involved in many different types of risk situations that require them to make decisions and take action. In part, these reflect the policy contexts which frame the identification of a risk situation and guide appropriate responses. For example, mental health policy and legislation provide a framework for assessing the risks that people with acute mental health symptoms pose to themselves and/or others, and require social workers in statutory mental health settings to take certain action.

However, while social policy plays a part in framing risk responses, social workers themselves and the organisations they work in also play an important role in identifying and responding to these situations. When examining a client's circumstances, social workers may draw on their own personal and professional knowledge when evaluating the risks the person may face. They may also be directed by organisational protocols or by the influence of the organisational culture on their behaviour.

A key concern might be what happens if a social worker underestimates the risks posed by a particular situation and the person is exposed to harm. There is no doubt that they may be concerned about the impact on the client; however, in an era of increased managerial control and accountability strategies that serve mainly to scapegoat (Ryan, 1998), they might equally be concerned about their own job. Even worse, they might be concerned about facing litigation for negligence, being hauled before a public inquiry or being castigated in the media. These factors, reflecting the individualisation of risk in society, provide a context for a defensive 'covering my back' approach to practice that could easily produce similar effects to the street-level bureaucracy, as discussed in the previous section and examined further in Chapter 7.

Risk Management

Despite the overwhelmingly negative discussion of risk and the common equation between risk and harm, at its basic level risk simply refers to chance – the chance of particular consequences occurring from each possible course of action decided on and taken: 'Risk is the calculus of probability by which one might say that a certain outcome is more or less likely to occur' (Duff, 2003: 287). Thus, dominant notions of risk derive from probability theory and statistics, which are applied in such diverse fields as gambling, insurance and engineering. The term 'risk management' has generally been used to describe this technical approach to risk, which in turn is grounded in modernist and positivist thinking. The focus of this work is on calculating the risks that people are exposed to and then informing them of these risks so that they can make rational decisions – weighing up costs and benefits – to avoid them.

Risk management in social work and social care has involved the development and application of specific tools to evaluate risk and facilitate risk decision making. While such tools can be found in a wide range of practice areas, they are particularly noticeable in child protection, where the dangers – for a wide range of stakeholders – of making mistakes are heightened. Actuarial tools are probability based and provide a numerical calculation to inform decision making (Broadhurst et al., 2010), such as those developed on the basis of decision theory, discussed earlier in the chapter. Another set of tools is assessment frameworks, which are usually based on consensus or evidence, in order to minimise the likelihood of error and reduce subjectivity (Broadhurst et al., 2010).

However, as we have discussed, rational decision making is often limited by uncertainty. Where there is insufficient information to evaluate the likelihood of particular consequences or where some consequences are unknown, the rational decision-making process in risk management is compromised. Sheppard (1995) highlights the difficulties in predicting particular outcomes in social work, especially in some areas (e.g. child abuse, domestic violence, elder abuse) where there is a lack of clarity in definitions and where there may be multiple and contested ways of measuring the outcomes of risk behaviour. A particular concern is the identification of situations when social workers get things wrong – that is, when we make a decision and take action in a way that underestimates the likelihood of a negative consequence (referred to in risk management as a false negative), or when we overestimate this likelihood (a false positive). In some circumstances, the former may lead to disastrous results, such as a child's death, while the latter may lead to overly paternalistic responses (Kemshall, 1998).

Subjective and Contingent Risk

Inevitably, individuals' experience of risk in their lives and our response to it will be shaped by other factors, not just a rational, scientific evaluation. And as might be expected, there have emerged alternative ways of conceptualising risk that draw on social constructionist and postmodern perspectives. According to Kemshall (2010: 1249), 'these critiques of the rational actor introduced the notion of the social actor and the concept of situated rationalities, namely rationalities embedded in place, time and network'. Thus, these approaches tend to emphasise not so much the technical or cognitive process of risk decision making, but the social and cultural contexts in which such decisions are made. For example, the contexts of the decision maker will influence how the risk situation is perceived. That is, the contexts determine whether or not, first, a situation is seen as risky, and, second, whether the risk is experienced either as an opportunity or as a threat. A range of factors can be identified as affecting an individual's subjective experience of risk (Slovic et al., cited in Ryan, 1998). These include familiarity – the more familiar the person is with the risk situation the less risk it seems to pose – and also shared consequences – if the effects of a risk decision are spread over a number of people, individual exposure to negative consequences may feel lessened (e.g. it may feel safer to make a team decision rather than an individual one). Our subjective experiences are unique and thus it follows that people will inevitably view risk decisions differently.

Post-structural approaches see all risk as socially constructed and thus 'the task becomes one of problematizing the discourses and practices around risk and how they shape subjectivity' (Houston, 2001: 222). In reviewing this approach, Houston notes that those who engage in risk behaviours are identified as breaching norms. Risk management strategies become active tools in the surveillance and control of particular groups. Most effectively though, surveillance is carried out by individuals themselves who 'choose' not to engage in certain behaviours because they are constructed through discourse as being risky and in need of correction. According to Kemshall:

> A key mechanism of this self-surveillance is self-disclosure, the postmodern version of Western Christianity's confessional. Such disclosure is seen as the first step in reconstituting the self as a new, remoralized individual, subjugated to the instructions of professional expertise. Seeking help, dealing with one's problems, changing one's anti-social thinking patterns, engaging in self-help and adapting healthier lifestyles are all part of this reconstituting self-surveillance. (2002: 123)

Social workers who act in overly defensive ways can thus be considered to be exercising this type of self-surveillance, potentially to the detriment of clients (e.g. acting in overly paternalistic ways).

At the same time that risk seems to be increasingly individualised – in the sense that blame and accountability for risk errors are laid at the feet of individuals – it is argued that risk is also increasingly globalised. Most prominently, as noted in Chapter 2, Beck (1992) argues that in late (reflexive) modernity individuals are more and more exposed to invisible and unpredictable global forces. The expansion of information and communication technology means that private information and behaviour are increasingly exposed (e.g. via hacking or CCTV). The expansion of world travel leads to disease threats (like bird flu) and the globalisation of liberal capitalism poses considerable threats, not least in terms of environmental damage. While effort is spent on controlling these risks – by focusing on individuals' behaviour – inevitably this is an unachievable goal. Beck's approach attempts to straddle the objectivist/subjectivist divide: he sees global risks as both real (and observable) and constructed through powerful discourses and coalitions. Increased reflexivity in late modernity provides the opportunity for people to become aware of the subjective experience of risk and to take an alternative course.

Although critiqued as being overstated (Houston, 2001), Beck's thesis is powerful because it captures an experience of the (post)modern age: that of the individual, stripped of the securities of the nation state, battling against global forces. Regardless of the empirical evidence for the case, the notion of the risk society has become a 'social fact' (Alexander and Smith, 1996), or at least a powerful discourse. According to Kemshall (2002: 15), 'risk as calculable probabilities is being displaced by risk as future uncertainty'.

The reflexive modernisation of risk discourse in social policy has had a major impact on human service organisations in Australia and in other countries, such as the USA and the UK, where contracted services now predominate. Public and community sector responses to high-risk or at-risk groups are also apparent in a new reliance on the use of administrative techniques to govern risk. Bureaucratic information sharing and contractual policy processes use several implementation and evaluation tools to conceive the everyday risk of clients and organisational risks. These include financial and social audits, performance appraisals, good practice standards, and research and evaluation techniques (Wearing, 2001: 135). The use of this administrative technocracy has legitimised pro-market agendas of neo-liberal welfare and, in several new and unique ways, commodified and normalised clients. One of the authors (Wearing, 1998) has argued that the new governance and construction of clienthood in social work is predominantly groups of risky, underinsured and difficult to manage categories of clients, for example 'high risk' sexual offenders or mental health clients, and 'risky' unemployed people who are non-compliant with job seeking or job training (see also Fawcett et al., 2010).

Although the organisations in which social workers operate tend towards risk management (as in risk minimisation) strategies, there are certainly opportunities for social workers to take on board some of the issues emerging from subjectivist approaches to risk. Davis (1998) overviews a risk-taking approach, which has been developed by those seeking to empower clients, including those with mental health needs. A key concern has not been so much false negative risk decisions, but false positive decisions where the risk of harm has been overestimated and service users have been subjected to paternalistic and intrusive responses. A risk-taking approach assumes that risks are a normal part of everyday life. Furthermore, risk taking is seen as a fundamental expression of human agency and a strategy to enhance autonomy and self-esteem. This approach has commonalities with user-led initiatives, as reflected in the social justice approach to organisational participation discussed earlier in the chapter. It is also commonly articulated as a characteristic of good leadership, as well as a key factor in enabling organisations to become more innovative and creative.

Where risk minimisation is needed, then, where possible, the focus of intervention should be directed away from the individual and onto their environment. Thus, attention is not so much on individual responsibility for social risk but on social responsibility for individual risk. In Practice Example 5.2, different risks are encountered which require different responses. The challenge for staff and the organisation is how to balance risk minimisation with risk taking.

Responding to risk in a mental health situation

Tall Trees House is a residential unit for young people with mental health needs. All 12 residents are male and under the age of 25. The unit is managed by a recently appointed social-work-qualified director who is responsible to a voluntary management committee. In the past few years, there has been a high turnover of staff in management and caring roles. The unit operates with few written policies and, in particular, lacks policies and procedures on the management of risk. Local social service agencies have expressed concerns that there is a lack of rehabilitation and activity programmes and that there is a need for more staff training.

Ewan is an 18-year-old man who has recently been placed at Tall Trees following a voluntary admission to a psychiatric hospital. Ewan's hospital admission came about after a series of acute psychotic episodes during which he experienced auditory and visual hallucinations; he was later diagnosed with schizophrenia. At the time, he had been living with his grandparents (his parents having died in a car accident); they found the incidents to be distressing and impressed upon him the need to seek help. Initially, they thought that his increasing social withdrawal had been due to his bereavement, as well as to the difficulties he was having with his school work. In the lead-up to his first major psychotic episode, Ewan had been away from home for a few nights and had, his grandparents later found out, been drinking heavily with friends. It even appeared that he had slept rough one night.

While at Tall Trees Ewan's health was monitored by staff and he was receiving oral medication. He returned to the outpatients department of the hospital once every three weeks for an injection. He enjoyed working around Tall Trees, particularly in the garden, and he has been learning the guitar at a local drop-in club.

Last week, Ewan absconded from Tall Trees. When he returned, it was apparent that he had been drinking and had been sleeping rough. For the previous week, Ewan had been refusing medication and some of his previous symptoms had been reappearing. He had refused to go to the hospital and had had a number of arguments with staff about this. He had also been involved in a scuffle with another resident over use of the pool table. On investigation with his grandparents, it became apparent that it will shortly be the third anniversary of his parents' deaths. His health has continued to deteriorate and yesterday staff organised for him to be compulsorily readmitted to hospital where a recovery programme is being provided.

In consultation with staff and health professionals, the director is developing a risk management plan for Ewan in preparation for his return to Tall Trees. This involves the identification of known triggers for Ewan's withdrawing and aggressive behaviour, such as anniversaries of stressful events and the use of alcohol. The plan also documents a series of strategies to facilitate appropriate risk taking, including supporting Ewan's recreational interests and a longer-term plan for him to find employment (including work training). There will also be a focus on maintaining his friendship network and educating his friends and family on his condition. For the organisation as a whole, the director has decided to initiate a series of risk-management meetings. The aim of these is to evaluate existing strategies to manage risk, including both risk minimisation and risk taking, and where these are ineffectual. In developing ways of better responding to these issues, emphasis is placed on residents maintaining and building social supports both within Tall Trees and outside. Protocols and training will be developed to assist staff working with potentially volatile clients.

Improving Risk Decisions and Responses

While there are enormous challenges in attempting to straddle subjectivist and objectivist approaches to risk (Houston, 2001), it is our view that social workers need to draw on both in making decisions in and responding to risk situations. However, in doing so, social workers need to bear in mind that the service user should be considered as at the centre of decision making relating to their own circumstances. This is not to deny the authority for decision making that social workers and others sometimes bring to risk situations – such as in child protection or involuntary hospitalisation – rather it recognises the centrality of the client's subjective experience of risk in all situations. Even when their wishes are overridden, as might be necessary in Ewan's situation, highlighted in Practice Example 5.2, their experience and decision making must remain at the centre of our work.

Drawing on critical realism (Bhaskar, 1991) to inform an approach transcending the objectivist/subjectivist divide, Houston (2001) argues that social workers need to be tentative about identifying causal factors in any one situation. They need to think critically about positivist instruments, understanding that, in being based on observed and measurable phenomena, they might not always pick up on the underlying or deep causal factors in people's circumstances. Understanding relies on the subjective accounts of those involved, but these too should not be treated uncritically, as people's experiences and perceptions are shaped by their contexts. According to Houston (2001: 224), a critical realist approach to risk work would involve a process of retroduction: 'constructing models that tentatively explain how certain events unfold'. This involves setting up tentative hypotheses grounded in well-established theory and research, then testing these by applying them to the situation at hand and seeing if they help explain the phenomena. Where hypotheses are supported, interventions should be developed; where they are not, alternative hypotheses are to be constructed. It is a careful and tentative searching for explanation within the individual's circumstances and environment that characterises this approach.

Even though rational decision making in risk situations may be an ideal, practitioner frameworks for making risk decisions are invariably more complex, mainly because they also involve balancing different personal, professional and organisational values, as well as possible biases and prejudices. For Kemshall (1998: 424), 'objectives and goals are often unclear or contested, leading to value conflict for the practitioner, and how these conflicts are resolved directly impinges upon decision choices and outcomes'. For us, it is important to recognise the socially situated nature of risk decisions, including the way social context influences the subjective experience of risk. An emphasis on decision making (particularly as it relates to important practice situations) as a relational and shared enterprise – and as grounded in professional relationships based in trust – helps avoid the individualising tendency in rational decision-making discourse, and the easy options of blame and scapegoating (Dachler and Hosking, 2013).

Ethical Decision Making

Social workers who themselves make or support others to make decisions in risk situations should also be informed by the ethical dimensions of the situation and their own ethical stance. In the final chapter of this book, we discuss some different approaches to understanding professional ethics in social work. At this point, it is useful to make a distinction between deontological ethics, which emphasises the importance of adhering to certain ethical principles (such as 'do no harm') regardless of consequences, and consequentialist ethics, which does consider the possible consequences when considering appropriate behaviour. Healy (2007) frames this as a distinction between universalism (where absolute universal commitment to certain principles is required) and relativism (where the culture/context is considered when weighing up options). Inevitably, as Healy (2007) suggests, it is the middle ground between these two positions that seems most suited to social work decision making: that there needs to be a commitment to certain principles and human rights, but that culture, context and consequences should also be taken into consideration.

Thus, decision making involves not only the collection of information about 'facts', but also the application of values and principles to understand what is right or good behaviour in the particular circumstance. Risk situations frequently involve ethical dilemmas, most obviously tensions between rights to freedom and safety. These tensions are at the core of social work and all social workers would probably have been exposed to a range of situations where such rights conflict. Importantly, though, our responses in these situations should not become ingrained or instinctive. Mattison (2000) argues that ethical decisions require systematic and careful analysis so that social workers can recognise the impact on their decision making of their own attitudes and values: 'The challenge is to use ethical self-reflection to learn about oneself as an ethical decision maker' (2000: 208).

One strategy that can be used to facilitate such learning and guide ethical decision making is the 'ethical assessment screen' developed by Dolgoff, Harrington and Loewenberg (2012). This can help practitioners identify: relevant personal and professional values that relate to the decision-making situation; potential conflicts of interest; alternative ethical options and their impacts; and which options have the best likely outcome. This approach is similar to the use of decision theory, discussed earlier, with the addition of value-based and moral considerations to guide the selection of particular options.

Naturally, how these considerations are applied varies according to the type of situation. Dolgoff et al. (2012) argue that the first step is consultation with the relevant professional codes of ethics and/or practice standards. However, in cases where professional codes of ethics do not adequately address the situation or where there may be tensions between two different principles, then the authors propose a particular order of ethical principles to guide decision making. Based on the work of key ethical theorists such as Rawls (1971), Dolgoff et al. (2012: 80) propose the following order (the most important listed first):

1. protection of life;
2. social justice;

3. self-determination, autonomy and freedom;
4. least harm;
5. quality of life;
6. privacy and confidentiality; and
7. truthfulness and full disclosure.

Hence, it is argued that, for example, protection of life and issues of social justice should take precedence over maintaining confidentiality. While this rank ordering of ethical principles can be valuable in helping practitioners to think through ethical dilemmas and appropriate responses, Dolgoff et al. (2012: 79) do note that this is a tool only and 'should never be applied blindly'. For Healy (2007), based on an earlier account of the work by Dolgoff et al., this approach inevitably reflects a western cultural bias towards individualism which prioritises individual independence, rather than interdependence within a group.

In Chapter 7, we examine the issue of accountability in some depth and in this context recognise that social workers' ethical commitments relate to a range of individuals, groups and organisations, including clients, managers, funders and society more widely. It is important to note here, though, that ethical decision making relates not just to the decisions taken around the well-being of individual clients, but also to the interests and rights of a wide range of stakeholders. While these relationships will be guided by codes of practice and organisational policies, dilemmas can be experienced that require the consideration of competing ethical principles and thinking through the right course of action. For example, in participating in decisions relating to the allocation of work among colleagues it may be necessary to consider that distributive justice (fairness in the allocation of work) is prioritised over individual freedom or autonomy.

 Reflective Questions

1 Identify a risk situation that you have been involved in and where you were required to make a decision and take action. Who were the different people involved in this situation and how might they have (subjectively) experienced the situation differently?

2 Using the above situation or imagining another risk situation in social work (such as that outlined in Practice Example 5.2), identify some errors that could be made. What are some examples of false positive (overly protective) errors and false negative ones (i.e. those that underestimate the potential for harm)? Is one type of error more common than the other in this risk situation?

Conclusion

Social workers should be actively involved in making decisions in and responding to risk situations. We need to be concerned with minimising the negative outcomes that individuals' risk behaviour might expose themselves and others to, as well as with identifying and responding to the risks that individuals' environments might in turn pose for them. We need to take a holistic approach to the client's situation, recognising that their risk exposure is an important, but only one, part of this situation. Where possible, we should be working with clients to facilitate risk taking in different parts of their life. Inevitably, social workers will be concerned not just with the client's exposure to risk but also with their own and their organisation's exposure, particularly if errors are made. This is a reality for social workers today.

From our perspective, it is necessary for social workers to be honest and critical of their own work, drawing on strategies such as ethical self-reflection, identifying how they influence decision making in these situations and how things could be better done next time. This involves reflection on the everyday activities of organisational life, as well as the 'big picture' and strategic decisions and actions. In the next chapter, we examine a force for facilitating such strategic decision making: leadership.

6 Leadership and Supervision

In this chapter we overview

- different approaches to leadership, including transformational and distributed leadership;
- power and gender in social work leadership;
- the contemporary context of social work supervision;
- different approaches to supervision, such as performance management and relational approaches;
- critical issues in supervision, such as supervising across difference.

Introduction

In recent years, increased attention has been given to leadership in social work, particularly within the context of the diversified health and community services sector, the opening up of more positions to people with vocational qualifications or life experience (Healy, 2004), and the rise of managerialism (Tafvelin, Hyvönen and Westerberg, 2014). As in the field of organisation and management studies, in social work, leadership is variously defined, although it can be characterised by a commitment to ethical practice and an ability to empower individuals and communities (Rank and Hutchinson, 2000), as well as by having vision, influencing others to act, being able to collaborate and problem-solve, and creating positive change (Holosko, 2009). Particular leadership approaches, especially transformational leadership, are promoted as aligned with social work values (Gellis, 2001; Mary, 2005). As in other fields, there has also been substantial interest in distributed leadership, particularly in the drive to develop learning organisations within the health and community services sector. The notion of distributed leadership is particularly relevant to recent social work graduates who, as newly qualified practitioners, may not be in a formal leadership position, but may well be called on to undertake leadership roles within specific contexts.

Every day social workers and social work managers adopt leadership roles through their supervision and mentoring of other practitioners, and thus may also model appropriate leadership strategies to these individuals. In both leadership and supervision practices, power is negotiated, and care needs to be taken with the way in which leaders and supervisors draw on their authority when working with others. Also, like leadership, the scope of social work supervision is very much influenced by the political and organisational context, and may well be limited where there is an emphasis on narrow managerial control or where time or other resources are limited. However, the potential for supervision – in its capacity to facilitate critical reflection and consider different ways of doing things – and leadership – particularly in the use of distributed leadership – to transform organisations is considerable. These are the grains around which the pearl of organisational change, morale and purpose can grow.

Leadership

Approaches to Leadership

Everyone probably has their own take on what leadership is and who can be considered a leader. For many, the image that is conjured up is of a charismatic hero, a change agent and a risk taker who knows how to exercise control when appropriate. As noted in Chapter 1, leadership is usually considered as something different to management. The former involves an orientation towards change and innovation, while the latter emphasises operational functioning and stability. However, as Lawler (2007) argues, it is still easy to conflate the two, especially as most of the literature on leadership is written for an American corporate audience with a strong emphasis on top-down management, rather than the inclusive and informal leadership patterns more accepted in human and health services. In social work, leadership has been discussed in relation to the need to promote the public image of the profession, the impact of leadership on social work staff performance, and the role of social work leaders in facilitating inter-professional activities. Social work's more inclusive approach to leadership has also been considered as a counterbalance to the influence of managerialism, with its emphasis on routinisation and de-professionalisation (Lawler, 2007).

Generally, though, our understanding of social work leadership is informed by the wider literature on this topic in organisation and management studies. In these fields, an explanation of what leadership is centres on how leaders influence organisational processes, enable group cohesion and accomplish organisational goals (Bargal, 2000). This understanding emerges from the three dominant approaches to leadership developed during the twentieth century: the trait approach; the style approach; and the contingency approach (Bargal, 2000; Parry and Bryman, 2006). It also informs the transactional approach to leadership with its focus on ensuring compliance through providing rewards.

The trait approach, as one might expect, focuses on the personal qualities or traits of the leader and 'implies that leaders are born rather than made' (Bryman, 1992: 2). The traits identified in research relate to physical appearance (e.g. height), abilities (e.g. fluency of speech) and personality (e.g. extroversion). This approach has been said to generate 'great man' theories because of its focus on innate qualities as demonstrated by great military and political leaders (Northouse, 2009), although this resonates further because the qualities identified as related to leadership – such as self-confidence and dominance – reflect those of idealised masculinity. The most obvious application of the trait approach is the use of personality tests in the hiring of senior management staff (Northouse, 2009).

From the late 1940s, the focus shifted to researching leadership behaviours or styles with a view to training people to become leaders. Two different styles that are emphasised in this research are the consideration style (where leaders are concerned about and thus trusted by their subordinates) and the initiating structure style (where leaders actively direct the work of subordinates) (Bryman, 1992).

The contingency approach emerged in the 1960s and emphasises the situational factors that enable different approaches to leadership. For example, Fieldler (1993) argues that relationship-focused leaders and task-focused leaders are effective depending on the degree to which the situation is favourable to them or the extent to which they can exercise control over the situation. A critique of both the contingency and style approaches to leadership is that they fail to acknowledge informal sources of leadership within organisations – that is, that people in less powerful positions can also exercise leadership qualities depending on the situation (Bryman, 1999).

While leadership research based on the trait, style and contingency approaches is still carried out and continues to influence organisation and management studies, since the 1980s a series of alternative approaches has emerged. One of these approaches has been widely employed within the military: transactional leadership. This approach focuses on the nature of the exchange between the leader and the follower where the leader provides rewards, such as status or resources, in return for compliance (Burns, 1978, cited in Bryman, 1999). According to Lawler (2007: 127), transactional leadership 'has a focus on stability, efficiency, formal authority, coordination, results and control'. It is perhaps more concerned with maintaining organisational functioning than with trying to energise or transform the organisation.

Transformational Leadership

In contrast to the approaches to leadership just described, transformational leadership characterises the role of the leader as a 'manager of meaning' within the organisation, rather than as a director of tasks. The leader is seen as influencing and reinvigorating organisational culture and morale by articulating shared values and defining the mission or purpose of the organisation (Bryman, 1999). In this sense, the literature on transformational leadership has much in common with the literature on change management and learning organisations.

The transformational leader motivates and inspires followers so that their aspirations become raised and are fused with those of the leader. Much of the management literature on transformational leadership has focused on the charisma of leaders and their capacity to generate shared values. Transformational leadership 'goes beyond transactional behaviors by developing, intellectually stimulating and inspiring followers to put aside their own interests for a collective (team, unit) purpose' (Gellis, 2001: 18). Bass (1985, cited in Bryman, 1999: 31) identifies it as involving:

- *charisma* – developing a vision, engendering pride, respect and trust;
- *inspiration* – motivating by creating high expectations, modelling appropriate behaviour and using symbols to focus efforts;
- *individualised consideration* – giving personal attention to followers, giving them respect and responsibility; and
- *intellectual stimulation* – continually challenging followers with new ideas and approaches.

In Sweden, a study of 158 social services employees found that transformational leadership was associated with two key employee attitudes: role clarity and organisational commitment (Tafvelin et al., 2014). This relationship was strongest when employees spent a lot of time with the leader and when they felt supported by their colleagues – highlighting the importance of organisational context for transformational leadership to have a positive impact.

In an influential model of transformational leadership, Kouzes and Posner (2012) map out a strategy for developing leadership capacity among senior staff. Their approach, while perhaps veering into the field of motivation psychology, is widely employed, especially in the USA. It involves leaders:

1. Modelling the way:

   - finding your voice: clarifying personal values;
   - setting an example: aligning actions with shared values.

2. Inspiring a shared vision:

   - envisioning the future: imagining new possibilities;
   - enlisting others: appealing to shared aspirations.

3. Challenging the process:

   - searching for opportunities: looking for ways to grow;
   - experimenting and taking risks: celebrating wins and learning from mistakes.

4. Enabling others to act:

   - fostering collaboration: promoting joint goals and building trust;
   - strengthening others: sharing power and discretion.

5. Encouraging the heart:

   - recognising contributions: showing appreciation;
   - celebrating values and victories: creating a spirit of community.

Kouzes and Posner (2005) recognise the potential lines of critique and cynicism that may be directed towards this transformational approach. In encouraging leaders, they argue that it is important for each leader to find their own voice and their own style. They need to build up social capital with staff, and often this flows on from doing what they say they will do. They also highlight the need to get close and listen to people and their concerns, to try to build a sense of community and look for opportunities to grow capacity within the organisation.

So what do people typically say that they value in a leader? According to Kouzes and Posner (2012), when asked this question, thousands of people surveyed world-wide indicated that they wanted their leader to be: honest (89%), forward-looking (71%), competent (69%) and inspiring (69%). For Kouzes and Posner (2012), the leadership qualities that individuals should be aiming for include being able to articulate a vision for the future, being entrepreneurial, treating people with dignity, communicating key messages about the organisation's priorities, developing trust and inspiring high-level performance.

In identifying a style of transformational leadership appropriate for public service work, Dunoon (2002) shies away from a focus on charismatic transformation, as this is seen as overly focused on an individual leader who, even if inspiring the organisation effectively, may render it vulnerable when he or she, inevitably, leaves. Rather, Dunoon – drawing on learning organisation ideas (Senge, 1990) – advocates a learning-centred approach to transformational leadership, which is primarily about capacity building within organisations. Part of this approach involves helping people to become self-aware, to clarify their goals and develop their own responses to organisational issues. It also involves building organisational capacity by helping groups to move beyond dysfunctional dynamics to 'achieve more creative and deeper understandings of the issues they face and build new insights as the basis for action' (Dunoon, 2002: 9).

Distributed Leadership

Dunoon's (2002) approach reflects the emerging literature on distributed or dispersed leadership, which recognises that leadership behaviours and practices are not solely the preserve of the formally designated leader. Dachler and Hosking (2013) critique the 'possessive individualism' of dominant narratives on leadership, whereby leaders possess qualities, such as charisma, and direct or influence subordinates as if they are objects. In contrast, and as acknowledged in the group work literature, leadership can be seen as a characteristic of group dynamics and can be shared between different members of the group, often for different purposes. According to Lawler (2007: 134), 'expertise and power do not reside with individual leaders but effective group dynamics are encouraged to distribute leadership functions across the group'. Here the focus shifts from the characteristics of the leader to the processes of leadership (Crevani et al., 2010).

Where there are formally designated leaders, Manz and Sims (1989) argue that they should be involved in developing the capacity of others within an organisation or a team to take on leadership responsibilities. Their conceptualisation of

'SuperLeadership' is about unleashing the leadership potential of an organisation's employees, and, in particular, their capacity for self-leadership. The need for SuperLeadership, Manz and Sims argue, has come about because organisations rely increasingly on teams of people working cooperatively together and developing their own knowledge and solutions to problems they encounter in everyday organisational practice: 'In many modern situations, the most appropriate leader is one who can lead others to lead themselves' (Manz and Sims, 1991: 18). Strategies for managers promoting this type of leadership include modelling self-leadership, encouraging self-set goals and creating positive expectations of employees.

Before proceeding further with this line of argument, it is worth raising a note of caution with regard to distributed leadership, or rather, how it can be employed for political purposes. According to Grint and Holt (2011), in the UK, distributed leadership is being promoted in local communities through social policy, informed by the Big Society initiative, to shift leadership responsibility from government to civil society organisations. They suggest that 'the assumption that the voluntary sector, for example, is adequately equipped in terms of leadership capacity or financially resourced to take over the reins from an undernourished central State is extremely dubious' (2011: 86).

Nonetheless, at an organisational level, the idea that leadership can be distributed throughout an agency is, for us, a more helpful understanding of leadership than the notion of the charismatic or heroic leader transforming the organisation from the top down. Such an approach not only recognises the agency of other members of the organisation, but it also acknowledges that few leaders/managers will be able to or want to live up to the ideal of the heroic leader, at least not all of the time. Even if other members of the organisation may not have the opportunity to exercise leadership practices, the recognition that there is such a potential within and throughout the organisation provides a greater sense of the humanity both of the members of the organisation and of the organisation itself.

From this perspective, the opportunities for social workers to exercise leadership functions and demonstrate leadership capabilities within human service organisations are considerable, even if they are not in formally designated leadership or management roles. Leadership abilities are increasingly seen as important for social work practice, according to Rank and Hutchinson (2000: 499), who define social work leadership as involving the communication of vision, guided by a code of ethics, 'to create proactive processes that empower individuals, families, groups, organizations and communities'. Healy (2004), in particular, advocates that social workers become practice leaders within the increasingly diversified human services labour market. However, a consistent theme in the literature on social work and leadership is the need for our education programmes to better prepare students to take on leadership roles (Healy, 2004; Rank and Hutchinson, 2000).

A similar argument could be made in relation to developing the capacity of social workers to be leaders and initiators of organisational change, as discussed in Chapter 3. Social workers would not have to be in a formal position of authority to participate in or lead organisational change. According to McDonald and Chenoweth (2009: 109), 'social work professional associations and individual social workers in specific organisational contexts can, if they choose, act as strategic and transformative leaders, and engage deliberately in a sustained process of *theorising institutional change*' (emphasis in original). Thus, social workers can take action to lead organisational change in line with social work values, drawing on social work and organisational knowledge and making use of practice skills. Like other leaders of organisational change, social workers would need to be mindful of the experience of change of other employees and stakeholders. They could also seek to develop change management initiatives that facilitate a culture of organisational change and learning that correspond with social work values. In Practice Example 6.1, we discuss the ways a social work manager implements a distributed leadership approach.

Encouraging distributed leadership

Jane works as a social worker in a neighbourhood centre, which is managed by Margaret, who has a management background. The centre routinely engages volunteers and runs a training programme for them twice per year. Despite this, Jane has been concerned that ethical issues involved in the everyday practice of the organisation (e.g. tensions around confidentiality and client records) are not fully acknowledged by paid and volunteer staff. She has also felt that paid and volunteer workers do not often have the opportunity to reflect on these issues together. In a recent meeting, she decided to raise these issues with the staff team. She suggested that the organisation set up regular group supervision meetings – involving paid workers and volunteers – during which ethical issues could be raised and debated. Jane offered to organise the first of these meetings. She was taken aback by the meeting's overwhelmingly negative reaction to her suggestion.

After the meeting, Margaret discussed with Jane the group's response. Together, they were able to unpick some of the issues that may have led the group to react that way. Through this discussion, Jane was able to consider the anxieties staff might feel in having their everyday work practices exposed to scrutiny by the group and the perceived threats to status and expertise that paid staff might feel if they were involved in such meetings with volunteer workers. From this discussion, an alternative approach emerged: peer support meetings among paid staff and the development of a mentoring system between paid staff and volunteers. Prior to the next agency meeting, Jane canvassed these ideas informally with both paid and volunteer workers and gained some tacit agreement. And despite debate at the next meeting, the agency agreed to Jane's plan with the modification that it should be regularly and carefully evaluated.

PRACTICE
EXAMPLE 6.1

In Practice Example 6.1, Jane demonstrated her own leadership capacity by encouraging staff to consider ethical issues in their practice and work more closely together reflecting on these. While her initial attempts to raise this were unsuccessful, Margaret displayed a commitment to Jane in supporting her ideas and encouraged her to consider alternative strategies. As in the SuperLeadership model, Margaret provided a climate of positive regard and expectation which stimulated Jane's leadership capacity.

Power and Leadership

The notion of power is inevitably intertwined with the concept of leadership. And the different approaches to leadership seem to reflect different understandings of power. In the trait approach, we see a more traditional understanding of power – something that is containable and can be wielded by those in authority. In the styles approach, power is potentially exercised through punishment and reward (behavioural conditioning). In the transactional approach, power is something that can be exchanged to ensure compliance. In the transformational and distributed approaches, it is possible to conceptualise power as something more fluid and more dependent on culture and context (more in line with both a relational and a postmodern understanding of power; see Chapter 2). These last approaches, in particular, embrace the notion of empowerment by enabling people throughout the organisation to take on greater leadership responsibility and thus exercise more influence and hence authority in that setting. Here, power lies in networked face-to-face relations, rather than in codified rules and procedures (Dachler and Hosking, 2013).

In terms of those in formal leadership roles, we can see different ways in which they exercise their power as leaders. These include:

- *legitimate power*: derived from position and role in the organisation;
- *coercive power*: the capacity to impose punishments;
- *reward power*: attempts to motivate by providing rewards – both material and symbolic;
- *expert power*: exerted by those who have special knowledge that can be imparted;
- *referent power*: arises from charisma, has capacity to motivate and instil loyalty; and
- *communication power*: has access to key information and can share or withhold this. (Adapted from Beckett and Horner, 2016)

As the above list suggests, power can be used by a leader both positively and negatively within an organisation. While the following are caricatures of leadership styles, they do highlight some of the negative ways in which power can be used (or avoided) by leaders:

- *the oblivious leader*: lacking direction, passive, avoiding responsibility;
- *the mis-leader*: conveying incorrect or mixed messages;
- *the put-downer*: using humiliation as a tactic;
- *the micro-manager*: over-involved, not trusting others;
- *the arrogant leader*: proud, overly self-confident, ignoring others' contributions;
- *the narcissistic leader*: manipulating others for personal ambition;
- *the loner*: aloof, unapproachable, behind closed doors; and
- *the charmer*: gaining personal acceptance from staff. (Brody and Nair, 2014)

A more positive approach involves the recognition that power exists in the relationships between leaders and, for want of a better word, 'followers' – but that, even so, people can be invited to share and participate in power-related processes, such as decision making. While some decision-making situations (such as emergencies) require leaders to take personal responsibility and delegate tasks to staff, other situations may call for a more participative style. Here, the leader may present ideas and options to staff and ask for feedback before final decisions are made. A more delegative style would involve the leader supporting staff to make consensual or democratic decisions about their own work practices, and for the leader to be one of the group. As highlighted by the contingency approach to leadership, it is likely that the context or situation will influence the type of decision-making style adopted by the leader.

While the sharing of power is at the centre of the notion of distributed leadership, and thus aligns with social work values, it is important to recognise the limits or constraints on this. Not least is the danger of formally designated leaders or managers denying or hiding the actual power or authority they exercise. Ray et al. (2004) argue that differential power relations – within society and specific organisations – are historical artefacts and deeply rooted. This may impede the way in which distributed leadership can be facilitated:

> If leaders do not act with respect to the organization's historical antecedents, codes of order and disciplined practices, they risk losing the support of their followers ... For instance, if, in an attempt to disperse leadership, traditional leaders de-differentiate their relationship with their followers, these followers may well see them as behaving inappropriately. In such a case, followers may react by seeking to replace the leader with a more traditionally oriented alternative. (Ray et al., 2004: 325)

The challenge for social workers in negotiating power in leadership roles, as in other areas of practice, is to seek to be honest and transparent about power relations, especially when they are empowered to exercise formal authority. There is also certainly scope to pursue organisational change – and possibly even conflict, as discussed in Chapter 4 – to promote increased equity in organisational life.

Gender and Leadership

In Chapter 1, we noted that social work is sometimes perceived as a 'semi-profession'. According to Meagher and Parton (2004), this suggestion that social work has never achieved a fully professional status derives from the caring and relational aspects of its work, which contrast with the value placed on control and mastery within the ideal types of professional and bureaucratic work. Clearly, the gendered dimensions of this contrast are not far beneath the surface, given that social work is a mainly female and gendered occupation (Meagher and Parton, 2004). And inevitably this is reflected in pay awards – typically much lower for female-dominated occupations than male ones (Alkandry and Tower, 2011).

While disappointing, it is perhaps unsurprising to discover that gendered social relations are as evident within social work and its labour hierarchy as they are in wider society. Of key concern is the disproportionate number of male social workers, in comparison to their overall representation in the social work workforce, who move into management and formal leadership positions within the health and social care industries. Pease (2011) documents a series of research studies that demonstrate not just this inequity, but also that women social workers still tend to earn less than their male counterparts in comparable organisational roles.

Despite this, there is some evidence to suggest that female as well as male social workers are promoted to higher income positions in the human services more quickly than, say, teachers or nurses who begin on similar levels of award wages in Australia and the UK (Australian Institute of Health and Welfare, 2011). Additionally, both female and male social workers are relatively well paid compared to semi-skilled and unskilled workers working on the front line of the health and social care system (e.g. in home care and support worker roles), and whose jobs may be more risk-filled in terms of work intensification, casualisation and health risks.

In wrestling with the question of whether or not we need more men in social work – wouldn't they just keep moving up the ladder quicker? – Pease (2011) argues that what is needed are men who embrace the caring ethos of social work, are critical of hegemonic masculinity and embrace pro-feminist practices. Even so, this would not negate all the complex barriers women face in negotiating organisational hierarchies, not least of which are career interruptions due to family and care-giving responsibilities (Eagly and Carli, 2007). Nor would it necessarily undo the historical institutional power relations, as suggested earlier by Ray et al. (2004).

While this highlights the ongoing challenges women face in taking up formal leadership positions, what can be said of the ways in which women do exercise their leadership, either formally or informally? A key concern is that the stereotypical image of leadership in organisations is that of the heroic leader, and, as discussed earlier, this typically has masculine qualities (Dachler and Hosking, 2013). Conversely, the qualities that women bring to leadership are often hidden or unacknowledged (Page, 2011). While it would be extremely dangerous to assert that this is the case for all women, it may be that some are able to lead in a different way because they are excluded from or on the margins of male leadership discourse: 'From this perspective gender offers an opening for transgressing dominant modes of being and acting, for individual leaders and as a basis for collaborative leadership' (Page, 2011: 320–1). According to Evans (2010), recent shifts in the corporate world have highlighted the value of certain leadership qualities which women may be more likely – either on average or stereotypically – to demonstrate than men. These include emotional intelligence, collaboration and negotiation skills, a capacity to empower people, attention to customer and employee welfare, and a considerate and caring style.

In terms of the different approaches to leadership discussed earlier, it is clear that these qualities, as ascribed to women leaders, have more in common with transformational and distributed leadership than the more traditional trait, styles, contingency and transactional approaches (Evans, 2010). Transformational approaches – in their focus on participation, empowerment and encouraging leaders to move beyond their own immediate interests – appear to be in line with more 'feminine' participatory approaches to leadership (Kark, 2004; Lazzari et al., 2009). However, how well this approach, in its emphasis on the heroic individual, sits with feminist principles is dubious (Lazzari et al., 2009). Distributed approaches appear more compatible with feminist values given their focus on relational practices and sharing power. Again, though, these do not exist outside of institutionalised gender relations, and thus the extent to which distributed approaches can challenge hegemonic masculinity in organisations and leadership may be limited (Lazzari et al., 2009). Further, Gray and Schubert (2016: 113) argue that a feminist approach to leadership should transcend management discourse (evident in the literature on women and transformational leadership) and 'be understood as a collective force aimed at social transformation and social justice, particularly through empowering women's development'.

Despite these tensions, the qualities that many women bring to leadership are well known to social work, despite the disproportionate representation of male social workers in formal leadership roles. One may look no further than the founding 'mothers' of social work, such as Mary Richmond and Alice Salomon. In a new wave of historical gender scholarship, women's leadership roles in the development of charitable organisations and what we now call civil society are coming to light (Netting and O'Connor, 2005). In the USA, for example, Lady Boards of Managers over-saw the development of many health and human service agencies between 1866 and 1900. While they were subsequently replaced by their male counterparts, 'ironically, the concepts of partnership, collaboration, cooperation and other positive behavioral attributes that are considered "new" in the management literature today were present in the "old" Lady Board of Managers design' (Netting and O'Connor, 2005: 457). In Australia, Hughes (2010) documents the substantial range of services provided by the Catholic Sisterhoods, a role which has been largely obscured in the writing of social work and welfare history. In the course of their work, they demonstrated high levels of leadership and management capacity, including administrative competence, indi-vidual consideration, generating a shared vision, facilitating strong organisational culture and contributing to the capacity building of others (Hughes, 2004).

The failure of leadership seems to be a common discourse in everyday life. Much political commentary in the media is focused on the leaders of the main political parties, their various shortcomings and their challengers. Similarly, in organisational life, there is often a focus – at least among workers – on the foibles of the organisa-tion's leader/manager. Inevitably, we each have some sense of what and who makes a great leader, and invariably our leaders in everyday life fall short of the ideal.

The challenge in understanding leadership for human service organisations is to move beyond these unrealistic and often overly male representations of leadership and to recognise the everyday leadership practices that enable people and organisa-tions to change. These practices may certainly be evident among formally designated leaders and/or managers, but they may also be apparent among other employees or organisational stakeholders. One of the common ways in which leadership capacity is put into practice is through professional supervision.

Supervision

Supervision has long been regarded as key to developing and maintaining ethical and critically reflective social work practice. Recent surveys have suggested that it is received by about 84% of Australian social workers (Egan, 2012) and 82% of newly qualified practitioners in England (Manthorpe, Moriarty, et al., 2015). Busse (2009) discusses the historical rise of supervision in social work in the USA in relation to the shift from the distribution of resources to the poor in the nineteenth century towards facilitating self-empowerment and personal development in the twentieth century. While in the former direct managerial control was needed, in the latter it became evident that the more complex and ambiguous nature of the work required more social work expertise and pedagogical guidance. In the process, supervision became an instrument in the professionalisation of social work (Busse, 2009). Since then, different models of supervision have emerged in different contexts, and it is notable that in countries such as Germany and Sweden the focus has been on external supervision, while in the UK and Australia it has been on social work line managers supervising subordinates (Bradley and Höjer, 2009; Busse, 2009; Egan, 2012). While external supervision does occur in the UK and other countries, such as Australia, it is usually voluntary and takes the form of a consultation, rather than being mandatory and linked to job performance goals.

For many years, the touchstone for conceptualising social work supervision has been Kadushin's definition, which focuses on the supervisor's administrative, educational and supportive functions (Kadushin, 1976). But, according to Kadushin (1976: 21), the ultimate purpose of supervision is to produce a high-quality service, both in terms of experience and outcomes, for service users. This is inevitably constrained by the boundaries of the organisation. Thompson (2015) and Morrison (2001) identify similar elements to social work supervision. These include *performance monitoring*: making sure that employees are carrying out their duties appropriately. While this is an essential part of supervision and one that cannot be avoided, Thompson (2015) argues that supervision practice should be wider than this. Thus, supervision should also include, as Morrison (2001) outlines:

- *professional development*: promoting learning and continuous professional development, e.g. by adopting a reflective practice approach;
- *staff care*: supporting staff and helping equip them psychologically to undertake the tasks involved in a social work role. This may involve an awareness and capacity to assist with the emotional aspects of everyday practice;
- *conflict mediation*: invariably supervisors are located between supervisees and the agency and thus they are in a key position to mediate disputes between the supervisee and others within the organisation.

The current neo-liberal and managerialist climate within human service organisations poses some particular challenges for social work supervision, and it has been argued that there has been a withdrawal of emphasis in supervision from professional development back to administrative or managerial control (Noble and Irwin, 2009). Not least has been the impact of resource cutting and work intensification, which means that in many agencies there may not be as much time for supervision now as there was in the past. On the other hand, it can also be argued that the increased focus on risk management or, more accurately, risk minimisation has led to a resurgence in supervision as a means of overseeing and monitoring practice

(Beddoe, 2010). In a study of 280 newly qualified social workers in England, more frequent supervision was associated with more confidence in managing and prioritising workloads, better engagement with the job and more of a sense that their professional practice had improved (Manthorpe, Moriarty, et al., 2015) – although it was identified as being less useful in managing stress and negotiating boundaries with clients. In a related study of line managers, there was little sense that supervision facilitated reflexive practice or enabled the transfer of theory into practice (Manthorpe, Moriarty, et al., 2015). According to King, Carson and Papatraianou (2016), increased managerialism has meant that social workers have had to look further afield to gain the support they need to negotiate the organisation. In their study of 193 human service practitioners, many sought advice and guidance from a diversity of colleagues, particularly in terms of educational inputs, such as gaining theoretical insights and discussion of ethical dilemmas.

Nonetheless, social work supervision remains an important part not just of the professional endeavour, but also of organisational development and change. According to Noble and Irwin (2009: 353–4):

> In many instances, supervision sessions (even those that are infrequent and conducted on the run) are the only remaining sites where professionals can explore, lament, review and strategize against the more negative changes in the current landscape that are affecting the nature of their work and the way needed services are being under resourced and becoming vastly inadequate for the growing need. It can also provide a much needed site for possible resistances to emerge as the real and pressing issues associated with current practice concerns are brought into discussion and personal and professional reflection.

However, such professional supervision may not necessarily be considered a challenge to organisational functioning; it can also be seen in a positive way as a contributor to organisational learning and change (Bradley and Höjer, 2009). This is especially the case if supervision can relate to other learning strategies within the organisation – such as seminars, group support or workshops – or where supervision is conducted within a group environment rather than in a private dyad. As reflected in a social work supervisor's account of supervision in Beddoe's (2010: 1286) study, the 'ideal supervision would create a safe environment for people to "discover their learning edge", build competence and utilise the energy generated by excitement and challenges in practice'.

Approaches to Supervision

Different approaches to supervision are evident within the social work literature and they variously emphasise particular aspects of supervision, as we have just discussed. These approaches are not necessarily mutually exclusive and, as Cohen (1999) suggests in relation to strengths-based supervision, different approaches might suit different supervisees, depending on their own perspective and style of practice.

In some human service organisations, the dominant approach to supervision is managerialist. That is, the focus of supervision is on performance monitoring and maximising organisational benefits, with less emphasis on a wider developmental or supportive role. It may be that this is more common in situations where social workers are supervised by a manager who does not have a social work or similar professional background. In Chapter 7, we examine in some depth the implications of a reliance on managerial approaches to supervision, especially for producing a restricted sense of professional accountability and responsibility.

A traditional social work approach to supervision is often referred to as problem focused (Cohen, 1999). The emphasis is on the supervisor providing advice and assistance to the supervisee in their day-to-day practice. Thus, inevitably, the focus is on resolving day-to-day practice problems. While this is an important part of supervision, arguably it reflects a reactive orientation and does not particularly stimulate the longer-term learning and professional development of the supervisee. Some of the games that Kadushin (1968) identifies as occurring in supervision can be seen as arising from this problem-focused approach, particularly where the supervisee unrealistically elevates or covertly undermines the supervisor's expertise (Cohen, 1999).

While much of the work that happens in supervision reflects a concern about problems – supervisees and supervisors are no doubt anxious to resolve difficulties that the worker may be having – other approaches to supervision have emerged that focus more on the supervisee's capacity to resolve these for her- or himself, rather than on the supervisor handing down advice.

Developmental approaches to supervision identify the purpose of supervision as enabling the supervisee to develop their own professional identity and to gain confidence in their own professional role (Itzhaky, 2000). In this way, developmental approaches see supervisory relationships as mirroring parent–child relationships. According to Itzhaky (2000: 530), 'while the aim of the parents is to help their children be independent, the aim of the supervision process is to create an independent, professional social worker, free of dependence on the supervisor'. Writers from this position, such as Itzhaky, commonly identify a series of developmental stages that reflect lifespan or child development stages, as conceptualised by lifespan theorists such as Erikson (1968). Commonly identified are characteristics of supervision that are dominant at different stages of the supervisee's professional development. For example, Itzhaky highlights the following stages:

- *Beginning stage*: the supervisee often feels threatened in supervision and feels unable to fully trust the supervisor, even though he or she may rely heavily on the supervisor for assistance. Performance may be low in this stage.
- *Intermediate stage*: the supervisee is feeling more confident and is drawing on a wider range of sources of knowledge from the environment, although there may be a gap between knowledge and performance. Supervisees are likely to respond more positively to feedback from supervisors in this stage; however, there may be some conflict as the supervisee struggles to become more autonomous.
- *Advanced stage*: supervision becomes a more flexible learning environment, with the supervisee being adept at taking the initiative and choosing between a range of alternatives. The relationship becomes more egalitarian.

- *Final stage*: the supervisee is now independent and feels a strong sense of his or her own professional identity, competence and style of practice. The supervisee is well placed to now take on the role of being a supervisor.

This approach highlights some of the different issues that might be facing supervisees and supervisors, and the need for different supervision styles depending on the stage of the supervisee's professional development. It also acknowledges the role of the supervisor as a supporter and encourager of change in the supervisee's professional life.

While psychodynamic approaches to social work may be less common today than in the past, because supervision is so important within psychotherapy and is so extensively discussed in the literature, these approaches have much to offer social work supervision. In particular, they offer insights into the emotional and psychological dimensions of supervision and the unconscious reflection of emotions, especially those relating to intra- and inter-personal conflicts, within the supervisory relationship. Having said this, it is important to bear in mind that there are likely to be quite different organisational and practical constraints impacting on social work supervision compared to psychotherapeutic supervision, particularly where the psychotherapy supervisee is in private practice.

One psychodynamic approach to supervision that has much to offer social work is the relational model. This model – as presented by Frawley-O'Dea and Sarnat (2001) and Ringel (2001) – seeks to move beyond the idea that the supervisor knows best and aims to encourage collaboration as the basis for effective supervision. According to Ringel (2001: 172), rather than seeing the supervisee 'as developmentally immature, or as a novice who is there only to learn from their supervisor's knowledge and expertise, both [supervisee] and supervisor contribute their insights and utilize the supervisory relationship to further mutual learning and growth'. This demands a high degree of honesty and openness on the part of both supervisor and supervisee and will inevitably lead to some feelings of vulnerability that should be explored and discussed. Other issues that are important in a relational approach reflect years of psychodynamic scholarship. They include such concepts as transference, which in supervision refers to a process whereby emotions are displaced from the supervisee to the supervisor (or vice versa), often because a powerful emotional memory has been evoked. Emotional caution and confidentiality both need to be exercised in the use of this approach, especially if a practitioner is being supervised by a line manager. There may be misunderstanding about the purpose and outcomes of such supervision, especially if the issues raised in supervision are related to management strategies, performance monitoring or the authority of another senior colleague in the same workplace. Supervision in psychotherapy is usually done by an independent paid colleague from another organisation or in private practice. It may be that this is also an appropriate strategy for social work supervision, especially if it is to be based on a relational model.

In line with the popularity of strengths-based social work, which draws on the work of Saleebey (1992) and others at the University of Kansas, a strengths-based approach is also promoted as effective for supervision. A strengths-based approach refuses to accept that people should be identified according to professional determinations of their deficits, problems or conditions. Rather, practitioners are encouraged to work with people to identify past sources of strength and resilience in their lives and to apply these to present situations (Cohen, 1999). Thus, according to Cohen, supervision from a strengths-based perspective would primarily focus on the successes workers experience in their practice, rather than on the problems and frustrations of their work. Supervision should not be reactive or crisis-driven; rather, it should be proactive and occur regularly at a predetermined time. It should also focus on enhancing professional development and promoting quality. Learning from success is the key. Research on strengths-based supervision in child welfare in the USA has reported positive outcomes since supervisors implemented this approach, including increased learning, professional development and critical thinking (Lietz et al., 2014). In Practice Example 6.2, a social work supervisor seeks to develop a more supportive and responsive relationship with her supervisee.

PRACTICE EXAMPLE 6.2

Different approaches to supervision

Kerryn works as a senior social worker in a community centre that provides both community development and counselling services to the local area. She has been supervising Hannah since she joined the team six months ago. Although Kerryn has enjoyed working alongside Hannah – she is a committed and diligent staff member – she feels that supervision hasn't been as successful as it could be. Most of the discussions they have had in supervision have revolved around particular problems Hannah encounters in her work and Kerryn has found it easy to fall into a 'teacher–student' type of relationship in these discussions. She has noticed that Hannah has seemed less motivated about work recently and she knows that she has been under stress lately, given the recent break-up of a long-term relationship.

When Kerryn talked to Hannah about her experience of supervision, Hannah acknowledged that while she feels more comfortable with managerialist and problem-focused styles, these were not going to help her address her reducing motivation at work. This acknowledgement allowed Kerryn the opportunity to explore some of Hannah's personal issues and how they were impacting on her work experiences. By discussing Hannah's work experience without reference to her performance, Kerryn was able to refocus the style of supervision towards more relational and strengths-based approaches. Kerryn was careful not to overly focus on Hannah's personal issues or to initiate some form of therapy. Rather, she spent time identifying and supporting Hannah's strengths in her practice and encouraging a more open discussion of areas for further learning.

Issues in Supervision

As our discussion of supervision approaches has highlighted, a range of issues commonly emerge in supervision relationships and consume considerable energy – often emotional – on the part of both supervisors and supervisees. Many of these issues relate to the negotiation of power and authority in the relationship, as is suggested in the developmental approach. Regardless of the extent to which a collaborative environment is created – as recommended by the relational approach – the supervisor, by the nature of their role, will always occupy a position of greater power in relation to the supervisee. That supervision usually takes place 'behind closed doors' raises the possibility that supervisors may sometimes exploit their position (Itzhaky, 2000).

Difficulties between supervisors and supervisees may sometimes occur where they have different styles of practice or different priorities in supervision (Korinek and Kimball, 2003). Conflict is not an unlikely event in supervision – although it is not inevitable – because such relationships involve a high degree of interdependency. For example, while the supervisee needs the supervisor to assist their professional development, the supervisor might in turn need the supervisee as a source of professional identity and work responsibility (Korinek and Kimball, 2003). Where there is a sense of different needs and incompatible goals then conflict can emerge (Korinek and Kimball, 2003).

Where learning is a key feature of supervision, differences in learning style – such as one person preferring to observe while another prefers to act – may produce challenges (Korinek and Kimball, 2003). Invariably, the key is to talk about these differences and for the supervisor to focus on what is most effective for the supervisee. Assessing learning styles by using a learning style inventory (e.g. Honey and Mumford, 1986) may be a useful strategy and may open up some discussion of difference between the supervisor and the supervisee.

Of course, there are other differences between supervisors and supervisees that may affect their relationship. Either party may feel powerful in the relationship depending on the context, as well as depending on their own personal identities, characteristics or histories, and their affiliation with disadvantaged social groups. For example, how might a woman in her late 20s feel supervising a man in his late 40s? Or how might a supervisee whose first language is not English feel about showing written work to a supervisor who is a native English speaker? Ideally, as suggested in the relational approach (Ringel, 2001), the pair should try to talk about these differences so that the power implications can be identified. Additionally, the differences may provide access to knowledge and resources that might not otherwise have been considered. Recent work on the value of culturally relevant supervision highlights the need for supervisors not to assume that they can gain 'cultural competence' when working across difference, but, rather, they should maintain open conversations about identity and culture to 'shape a supervisory relationship that encourages transparency, collaboration, and an exchange of ideas' (Hair and O'Donoghue, 2009: 76).

Power issues in supervision are also evident when a supervisee's performance is being assessed. Although supervision usually involves an ongoing assessment function, assessment may come into sharp focus at particular points in time, for example when a performance appraisal is being conducted or when a supervisee applies for promotion. As in practice teaching relationships (O'Connor et al., 2006), for us it seems important that supervisors are upfront and open about points where a supervisee's performance is being formally assessed. If supervision includes professional development, support and conflict mediation, then hopefully the supervisee feels secure enough to trust the supervisor and to be honest about mistakes made or difficulties encountered. However, if the supervision is primarily about performance monitoring or has been overly problem focused, then it is possible that supervisees may seek to conceal such information in order to protect themselves (Itzhaky, 2000).

Social workers are not always fully prepared to take on supervisory roles within human service organisations (Cousins, 2004). While most of us have experienced supervision – sometimes good and sometimes not so good – not so many social workers have undergone post-qualifying training in supervision. One of the difficult issues that new supervisors must face is the authority that accompanies the role. As Cousins (2004) argues, trying to delegate such authority or pretending that it doesn't exist denies the reality of the situation and fails to best serve both the supervisee and the organisation. Going to the other extreme and excessively asserting one's authority or expertise over that of the supervisee is equally – or arguably even more – damaging. Korinek and Kimball (2003) present a range of strategies for supervisors to try to minimise conflict in supervision relationships, such as having a clear supervision contract and adopting a supportive attitude that emphasises strengths rather than deficits.

Just as some social workers may not be fully prepared to be supervisors, so too might some not be ready to be supervisees. While all newly qualified workers should have received supervision in the form of practice teaching and assessing while doing their social work degree, unfortunately such supervision may not always have met expectations. Additionally, the increased organisational accountability that comes from being an employee supervisee as opposed to a student supervisee means that supervision in paid employment is often a different experience.

So, how can supervisees get the most out of supervision? First, we would argue that it is important to stay focused on the purpose of supervision in paid employment: that is, to promote high-quality practice with service users and communities, in line with organisational constraints. It is necessary to be clear that supervision is not about personal issues, except where these affect practice. Thompson (2015) offers some other useful suggestions:

1. *Be honest*: try not to keep secrets or engage in game playing.
2. *Be prepared*: make sure the time spent in supervision is quality time.
3. *Be assertive*: if things are not going well then it is important to speak up.

Supervisees need to be committed to maintaining a good working relationship with their supervisor and recognise that this is necessary even when they may be quite different from their supervisor or when they might not see 'eye to eye' on some issues.

Conclusion

It is easy to wax lyrical about the value of supervision in social work, particularly for beginning practitioners, in negotiating the complexities of practice, the tensions between professional and organisational roles, and making sense of what social work is all about. However, it is important not to forget that, like leadership, supervision is imbued with power relations and that the potential for abuse of authority is considerable. Unlike other leadership practices, supervision often occurs in a private environment where there can be highly charged emotions, conscious and unconscious, impacting on the relationship. Also, clearly, there are many approaches to supervision in different organisational settings, some of which may have little concern for social work values or professional autonomy. Nonetheless, supervision can facilitate critical reflection, develop effective practice strategies and encourage increased accountability and responsibility taking. These last two are the focus of our next chapter.

7 Accountability and Participation

In this chapter we overview

- defining accountability;
- codes of practice and quality standards;
- managerialism and accountability, including new accountability techniques;
- accountability and participation for service users and front-line staff;
- social innovation and participatory evaluation;
- service user movements.

Introduction

How is social work accountable and to whom is it accountable? How is a social worker required to demonstrate competence or professionalism within organisational contexts? The newly qualified social worker may quickly learn that there are professional ethical and operating principles that require them to act in different ways to those prescribed by organisational roles and responsibilities. What tensions are there between a social worker's 'felt' and professional accountability and the organisational or public accountability systems? These views of accountability can also be further confused by significant trends of privatisation and marketisation of services where accountability is linked to financial audits and the drive to quantify outcomes in performance and outcome evaluations (Burton and van den Broek, 2009; Ebrahim, Battilana and Mair, 2014). We have linked these trends to managerialism's influence and bureaucratisation in social work and social service delivery in the last two decades. Across English-speaking welfare states, social services have been subject to increased scrutiny in cost–benefit analysis, outcome-based evaluations and staff performance measurement in what has been called an 'era of accountability' (Kettner, Moroney and Martin, 2013). A social worker may have to choose between following personal views based on what is the responsible thing to do, and following official views that effectively encourage covering one's back and compliance (possibly inadvertently) with malpractice or workplace activities which they do not agree with ethically.

Understanding Accountability

Several writers in the social work literature have addressed both the philosophical and practical dimensions of accountability (Banks, 2002, 2004; Munro, 2004, 2005; Ospina, Diaz and O'Sullivan, 2002; Walker, 2002). Questions about accountability have also been raised in relation to the tensions between the professional values in social work and the increasing use of user-pays and market-based service delivery. Typically, these tensions involve a concern for process issues, such as quality of care, versus a concern for outcomes and efficiency. In such a climate, social workers need to guard against the drive for short-term efficiencies that can override longer-term effectiveness in programme delivery.

Organisational change brings with it important questions for professional ethics and accountability. Recent management and government reforms in terms of assessing, monitoring and ensuring quality control in human services have identified performance accountability as a key concern. This form of accountability focuses on monitoring the performance of staff in terms of their roles, responsibilities and duties. Will this satisfy the critics who want social work to maintain better standards and quality in their interventions? Social work will increasingly be subject to exacting standards as management and organisations 'drill down' into the fabric and interactions of organisational life. Further, the need for systems of professional and expert accountability in part results from social work becoming a high-profile profession, given the social problems, issues and risks it must confront and their severity as perceived by the community and the media.

The forms of accountability in social work and in human service organisations are multiple. One area of complexity is the sources of authority that hold social work to account as these are diverse in nature and significance. Banks (2002: 30–3), for example, based on actual cases, argues for four forms of social work accountability. They are:

- *technical*: accepted knowledge and skills about what works and how to do things;
- *procedural*: sets of rules and procedures about how to do things;
- *managerial*: orders or requests from a service manager; and
- *ethical*: accepted values and what is right or wrong.

The combination of these forms of professional accountability for social work can create confusion for newly qualified workers and needs to be weighed up in ethical decision making. Part of the key to understanding how such accountability practices work is to follow the activities and understand the actions of social work in specific organisational contexts. Further questions are raised by focusing on how staff and clients experience the organisation. Can and should staff members participate in the decisions usually made by managers? Specifically, can clients as users of services also participate in management and programme decisions?

In Chapter 1, we argued that social work's commitment to social justice marks it as distinct from other professions. Such professional action marks out the domains of intervention and change for social work involvement. Social work is involved in many areas of activity that make the profession multifaceted and multi-layered. Issues of accountability are multiplied by the audience to which social work finds itself accountable.

In a later section of this chapter, and following Corbett (1991), we explore the concepts of responsibility and accountability – upwardly to the organisation, downwardly to the client, inwardly to the profession and outwardly to the community. Some difficulties and tensions are apparent when using Corbett's model. For example, social workers might be involved in 'blowing the whistle' on illegal or unethical organisational practices that could include fraudulent use of funding or misrepresenting the extent of personal or familial problems. Following an examination of Corbett's model, we highlight two different forms of responsibility: passive responsibility or being held to account for past actions, and active responsibility or being more responsible to ensure future behaviour is appropriate (Bovens, 1998).

The term 'accountability' also has a strong source of meaning in legal science; that is, it is defined in legalistic terms as liability for conduct or action. This form of accountability is about who bears responsibility (Bovens, 1998). Why did you do it? What is to be done? In order to feel responsible and take responsible action, we are answerable to formal, informal and metaphysical forums (e.g. tribunals, appeal systems and/or the law). So accountability is the classical form of taking responsibility. Personal and systemic forms of being held to account are different and sometimes overlapping phenomena. The dimensions and interactions of felt and system accountability are key to understanding human service organisations and professional practice (Ebrahim, 2005). The added dimension of 'negotiated' accountability between organisation and community in social services has featured strongly in the customer- and consumer-based rhetoric of service organisations in recent years.

Audits and Codes of Practice

One crucial dimension to social work accountability is the tension between professional and organisational agendas, especially around professional values and identity versus desired programme and organisational outcomes. This can raise issues and sometimes conflict about what knowledge base constitutes professional identity and what are the core values of the profession. Codes of ethics offer suggestive guidelines for ethical decision making and behaviours that can help cohere with professional identity. The British Association of Social Workers' *Code of Ethics for Social Work* (BASW, 2012) identifies the need for social workers to be prepared to act as whistleblowers, thus acknowledging the potential for conflict between the values of the profession and the immediate interests of the organisation or powerful individuals within it. In this context, being prepared to engage in everyday action for change may involve quite drastic action that puts one's own job at risk.

Interestingly, codes of ethics are only directly applicable to members of professional associations, and thus breaches of these ethics can only be investigated with respect to members. In countries such as Britain and Australia, membership of the professional associations is typically low and thus one is left wondering about the utility of such codes. Nonetheless, they do provide a touchstone for appropriate conduct in professional relationships. The updated Australian Association of Social Workers' (AASW) *Code of Ethics* (2010) is a useful case in point of how an explicitly outlined code of ethics can set a clear framework that strengthens the integrity of practice.

In countries, such as New Zealand and the UK, where social work is a registered profession there are additional standards or codes of conduct to which social workers are held accountable. (Registration of social work in Australia has yet to be achieved despite a long-running campaign by the AASW.) Following the abolition of the General Social Care Council in 2012, a set of standards of proficiency was developed and published by the replacement regulatory authority, the Health and Care Professions Council. In the area of adult social care, a voluntary code of conduct replaced the previous code of practice. In the other countries of the UK – Wales, Scotland and Northern Ireland – the Care Councils were retained and continue to take responsibility for the revision of codes of practice and conduct.

Space does not permit a full account of British regulatory codes that relate specifically to social work and social care. However, examples from the *Standards of Proficiency: Social Workers in England* (Health and Care Professions Council, 2012) include being able to practise safely, within legal boundaries, as an autonomous professional, in a non-discriminatory manner, and to understand key concepts in the professional knowledge base. The changing nature and role of non-profit contracted service organisations in the provision of services have increased the need for British social work to comply with such quality assurance measures. This may be a trend in Australian social work in the future, with national standards developed by the AASW in areas such as mental health, school social work, and supervision, as well as organisational codes of conduct in areas such as child protection and community services (e.g. New South Wales Family and Community Services, 2013).

Importantly, many social workers will find themselves working within organisations that adopt traditional accountability concerns around finances, internal controls and regulatory compliance and what is called 'negotiated accountability' with client groups and the community (Ospina et al., 2002). Negotiated accountability comprises collaborative and partnership approaches to service delivery. This approach also coalesces with a managerial 'customer service' ethos, which influences social services. The perceived and actual discretion exercised by professional and related workers, particularly in non-profit organisations, has been either undermined or constrained by managerialist accountability mechanisms and increased outcome evaluation (Carson, Chung and Evans, 2015). Front-line workers will have to work smarter to maintain discretionary skill and expertise in the wake of managerial reforms and performance accountability in their jobs.

The main political, social and administrative context for increased public and professional accountability and performance in the delivery of social work services is the rise of what Power (1997) terms the audit society. As Munro (2004: 1091) points out:

> To some extent, the audit system is not a cause but a symptom of what is essentially social change. Professionals are given autonomy when the government and the public trust them to perform well. Auditing is introduced when the trust is lost and professionals are asked to make their practice transparent and accountable. Society's increasing distrust of social workers is part of a far wider process affecting professionals and officials.

Modern governments use strategies of new public management or managerialism, such as increased financial auditing, in their efforts to control the efficiencies of services. There is a stronger ethos of customer service and value for money with the introduction of user-pays models and privatisation in services. The audit provides a way that services can be held to financial and administrative account. Some of the problems with this management approach, as the quote illustrates, are how autonomy and flexibility of professional services and trust between providers and users of services can be maintained, given the watchdog-like imposition of these measures. At a 'big picture' level, it is therefore important for social work to understand accountability measures in the context of social change and shifting societal arrangements.

The use of audits and competency and quality standards in professional work raises new questions and difficulties in organisational contexts. In the next section, we explore how some of these new standards are often contradictory in purpose: imposing a top-down monitoring of actions, while asking for more front-line flexibility and risk taking by staff.

Competency and Quality Standards

In social work practice in organisations, we can say that accountability is affected by three main levels of organisational activity. First, 'one-on-one' encounters in social service organisations are the most visible level of relationship either between staff or between staff and clients/communities. Second, there is the level of formal performance standards and indicators and other requirements for workers or managers to fulfil their roles in the organisation. Finally, there is the level of external accountability, for example to funding bodies, which extends beyond individuals or formal internal organisational arrangements. Confusion about what priority should be given to each level of accountability can lead to multiple and often competing senses in which an individual social worker is, or feels, accountable (Walker, 2002: 62–3). This makes it difficult to discern whether evidence-based practice and best practice, as detailed in Chapter 1, is a professional movement or a political outcome of managerialism, or both. This is further explored in the next section.

A further dimension to social work accountability is that social work itself is a professional community that has values and standards set by formal training, education and other socialisation processes. These educational representations of social work in particular can conflict with organisational or societal views about how the profession is held to account (Banks, 2002, 2004). For example, the societal and media-driven expectations of social work might be to manage and solve social problems like poverty or domestic violence, whereas educational agendas might expect social workers to advocate on behalf of poor people, or women as victims of domestic violence. The new accountability of social work is evident in detailed procedures and monitoring systems that both regulate and account for practice. The complexities of ethical reasoning and justifications for social work's actions in organisations cannot be adequately addressed here (see Munro, 2005 and Chapter 9 for some limited discussion). However, there is little doubt that in today's climate of restrictive budgets and staff shortages, quality resources for information gathering and sharing may be in short supply. Nonetheless, service users have a right to both information on professional performance and a level of sensitivity and appreciation of their circumstances. If social work's monitoring and compliance systems are increased under the 'new accountability' of managerialism, it is likely that the sensitivity of intervention, say to cultural differences, will lose out. Chapter 8 will address some of these issues and examine evidence of work pressure and work intensification based in performance appraisal and monitoring in human services.

Central to current debates are the issues of quality standards and professional competence. These relate to the second level of accountability: performance accountability. During the 1990s, the construction of competency in social work was a key debate in social work and social work education in particular. Coulshed and Mullender (2001) discuss the tension between standards of excellence that encourage professional autonomy (and thus active responsibility) and the restrictions of top-down competency-based approaches that limit risk taking and innovation. In the last decade or so, British government agendas have appeared to want to secure top-down regulation over bottom-up autonomy and initiative by using performance indicators and national standards frameworks. In this scenario, service organisations are not 'freed up', as the politicians claim, but are subjected to more constraint by hierarchies and authority. This has been demonstrated through the use of audits to secure top-down financial and performance accountability in social work (Munro, 2004).

A central question then is how can quality practice be achieved in social work? Competency and professional autonomy need to be situated in the context of organisational practice and the organisation's socio-cultural connection to local community life. In order to work effectively, managers and front-line staff, including social workers, need to have clear boundaries with clients and maintain their sense of practice integrity with the community, using clear guidelines and ground rules for practice. In a general way, codes of ethics and codes of practice can enhance such work if used flexibly. Additionally, front-line staff, in particular, need to enhance their own autonomy with good practice supervision and in-service training to sustain quality services.

The question of quality practice can also depend on the perspective taken in achieving organisational and professional goals. The metaphors and theories of organisations (discussed in Chapter 2) can be linked to these issues. How we see ourselves in an organisational setting, and under what operating principles, can determine choices and decisions in these contexts. For example, the machine metaphor of Taylorism versus the constructed other metaphor of postcolonial theory give different understandings of how clients from different racial backgrounds are managed or encountered by human services and social work. Theories of accountability in social work can link to these organisational metaphors and other important creative areas of social work, such as programme design and clinical practice (Banks, 2004; Webb, 2001).

 Reflective Questions

1 How can codes of practice be linked to demonstrating effective and quality social service delivery in organisations?
2 What values and intervention strategies across the micro, mezzo and macro levels of practice will contribute to the effectiveness of small to medium-sized organisations with their clients and local communities?

The Impact of Managerialism

It is important to understand that the new agendas for accountability in organisations are a response to wider social policy trends and economic and political developments in service delivery in Anglo welfare states. The post-World War II welfare state has, in recent years, become increasingly market oriented – commonly associated with neo-liberal ideology that embraces global free markets and private sector performance management techniques. This ideological emphasis on creating more room and authority for free markets has resulted in shifts towards greater selectivity, residualism and privatisation in social services delivery. In the UK, the Global Financial Crisis of the late 2000s provided the justification for the escalation of these neoliberal strategies under the guise of 'austerity measures'. In Australia, new accountability agendas also reflect a conservative form of communitarianism developed in national social policy that relies on the language of social capital, social enterprise and capacity building in communities. Nonetheless, the worldwide trend towards privatisation and user-pays services has resulted in a smaller public sphere for debate and accountability on social welfare issues.

As suggested in earlier chapters of this book, there is now an ethos of extensive managerialism in the public sector and social welfare services that emulates many private sector management developments. This trend has had a major effect on social work's ability to deliver effective services in a period heavily focused on cost efficiency. Many writers have been critical of the mismatch between this private sector ethos and the common values and core focus of social services (Briskman, 2003; Ife, 1997; Thompson, 2000; Wanna, Butcher and Freyens, 2010). One social work critique of managerial strategies sees them as imposing certain modes of practice:

In managerial discourse, social workers are seen as largely accountable to their organizational superiors, namely managers and supervisors, through normal bureaucratic channels. [This] … requires that social workers 'do as they are told', following policies, procedures and regulations laid down 'from above'. (Ife, 1997: 53)

This *managerial discourse* is perhaps the most common one used when social work is held to official account. However, Ife also mentions three other competing discourses:

- *market discourse*: defines accountability by customer choice or satisfaction/consumerism;
- *professional discourse*: defines it as a duty to the client (not customer); and
- *community discourse*: the worker is held to account through democratic decision making, for example in community management committees, collectives or service user participation.

The argument could also be made that managerial discourse has intensified in recent years and has unfolded from earlier models and theories about 'good' management practices, such as the TQM movement of the 1990s (see Chapter 1).

Ife's (1997) model is useful for understanding how competing discourses can sometimes overlap and run parallel in human services and in social work. Ife (1997: 57) claims that social work can be 'practised within any of the four discourses', and he explores the possibilities and contradictions of such practice as assessed against hierarchical to anarchistic, and positivist to humanist, dimensions. In terms of critical organisational theory, all these discourses have a purchase on organisational practices, but some discourses dominate more than others in the current system. The political and policy implications of such discourses in social work and human services are even more apparent 20 years after Ife (1997) proposed his model.

The depoliticising of human services work is not a new effect of top-down managerial approaches. Since the early 1990s in the Australian public service, for example, there have been clear programme agendas and guidelines relating to the performance of staff using new accountability practices: 'Accountability is defined as existing where there is a direct authority relationship within which one party accounts to a person or body for the performance of tasks or functions conferred, or able to be conferred, by that person or body' (Management Improvement Advisory Committee, 1991: v). This definition heralded the new organisational theme of 'performance' as a key to accountability in Australia's public and social service cultures. 'Performance' accountability is dependent on many factors, such as the generosity of resources, workplace morale and the nature of relationships established between people in any organisation. The frustration for many public sector employees today, including social workers, is that there is little regard to questions of how performance is governed by accounting and auditing techniques. Social workers increasingly find their time taken up with the filling-in of performance data sheets and accounting for their daily activities in new performance-monitoring systems.

Wanna et al. (2010: 272–5) argue that the cultures and behaviours of public sector organisations cannot always produce a performance culture, despite utilising the tools of performance measurement and review. Managers do not always have control of organisational inputs and outputs or, for that matter, of final outcomes. As argued in Chapter 2, imagining metaphors that shape stability and change means that the actual social impact of human service organisations programmes can result from a combination of internal and external criteria and contextual complexities. Human service organisations have varying missions and multiple programme objectives that can increase the multidimensional nature of service and programme impacts, and make evaluation of service performance and effectiveness more difficult. Wanna et al. (2010: 275–7) also list some perverse negative effects as possible outcomes of performance management. These include:

- what is called 'gaming the numbers', which provides an incentive for gaming behaviour to be rewarded for meeting criteria such as performance or efficiency targets;
- a blocking of innovation or risk taking from an undue focus on seeking out funding 'cash cows'. This practice encourages the status quo by reproducing existing practice or blocking ambition as funding for services in the UK and Australia are often associated with private organisations 'skimming' or 'creaming off' highly funded users as clients;
- a veiling of actual performance, notably by aggregated data for large organisations that do not recognise the context of organisational practice, such as the establishment of long-term relationships with mental health clients that is made particularly difficult by both their disabilities and typically socio-demographic isolation. Examples of measures of effective performance here might actually be the client's ongoing social stability in housing and their physical and mental well-being, rather than the number of times a social worker has phoned, seen or referred a client.

Another perverse negative effect of performance management can be to drive out professional attitudes and discretionary risk taking, particularly when cooperation and trust, rather than competition, are needed in service delivery. We have mentioned the effects of performance monitoring elsewhere as encouraging a 'defensive social work' that does not take risks or challenge existing poor practice. Further, the copying of 'best practice' performance-based models does not necessarily lead to new learning and/or innovation. On the other hand, those organisations that do demonstrate efficiency or best practice may have their budgets cut to meet the new 'benchmarks' they themselves set for desired efficiency.

A further undesirable side-effect of putting greater pressure downward on frontline professional and other staff is that hostility and negativity in the workplace over lack of and ineffectual resources can lead to situations of possible abuse and blatant bullying. This is not a new phenomenon to social work relationships, and is usually more common in hierarchical settings such as hospitals (Collins, 2001). Space does not permit a full discussion here of this complex issue of conflict management and bullying in the workplace. Needless to say, processes of natural justice between conflicting parties and their grievance claims are often not dealt with in appropriate ways in the organisation, if at all. The result can lead to a need for workers to go outside the organisation and effectively 'whistle blow' on colleagues, management or the agency itself. This is a fraught ethical and legal strategy but one that is increasingly common across both non-profit and for-profit agencies in health and human services (Avakian and Roberts, 2012). The need for whistleblowers is enhanced when lucrative and partially secretive contracts for services and largely unregulated/self-regulated organisations are involved as providers of social services, as is the case now across English-speaking welfare states.

The language of performance management does not match the complexities of human service delivery and creates the paradox of perverse outcomes. All of these perverse effects add up to a difficult trajectory for organisations engaged with performance management in social work and the human services. The managerial undermining of trust and cooperation between front-line service agencies leads to compromise over policy goals and effective governance, and networking of these organisations. On this basis, effectiveness of performance may depend as much on the health of organisations and their specific programmes in any one sector or policy domain, and the resources available in that sector, as it does on tighter performance appraisal. Is there some autonomy and space for organisations to work within such constraints? Some authors have argued that there is some flexibility within 'social enterprise' strategies for innovation and 'third way' models of service delivery that can challenge and move beyond such perverse managerial and essentially neo-liberal or market-oriented effects (Barraket, 2008; Melville, 2008).

Research and Managerialism

Government-led reforms have instituted accountability techniques in line with the shift towards managerialism. In particular, the increasing use of research and evaluation instruments to measure standards and quality in human service organisations has raised difficult issues for professional social work. One key tension emerges between organisational (formal and informal) trust in professionals' work and mechanisms of formal accountability (Ebrahim, 2005; Munro, 2004; Walker, 2002). We have discussed the links between managerialism and new accountability as the general context for breaking or establishing new relationships between service providers and users. The social work profession has adopted feedback loops in organisations, such as client satisfaction surveys, to help evaluate programmes and professional effectiveness within these organisations. The new focus on performance in managerial approaches raises both anxiety in staff about their actions and also decreases risk taking on behalf of clients.

Munro's (2004, 2005) work on child protection points to organisational contexts as central to understanding good practice and professional accountability in social work. This raises questions about workers' knowledge and experience in organisations so that they can appropriately account for and reflect on their practices. The political driver for evidence-based practice (EBP) across professions such as medicine, nursing, psychology and social work is the new accountability and auditing agenda that Munro (2004) alludes to. The increased emphasis on EBP is in line with the introduction of quality and competence standards in British and Australian social work. Should 'evidence' be used as a criterion for judging the competence or standards of professional social work in organisations?

Social work, as a profession, has always been concerned with an adequate knowledge base for the kinds of occupational tasks and activities practitioners are involved in. Evidence can be understood as a narrower term referring to particular types of knowledge acceptable to a profession such as that gained from empirical research, government reports and academic theories, and arguments in particular disciplines like psychology and sociology. Further, the debate in social work on EBP appears to be centred on how positivistic and 'scientific realist' notions of evidence govern professional work. As discussed in Chapter 1, some argue that this is a narrow and unhelpful focus for a profession that needs a holistic understanding of human beings and human interactions (Larner, 2004; Webb, 2001).

In an Australian study, EBP was seen by social workers in a multi-disciplinary health team in rural Victoria as incompatible with their humanist knowledge base, which focused on the clinical experience of clients (Murphy and McDonald, 2004). In this study, non-social work team members, such as nurses and physiotherapists, de-legitimated social work by saying that it seemed to have little or no evidence for its practice. The important organisational context here was the introduction of EBP in health and the exacerbation of the divide between those with a bio-medical focus and the health-related professions, such as social work, that did not have access to such tangible knowledge. The problems were intensified by the dominance of the medical model in health settings and the social effects of undermining social work knowledge with bio-psycho quantitative science. The reach of 'medicalised governance' of local health services – even in rural settings such as the focus of this study – means that the medical model, including its reliance on positivist and quantitative science, can de-legitimise social work's humanistic knowledge base and experiential emphasis (Wearing, 2004: 264–5).

How can social work offer its own and often unique perspectives on human service organisations through research and pursue a commitment to improving the quality of our practice? There is a variety of methods related to practice-based research that can yield new insights into change and cultures in human service organisations. These alternative ideas on how to determine good practice and useful knowledge in social work are based in humanistic, existential and postmodern views, as several of the critics of EBP have claimed (Larner, 2004; Murphy and McDonald, 2004; Sellick et al., 2002; Webb, 2001). These include a reliance on experiential and practical knowledge to form on-the-ground judgements and decisions in practice.

One source of experiential knowledge of clients comes from service-user-based research and participation in health and social care organisations. We suggest in later sections in this chapter and in Chapter 8 that service user participation in service delivery and research can have a major impact on human service organisations, their governance and management structures. There have been stronger parallels in health services. Over the last 10 years or more, one area that has demonstrated a useful re-orientation of research practice is mental health research, which has sought to actively elicit service user views. Again, these areas are used as an example in later sections of this chapter and in Chapter 8. In Practice Example 7.1, research findings are used as a basis for developing holistic practice with service users.

PRACTICE EXAMPLE 7.1

A refugee mental health and counselling centre

How can research be used to understand the outcomes and practices used in organisations and their effectiveness? The Refugee Mental Health and Counselling Centre works with refugees and asylum seekers to empower them in terms of psychological difficulties and needs. There are social workers, specialist youth and children workers, psychologists and a psychiatrist working as counsellors and therapists. The organisation therefore requires complex inter-professional practice and referral systems in order to work with the needs of refugees and asylum seekers.

In working with this client group, centre staff assess and write up psychological reports and advocate on behalf of clients for citizenship status and in other legal matters. Using evidence on the mental and physical health needs of refugees and holistic practice, the workers are able to better understand and work with their clients and families. Among other issues, mental health concerns for this group can result from the loss of and separation from loved ones. On the basis of prior research, other general life issues that have been identified include:

- money;
- finding employment and being under-employed;
- finding secure accommodation;
- education;
- learning English;
- maintaining cultural practices;
- developing a social network;
- experiencing discrimination and racism;
- tracing friends and family still in danger; and
- supporting friends and family overseas through remittances and sponsorship. (STARTTS, 2004: 17)

Thus, the centre adopts a holistic approach to clients' psychological and physical needs. Appropriate settlement is seen as a crucial part of this approach. So too are partnerships across a wide range of organisations in order to develop a coordinated response to clients' complex needs (STARTTS, 2004: 17).

Practice Example 7.1 outlines a hypothetical refugee mental health organisation that deals with the complex health, mental health and cultural needs of refugees and asylum seekers. The holistic and self-empowerment approaches taken by this organisation are underpinned by values and process models that loosely base their knowledge for practice on experience and research in working with refugees. Health, mental health and socio-cultural understandings of refugees can be based in research on their needs and is immensely useful in enhancing the quality of such services. This knowledge base would be made evident in the centre's literature and in the aims and mission of the organisation, thus encouraging a flexible and holistic wellness model, and making practice transparent to service users. There is some qualitative evidence that social work's supervision culture is better supported in Australia than the UK and that the demands of social work in the refugee and asylum seekers area require greater training and education, and support for social work supervision (Robinson, 2014). Recent Australian writing in the area has emphasised the importance of a critical reflective and reflexive practice for supervision that incorporates not only the client system but also the worker, agency and community systems. It is argued that this will provide a systems analysis to better understand the grounds and issues of social work supervision (Connolly and Harms, 2012: 169–76). Chapter 6 has addressed supervision in greater detail. What we are emphasising here, in the context of accountability to and participation of clients and communities, is the need to consider systems and their interrelations as a whole in order to develop good practice in social work supervision relationships.

Public Accountability and Social Work

A broader way of talking about social work accountability is to link organisational and professional accountability to public policy processes. Social work has, like other professions, been at the mercy of recent policy changes to public service accountability (Burton and van den Broek, 2009; Treen, 2015). We have emphasised in the previous section the use of accountability techniques in line with managerialist agendas in policy making. The issue of public accountability looms large in services that are contracted out, and in many cases where accountability criteria are set by governments. For service providers, these are sometimes difficult to comprehend and unwieldy. Consider the many issues that occur in public policy cycles where there have been tragic consequences for clients or families in the delivery of services, such as in the areas of ageing, disability, homelessness and mental health, to mention only a few.

From a critical point of view, key actors in service delivery such as politicians, the media and senior public servants are involved on a regular basis in attempts to gloss over and revamp the standard setting and performance accountability of social services. Politicians, for example, are clever at image-managing the perceptions of their policies, even to the point of lying and not seemingly being held to account for these deceptions. Media and official attention on social problems, such as child abuse, can manufacture incorrect and untruthful claims about the role of social work and its responsibilities. This style of public accounting and accountability of social work has a long history, and while it may often have beneficial effects, it may also need to be challenged and better understood. It has been most notable in highly visible and controversial areas such as child protection and child abuse in both the UK and Australia, as illustrated in the following case.

An example from real practice that illustrates these different dimensions of responsibility and accountability is the well-known Orkney Islands child abuse scandal of the early 1990s. The social workers involved were the target of a blame and accountability discourse in the media and official accounts of the time. In this case, responsibility as cause was the main way blame was attributed without full liability and legal culpability being imposed, despite the settlement by Orkney Islands Council with the families. In this way, the local council social workers had moral responsibility for mis-information about the families and this became the way in which legal and moral blame was attributed. Eventually, the Orkney Islands social services accepted financial and legal liability for the case, given the uncertainty over the reality of the allegations (Munro, 1998; Turbett, 2004). The Wood Inquiry (Wood, 2008) in New South Wales, Australia, and the Munro Inquiry (Munro, 2011) in England both made suggestions for change to the child protection systems.

The Orkney Islands case raises interesting questions about the responsibility of the Orkney Islands social services as an organisation and the decision making and professional judgement exercised within it. Why wasn't more information collected on the families before a decision was made to remove the children? What legal advice and personal and legal risks to employees were considered by the agencies in taking up the case? Who took responsibility for decisions? Did the Orkney Islands social workers act in an over-zealous manner? Or were they right to adopt a strong protective approach? These are questions of both an ethical and an organisational kind. They can be linked to our discussion of false positives and false negatives in Chapter 5. As Turbett (2004) points out, whatever the specifics of practice in the area, the subsequent debate has generated useful and critical insights into the nature of and guidelines for practice, particularly in rural social work. In the work of authors such as Munro (1996, 1998, 2005) and Turbett (2004), we see the fruits of efforts to come to terms with inquiries into the professional conduct of social work, especially in child protection. The Orkney Islands case, along with other high-profile child abuse cases in public life and the media in Britain and Australia, have provided a useful reflection on and, in some cases, correction to, the avoidable mistakes of the past (see Parton, 1985; Scott and Swain, 2002).

As highlighted earlier in this chapter, Corbett's (1991) framework for public sector accountability identifies four broad dimensions to organisational accountability in the human services. This framework can be applied to the Orkney Islands case and others in human service organisations for, say, older people, people with disabilities and the unemployed. The framework raises questions about social work practice, either directly or indirectly, in terms of upwards, downwards, inwards and outwards accountability processes and techniques.

Upwards: accountability to the government executive and parliament. This is the traditional model of accountability in a Westminster system. In the case of the Orkney Islands child abuse allegations, the Clyde Report (1992) to some degree settled the case, or at least was the official account. This report established a consensus within the professional literature. Munro (1996), for example, quotes this as definitive in the outcome for the profession and the ongoing analysis of the case. Upwards accountability can produce useful consequences for change in organisational policies and procedures, notably in child protection. Another example is Parton's (1985) account of the death in January 1973 of a 7-year-old girl, Maria Colwell, at the hands of her step-father. The subsequent inquiry into her death meant issues in the quality of social work in child protection and work with families could be explored, as well as giving 'social work a jolt' (Parton, 1985: 82).

Downwards: accountability to the user, client and consumer, as in traditional community development and the managerial model. In the Orkney Islands case, certain questions can be raised that pertain to the accountability of social workers to clients and families involved or potentially involved. How might decisions made and actions taken have been different if there had been a clearer focus on clients' rights? How could a more caring and flexible approach have avoided a defensive 'covering one's back' response (Turbett, 2004)?

Inwards: accountability to the organisation includes processes of internally driven evaluations and internal audits, peer reviews and other internal monitoring. In the Orkney Islands case, such ongoing processes were in existence but they were obviously not thorough and systematic enough to pick up on poor rural social work practice (Turbett, 2004). Internal evaluation and review usually involve both informal and formal reflection on policies and practice by all staff. This can also lead to more formal processes of external evaluators running process evaluations that focus on the explicit objectives and design of programmes or practice in the organisation. Kettner et al. (2013: 7) argue for the 'programme logic' model – one that addresses inputs, process, outputs, outcomes and impacts as separate and then connected entities – as the best way to evaluate social service programmes. We agree with this argument for using programme logic to evaluate and suggest that education of staff in the model is developed. The hope is that, if used extensively in organisational practice for social work, a more reflexive and aware 'inward' evaluation and accountability could be established. This increased awareness of programme effectiveness (or otherwise) would give a sense of programme legitimacy and, over time with careful development, boost the key ingredient of 'office morale' among colleagues (Wearing, 2016; Urquhart and Wearing, 2016).

Outwards: accountability to the public. This may involve leaking certain details or information to media outlets or those with no direct stake in an issue, such as the Scottish press in the Orkney Islands case. An increasingly reported form of outward accountability in service cultures is 'whistle blowing' on illegal and unethical activities, giving media and public attention to policies and programmes. In the Orkney Islands case, the parents themselves and local groups in some cases were also exposed to outside scrutiny.

In professional practice, responsibility is a more all-embracing concept than accountability. One can be accountable without taking responsibility as in 'just doing our job'. However, we cannot be responsible without demonstrating accountability (Bovens, 1998). This is an important logical step for the social work profession because integrity is maintained by taking responsible actions and not just by being accountable. We return to the ethical agendas of responsible social work in our final chapter.

The current politics of service delivery dictate that professional actions need to be documented and articulated to demonstrate, in particular, performance accountability in organisations. Writers such as Munro (2004) place the audit as central to these new modes of accountability that foster a change in the sense of the profession's responsibilities. The difficult question here is: how can social work practice be audited? Government policy in Britain and Australia usually means that audits are conducted as an opinion or 'judgement' based on financial and quality assessments of organisational and programme effectiveness. The British government introduced the concept of 'best value' in quality auditing. It includes the key elements: accountability, transparency, continuous improvement and ownership (Munro, 2004: 1080). Munro suggests that, in the 1990s, social work as an intangible set of humanist traditions that were 'autonomous, private and idiosyncratic' was an auditor's 'worst nightmare' (2004: 1080). This has perhaps changed in the last decade, with a stronger emphasis on tangible outcomes and performance-managed professionalism, though the jury is still out on whether or how the effectiveness of interventions has improved.

Efforts in recording and using new information to improve or create better social work practice have come about in the last two decades. One potentially positive step is the social work ethics audit, which can lead to greater reflection on ethical issues in social work practice (McAuliffe, 2005). The ethics audit is a documentary process administered to practising social workers around ethical decisions they make in their practice. Another example of a similar strategy is critical path analysis (Kemshall, 1998). In a similar vein, the use of critical incident analysis in qualitative focus group research and in process evaluation can enhance critical and reflective learning internal to an organisation and in inter-organisation exchanges (Thomas, 2004). A discussion of critical incidents can allow a space for front-line and professional workers to voice and reflect on their own cases and for this to feed back into front-line practice and management (Wearing and Edwards, 2003). The purpose of these efforts seems to be to emphasise professional effectiveness rather than managerial control. However, it is probably more common for a mismatch to occur between the rhetoric of quality standards and the actualities of organisational and ethical performance in social work.

The challenge for organisational understanding in social work is to identify how non-profit and for-profit service organisations are publicly accountable given they are not government organisations. They are, however, doing social welfare work on behalf of governments for citizens. In the managerial approach, relying as it does on private sector accountability techniques, the political and public impact of contracting out services is muted and 'deals' done over the privatising and commercialising of once public services are kept behind closed doors in the 'corridors of power'. This is clearly undemocratic in the sense that service users and staff have few rights to appeal poor service practice except by resort to law (e.g. in the UK, utilising case law to assert rights to services funded by local authorities). At least in acknowledging the politics of service accountability, individuals are then given some responsibility as 'clients', 'regulators', 'participants' or 'litigants' who are active in the service system.

Hughes (1994: 253–4) predicted over 20 years ago that managerial measures for accountability would replace the older democratic political model of accountability. This is somewhat shaky today given evidence of the failures of wholesale contracting out and privatising of service areas, including transport, aged care, employment services and education, to mention a few. Governments are backed by a sound basis in law and eventually someone is accountable in organisational hierarchies and beyond in the human services.

Social Innovation and Participatory Evaluation

One of the features of new social programmes in social care and human service delivery, as funded by both the UK and Australian governments, is that stricter measures of public accountability, especially in the form of outcome evaluation, are applied. The renewed focus on outcomes arises directly from managerial concerns for measuring 'concrete' effectiveness and efficiencies or 'value for money', and in many cases from encouraging the managerial ideology of 'doing more with less' (Burton and van den Broek, 2009). These outcomes are tied to methods of research and evaluation that fit with quantitative measures of outcomes. In several ways, these 'metrics' run counter to a traditional social work concern with processes within services and programmes that are often oriented to qualitative evaluation (Alston and Bowles, 2003).

There is, however, a tension between the use of these metrics and service providers' ability to innovate for change in an organisation. The often strict and lean criteria for outcome-based evaluation require lateral thinking and creative ways to evaluate programmes so as not to lose them. In many cases, little flexibility or 'space' is allowed in the funding criteria for service providers, including social workers, to create both innovation in delivery and alternative modes of service delivery (Carmen, 2010). However, it is possible for social workers to consider more broadly the options for designing and evaluating programmes that facilitate participation and accountability. In combining social innovation in programme design and organisational delivery with participatory evaluation, a democratic or bottom-up model of 'accountability' of services emerges that ensures the inclusion of client and front-line voices. Thus, a key theme that needs to be addressed for social work in organisations is how to ensure 'bottom-up' participation in evaluation. This partly relies on who will ask the questions in the evaluation and whether they are open to the voices of clients and front-line staff. 'Program evaluators are inevitably on somebody's side and not on somebody else's side. The sides chosen by evaluators are most importantly expressed in whose questions are being addressed and, therefore, what criteria are used to make judgments about program quality' (Green, 1997, cited in Neuman and Kreuger, 2003: 420–1). There are many forms of evaluation, not least of which is a feasibility evaluation that is required to make explicit the objectives of programmes before any further evaluation can be carried out.

One approach to evaluation that embodies the social work ethic of self-determination is that of empowerment evaluation that allows clients as participants to also take part as evaluators. Empowerment evaluation requires a number of criteria to be met such as: stakeholder ownership; stakeholder involvement; participatory group techniques; a multi-method approach; and the evaluator's help to redefine the role of stakeholders. This could be a very useful approach if an organisation is already working closely with service users and has volunteers from the community who are ex-clients. Within the empowerment model, there is an explicit participatory framework and commitment to voicing the views of those involved in the evaluation: 'Empowerment evaluation … [is where] the users of the evaluation can maximize their participation in and gain from the evaluation process … the more participation in decision-making processes the participants have, the likelier they become to commit to and invest in the decisions' (Smith, 1998: 256). The most recent thinking on social innovation and evaluation tends to suggest that forms of empowerment evaluation are best followed when certain stages can be fulfilled. Fetterman et al. (1996) have suggested four stages of empowerment evaluation:

- Take stock of concerns and resources.
- Plan a vision that all are dedicated to, and develop strategies and action plans.
- Implement strategies and action plans.
- Generate outcomes to document competence and progress.

These general stages demonstrate the traditional pattern of participatory evaluation with the added dimension of including how clients are empowered by the evaluation.

Certain operational conditions will also need to be fulfilled for a successful empowerment evaluation, which include using the evaluator as teacher and allowing time for stakeholders to be heard and recorded. Further, a working partnership of evaluators, practitioners and consumers is required, and participants should be compensated and management provide support for the process and the dissemination of results (Smith, 1998). These criteria for empowerment evaluation lead into larger issues in programme evaluation. For example, the question of whether evaluation should be done by independent/external or internal evaluators is a vexed one. Evaluation methodologists usually suggest internal evaluation as a way that organisations can have some control of what is evaluated and how, and keep the financial costs down. External and independent evaluation often requires financing from the programme funder or another body, but does have the advantage of providing independent advice. Other issues to consider are: the scope of the evaluation; how much it focuses on outcomes; difficulties in defining outcomes; whether different interpretations of 'effectiveness' are considered; the impact of hidden agendas; the need to maintain programme integrity; the complexities involved in the delivery of programmes; and whether the overall programme content and delivery make sense in the context of the objectives of the organisation.

Practice Example 7.2 brings several themes together in evaluating organisational practice, including interdisciplinary care, social innovation and user participation. The example used is a growing aged care organisation that is moving from autonomous professional care to more integrated and performance-managed care. Such a change could bring with it the paradoxical and perverse outcomes mentioned in relation to performance management in the public and social services in general. Further, such a transition and shift in care could apply across a range of other service areas, including mental health and health services, and so is an opportunity to reflect practically on processes and outcomes to which social work can make a significant contribution.

PRACTICE EXAMPLE 7.2

Evaluating social innovation in Oasis Aged Care

Is it possible to encourage social innovation and risk taking by social workers and participation by service users in performance-managed organisations? If so, how? Using a participatory evaluation framework such as empowerment evaluation can create significant social innovation and feedback into organisations regarding the needs and concerns of clients or service users.

Oasis Aged Care is planning to move from a residential nursing home attached to a private hospital to a full-scale aged care facility that includes age-blended accommodation and specific residential and community services for people aged 55 years and older. Many of the social workers in the service are traditionally engaged in palliative and hospice care, although they also see a strong case for their involvement in community and respite care as well.

As is the case in the hierarchies of other health/hospital settings, social work often finds its role subordinated to the clinical professions such as medicine, psychiatry, senior nursing or physiotherapy. The division of labour in the health profession can mean that there are perceived overlaps and competition in terms of health and social care (Wearing, 2004). A key issue is the different forms and competing ways in which these professions are accountable and responsible. There are some indications, however, that a degree of autonomy and also integration for social work can be enhanced through interdisciplinary care and cooperation (Hudson, 2002; Hughes and Heycox, 2010; Lymbery, 2006). In social work's case, it needs to come to terms with what are the tangible results and processes that are delivered by the profession for clients, thereby indicating effectiveness in service delivery. While the organisation may evolve into a more complex structure, the values of respect and capacity building for local communities and clients need to be the focus (Doherty et al., 2015).

There is concern among the social work unit that their programmes and practice will not be valued in the context of what is predominantly the provision of bio-medical and nursing care services for older people. In particular, it is feared that the broader grouping of families who are providing home-based care but rely on the facility for respite, and the aged care users themselves, will have little voice in the rapidly changing service. The senior social worker, with the support of the unit, decides to implement an empowerment evaluation that will bring social work's concerns and the experiences of the aged care clientele into the picture for senior management and the emerging organisational change agenda.

Following the four steps outlined in this chapter, evaluation of and subsequent feedback to the organisation and service users raise a number of options that will increase the profile of social work in aged care. These include developing strategies to sustain and support carers. A major focus is for carers to gain assisted enrolment in meditation, dance, music and fine art courses in the community to overcome isolation and develop informal social supports. Another outcome is to increase the number of outside visits, picnics and leisure trips by the residents to facilitate a better quality of life. The main redefined role for social work, however, is to develop and implement psycho-educational classes for partners, family members and carers on dementia and Alzheimer's disease.

User-led Participation and Anti-racist Social Work

How have social workers and the organisations they work in become more accountable to clients and local communities? A significant and related issue to public accountability is re-emphasising the democratic and citizenship rights of clients and their families in service delivery. The example used here to illustrate some of the difficulties with participation is anti-racist approaches in social work practice. The hotly contested debate in Australia over socio-cultural citizenship for Indigenous and migrant communities is evidenced in struggles around the 'stolen generations' and the detention and repatriation of recent refugee arrivals. These examples demonstrate that where global issues of 'race', migration and destination or host community intersect, there is a 'postcolonial contact zone'. Front-line workers in human and health services in Australia and elsewhere in ex-colonial welfare states often find themselves at the initial point of this contact zone. Similarly in the UK, social workers are increasingly thrown into the front line of the immigration debate. Legislative requirements mean that local authority social workers may be forced to report people trying to access services who may be in the country illegally (Humphries, 2004). More broadly, the anti-racist approach has a strong tradition in the UK and has been used as a principled basis for the inclusion and participation of black and minority ethnic groups in services (Begum, 2006; Dominelli, 1997). Some organisations demonstrate flexible spaces for cultural identity politics and practice that enable culturally appropriate participation of service users. Thus, there is a degree of democratisation in some human service organisations that include in their processes the rights and needs of the racialised 'other'. For example, when local communities' views and identities are considered and given credence in organisational policy and processes, there are possibilities for alternative programmes that include 'the other'.

Developing programmes in this way can mean they are deeply connected with non-white user identities and, if applied more broadly, with minority and host community cultures. Community-oriented (downwards) accountability and participation offer far-reaching and culturally sensitive ways of practising that move social work away from traditional casework or community work models. Alternative models require the appropriate devolution of power to client groups by increasing democratic participation in organisations. Begum (2006: 16–20), for example, lists three major factors that can enhance participation by black and ethnic minority service users in the UK:

- a strong history of self-help and direct action by black and minority ethnic communities;
- black and ethnic minority service user participation does work when properly supported; and
- having social care professionals working with black and ethnic minority service users as allies, advocates and brokers.

Some of these styles and histories of partnership between users and providers of services are also apparent in the disability rights movement in the UK (Carr, 2004). Carr (2004: 5–6) extends her review of service user participation beyond simply involvement in services to one that is concerned with the human rights and social citizenship of various groups, including black and ethnic minority communities, children, older people, people with disabilities, and so on. There is also a need in service delivery to include different kinds of advocacy at the mezzo level for changing policy within the brief of professional social work. This can include 'social advocacy' or action aimed at aiding social groups, and 'agency advocacy' or actions aimed at changing organisational and inter-organisational systems to enhance better service delivery (Levin, Goor and Tayri, 2013: 523–6). These are important dimensions to organisational practice for social work, albeit difficult to maintain under neo-liberal conditions of resource and budgetary constraints, and measures for economic efficiencies.

The broad related issue to that of participation and ownership in service delivery is that of cultural sensitivity. Social work education and practice theory in Australia and Britain is predominantly white and Anglo-centric, but many social workers, managers and other staff in the human services today come from diverse ethnic and cultural backgrounds, and their participation also needs to be considered in such organisations. Nonetheless, the ethno-centric and mono-cultural content of social work education is reflected in the hierarchies and power base within the social work profession. In order to help counteract such bias, there is a variety of organisational sensitivities and procedures that social workers can take into account. One suggestion is the principle and strategy of equalising action where social work advocates justice for black people and through equalising actions to redistribute power and resources towards non-white others (Dominelli, 1997: 162). There can be multi-dimensional and multi-layered factors that contribute to misunderstanding and misperception in the delivery of social programmes and social work as a professional service to ethnically diverse and minority group clients.

One example that is useful is cross-cultural work. Issues of racism and prejudice in service culture, norms and values can often be apparent if a social worker comes from a white or different background to service users and the organisational structure is white-centric. Thompson (1993), among others (see also Dominelli, 1997), has addressed these issues in terms of anti-discriminatory practice. Social work has a responsibility to challenge racial inequality and prejudice in broader society and how racism is institutionalised in human service organisations. How can an anti-racist, anti-discriminatory and participatory practice be developed in organisations that can then respect and enable the needs and rights of others? How can front-line and professional workers in organisations conceive their identities as in opposition to social constructions objectifying and 'othering' the user or client? In terms of urban Australia, Baldry et al. (2006: 372) address such issues for Aboriginal people through information sharing. They suggest that:

- managers, policy makers and ministers should talk genuinely with Aboriginal people and organisations;
- staff members should have the appropriate skills to work with Aboriginal clients;
- a summary of departmental policies in plain English should be made available – clear explanations need to be given regarding what went wrong when a form is incorrect; and
- information should be shared among and between government services and non-government organisations (NGOs) in order to ensure holistic responses.

We return to some of the concerns of service users or clients such as Aboriginal people, ethnic minorities, people with disabilities, children and older people, and their experiences of human service organisations in greater depth in the next chapter. Some of these cross-cultural and 'race'-based issues are addressed in models for practice rooted in anti-bureaucratic and participatory practice. Social workers and other front-line staff can improve service quality for oppressed groups, and create less racist and discriminatory practices and more effective learning organisations. They can also, given the diversity of backgrounds of social workers themselves today, challenge discrimination based on 'race' in the workplace. Principles such as equalising can also be applied to sexist, homophobic and locational oppression and prejudice when encountered in practice. Also, the insectionality of oppression around factors such as social class, gender, race and location can enable an understanding of the complex dimensions to oppression. In her review of the effectiveness of service user participation over a 20-year period in the UK, Carr (2004: 13–14) notes that organisational commitment and responsiveness are slow or not occurring, even in response to the legislated requirements for user participation. However, there is still hope that such change will bring greater accountability for service users and the broader community.

The Impact of Service User Movements

How has social work contributed to and become a part of the ethos of consumerism and/or participation? There have been debates in social work education and in practice that relate directly to the inclusion of users in service delivery research and decision making. One of the authors of this book has argued the case for rights-based and participatory practice for youth service delivery and the importance of youth–adult collaboration on programme knowledge, design and delivery (Wearing, 2011). The forerunner to these debates in such areas of service delivery is found in the inclusive arguments of the mental health and disability rights movements and their effects on social work.

Beresford and Croft (2004) have argued that the key changes for consumers or clients of services have come from disability rights movements and other social activism (Beresford, 2000; Croft and Beresford, 1997). Croft and Beresford (1997: 276) define the parameters of the service user approach from service users' perspectives and the social model of disability by stressing:

- 'support for service user to be able to participate on equal terms';
- equity in treatment of service users, regardless of age, class, 'race', disability, sexual identity or gender; and
- 'recognition of diversity, for example, people's different ways of communicating non-verbally, in pictures, by signing or in minority ethnic languages'.

Beresford and Croft (2004) provided a critique of social work approaches as needing to embrace service user perspectives, given the prioritising of learning from user experience (e.g. in education accreditation standards). Such an approach can be adapted to macro-practice issues in organisational settings as suggested by anti-racist social work. We also argue that assessing clients' lived experience of social work practice in organisations – particularly in terms of process and outcomes – is central to the self-evaluation of the profession. There are several models from practice that would assist these processes. For example, the task-centred approach seeks to gauge what tasks are completed when and where by social workers in a very straightforward and practical strategy, involving professional review and support for organisational learning (Marsh and Doel, 2004).

Task-centred practice involves the judicious use of three sources of knowledge: that from research; that from practice experience, and that from the views of service users and carers. In a social work agency it will usually involve setting this knowledge in the context of specific policies, and it will often involve some aspect of the law. Balancing up these from different sources is far from easy. Doing so in a stressful situation, where there are often important consequences for the lives of the individuals is particularly difficult. (Marsh and Doel, 2004: 153)

A detailed discussion of user-led research is not possible here. It would appear, however, that both individual and family views require consideration and give clients a voice in some organisations and areas of service delivery. We have suggested in the sections on accountability and participation that new ways of doing social work in organisations that take account of the clients' and front-line staff's perspectives are possible and achievable. Such reform measures that re-position the user as central to professional and organisational practice in health and social care services need to be tempered with caution, as the ideology of consumerism is often used to support the hyper-managerialism and economic rationalisation of certain units or areas of service delivery. Reform of organisational processes, procedures and structures may be possible in human services in using such guidelines as operating principles. We have suggested advocacy and empowerment models from service user movements and anti-racist and anti-oppressive practice to give some basis for this internal reform.

 Reflective Questions

1   What dimension of upward, downward, inward and outward accountability do social workers need to be aware of in the lessons learned from the case outlined in Practice Example 7.2? How can innovation improve the position and participation of clients or users? How should social work and related services be reviewed and evaluated to improve practice and organisational learning?

2   How can social workers improve sensitivity to cultural diversity among clients in service delivery? For example, what organisational structures and processes need to change to enable Dominelli's (1997) 'equalising principle' to impact on both staff and clients?

Conclusion

This chapter has discussed both accountability and participation in relation to human service organisations and social workers' possible roles as active and responsible change agents both for user and staff participation in such services. We consider these roles to be important for the profession in working with organisations and organisational change. Some authors have suggested general work-based strategies for dealing with change. Bovens (1998) argues that making a virtue of responsibility is useful when dealing with the vague and harsh realities of organisational change and accountability. Munro (1996, 1998) and Munro and Hubbard (2011) advocate giving more time and better working conditions to social workers to allow for considered decision making, self-critical judgements and organisational learning. Following such strategies can realise a good general and ethical basis for improving accountability and participatory practices.

A further set of questions arises from new managerial agendas. How can social work keep its professional integrity in the face of public and management pressures? How can social work survive managerialist cultures and implement principles and insights from practice wisdom and experience? In using child protection, aged care, participatory evaluation and anti-racist practice in this chapter as examples of social work expertise, we can expand on the developments for other areas of social work. Such practice areas could include work with offenders, HIV-positive clients, and call centres in the areas of child abuse, youth suicide and depression.

In becoming more accountable and more responsible, a fine-grained understanding of how staff and service users experience organisations is necessary. In the following chapter, we examine these experiential dimensions of organisational life in detail. In particular, we recognise that organisations are experienced at different levels: from the life-worlds of the individual and client through to the networks of interaction and social care delivered at the community level and institutions at the societal level. This will help establish our concluding arguments that organisational practice for social work requires a unique blending of micro, mezzo and macro practice orientations to be competent and effective.

8 Experiencing Organisations

In this chapter we overview

- stressors, issues and problems for staff and clients in human service organisations, including work intensification;
- voice, learning and experience in organisational practice;
- five levels of organisational experience, ranging from the client and individual level to the community and society level.

Introduction

Human service organisations are faced with many of the market-based dilemmas and problems that beset private sector and corporate organisations. These organisations have in many ways done away with old bureaucratic hierarchies and processes. There remain, however, significant challenges, such as overcoming possible corporate restructuring, which could include 'the removal or diminution of career ladders, greater insecurity, and the intensification of work for the survivors of restructuring' (Thompson and McHugh, 2002: 179).

How do human service organisations adapt to these demands and challenges? What has been required is a shift to models of service delivery that involve stakeholder interests, networks and claims for a participatory and anti-hierarchical approach, combined with organisational learning. It also requires levels of learning and unlearning to cope with large organisational reform and change in current social policy climates. There is even the more radical idea that the sheer juggernaut of knowledge and innovation now impacting human service organisations – through movements such as evidence-based policy and practice – requires 'non-learning' and spontaneity for workers to cope with the contradictions and dilemmas of work (Avby, Nilsen and

Ellstrom, 2015). Such organisational mindfulness, awareness and competence to act with authenticity and spontaneity may counter some of the everyday work stressors and scarce resources created by the neo-liberal welfare state (Wearing and Hughes, 2014). This need not separate, as organisational theory does, learning from non-learning organisations, as all human service organisations have the capacity to embrace flexibility and contradiction and to counter the managerial trends of formalisation and standardisation (Clegg, Kornberger and Pitsi, 2008: 364–5).

More than a quarter of a century ago, a leading writer on adult learning, Malcolm Knowles (1990: 163–6), sounded warnings for 'adult learners' that significant social changes such as personal computers would affect our ability to learn and adapt in organisations. Today, even more so, it would seem that social workers need to be both organisationally aware and ready to learn, and prepared to unlearn outdated or plainly mistaken practices that have the habitual and routine tendencies of bureaucratisation, for example, and that actually obscure the harsh realities of front-line work and hinder effective service delivery (Silverman, 2014). One macro issue that social work practice could increasingly focus on in organisational work is the need for prevention work with marginalised and vulnerable populations (Manthorpe, Cornes, et al., 2015). Another key area for social work awareness is exemplified by the concept of 'accurate empathy'. Such empathy is practised in highly complex and socially differentiated societies, such as the UK and Australia, where categories of social identity are shifting and any set 'pigeon holes' of oppression and discrimination are difficult to define, except in the most extreme circumstances of hardship and inequality (Wearing and Hughes, 2014).

We suggest that taking account of people's experiences as both users and providers in human service organisations will bring more of the 'life-worlds' of these people into perspective. Grunwald and Thierch (2009) provide a framework for this in their discussion of the social construction of reality as resulting from the social world of everyday experiences, and notably, in our case, those that the social worker is active and involved in constructing. This is similar to the everyday interpretive world offered in symbolic interactionist and phenomenological understandings of organisational processes and change. That is, the human change agent, whether social worker or related front-line worker, is always learning and renewing their skills and understanding of the social and personal realities of clients and the networks of those working around them in organisations. This is effectively a life-long learning and continuing education model. The point of view of actors and their experiences of and within changing organisational forms is crucial to informal and formal organisational learning and feedback on effective organisational action.

Experiencing Service Work: Stress, Restructuring and Limited Resources

The quality of care provided in human service institutions depends in part on how caring and compassionate the professional caregivers are, but it also relies on their flexibility and openness to change. New problems and solutions are constantly emerging in education, mental health, nursing and other fields. Professionals who have become set in their ways, who rigidly practise as they always have, aren't likely to provide effective – or humane – service (Cherniss, 1995: 77). In a climate of neo-liberal managerial reforms and the resultant organisational restructuring, issues around the pressures on professional work, including work stress and worker well-being, are heightened. What emerges in the change process is the need for professional social work to remain committed to values and a skill base that enhance the lives of clients and facilitate change in organisational environments. However, there are important work-stress issues to overcome in such change processes. One study indicated that staff in child and family social work had a lower level of job satisfaction, higher stress levels and greater absenteeism than the norms for other occupational groups (Coffey, Lindsey and Tattersall, 2004: 736).

We have indicated in prior chapters how recent organisational change in the human services impacts on staff, including social workers. The key impact on work identity is the general 'work intensification' of service work (Willis, 2005). This refers to the placing of more responsibility on workers to do more within the same weekly hours and often with the same or fewer resources at their disposal. Some, if not most, of this impact is attributable to managerial changes and the restructuring of human service organisations. A multitude of factors contribute to work intensification, including superficial interaction by telephone to optimise output and efficiency. This is evidenced in child protection call centres that have partly replaced face-to-face professional counselling (van den Broek, 2003), and in increasing aged care workers' administrative workload, thereby inhibiting their effective caring work and leading to burnout, absenteeism and turnover (Stack, 2003).

There is also evidence that managerial reforms have undermined traditional advocacy and policy roles in church-based human services (Winkworth and Camilleri, 2004). Thus, the empirical evidence suggests that social work will have to work harder to make advocacy and empowerment activities a priority in the face of organisational restructuring and managerial changes.

A flexible approach to social work is needed in the face of these emerging equity questions of protecting clients' rights to quality programmes and front-line staff's entitlements within organisations. International studies have highlighted workplace support, quality improvement measures and supervision as positive moderators of stress in work experience. A meta-analysis of 25 articles in the USA claims that sociological, economic and psychological studies have not yet developed a single unifying model for the process of staff turnover in human services and related work areas such as mental health (Barak, Nissly and Levin, 2001: 628). Arguments about gaps in research knowledge apply even more when the weight of change is considered in employment conditions, monitoring, auditing, compliance and accountability. Studies in Britain and Australia have emphasised that employees and their organisations in the human services will experience further difficulties if unprepared for new workplace changes and rationalisation (Coffey et al., 2004; Spall and Zetlin, 2004). Researchers have also found that front-line staff in contracted service organisations in family support work, for example, 'experience acutely' the changes in performance measures and other associated new work regulation (Spall and Zetlin, 2004).

These developments in human and social care services are paralleled in health, where social welfare spending is larger and where, in the UK and Australia, the impact of managerial reform on services has been felt for longer. There is a considerable body of Australian and British research on health services that has revealed some of the hidden social costs of managerial reform. One significant study of the effect of budget cuts in a public hospital in South Australia found that the work burden increased and the work intensified. Staff reductions fell on nurses and lower-level employees such as administrative, catering and cleaning staff. Early career doctors and all team-based staff were also affected by these changes in the workplace (Willis, 2005: 266). This study also revealed costs in injury, illness and staff turnover from the introduction of managerialism (Willis, 2005: 266). The privatising and outsourcing of public sector delivery in health is now matched in human services, although similar research on human services remains scant.

It is clear that changes in funding and other measures have increased pressures on staff, including a pressure to perform and be held accountable to middle and senior management (see Chapter 7). As already mentioned, this work intensification decreases a sense of autonomy and increases management control and work stress. It also raises questions about the degree of autonomy, support and supervision for front-line staff, in particular, in these organisations. There is a feeling that under pressure from managerial changes the front-line worker's and professional's discretion and autonomy may be hampered or restricted by centralised and hierarchical governance structures.

One of the most important issues this raises is workplace stress for social workers and other front-line practitioners. How can professional development and learning in human service organisations help to protect workers from overwork and stress? There are many self-help and popular texts available on stress in the workplace. For example, Warren and Toll (1993) provide some helpful tips on workplace stress, and in general provide a more humane perspective on the often dehumanising aspects of working in the caring professions. How such issues are managed in the workplace is also important for the health of the organisation. Social workers are commonly some of the worst offenders in not setting boundaries and time limits on their paid work. Over-involvement in clients' issues or feeling that extra work time outside of designated work hours is needed in order to establish effective practice are common professional conundrums. In some cases, good social justice work, counselling and advocacy will involve extra commitment. However, is it not better to think of the longer-term sustainability of effective work with realistic time limits than to burn out or become a workaholic? Rather than have people off sick, it is important that human service agencies adjust their expectations of staff according to staff needs and pressures. Dealing with such issues of work experience helps in managing the workplace and can build morale and job commitment through careful and fine-detailed attention to staff experience.

Work-related stress is just one area affected by organisational restructuring and managerial change. Other related issues of occupational health and safety include physical, psychological and emotional risks. This is especially important in service delivery in the human services where the health and well-being of staff flow in to their interactions and communication with clients and other stakeholders.

Sharing information, letting people know what is happening and what is expected of them, and listening and responding to what they say are important tools in the management of stress. Lack of communication, either at work or in personal matters, will act as a constraint (Warren and Toll, 1993: 120). Staff can also be subject to 'bullying' or undue work pressure by supervisors or colleagues, or experience a lack of adequate supervision for the complexity of tasks they are required to fulfil, or a general lack of support for and flexibility over personal, family and health issues. As the majority of the human service workforce is female, these issues are inevitably gendered. In this sense, human service restructuring can impact most heavily on women, especially those with young children in their care or those who care for other family members. Poor staff management practices can lead to high turnover of staff and increased sick leave, low morale and resultant ineffectiveness in service delivery (Barak et al., 2001).

Workplace stress and bullying in a human service organisation

In a local social services office, the caseloads of front-line staff, not all of whom are qualified social workers, are increasing by the month. The new social work qualified team leader, Noor, is a dedicated professional but relatively inexperienced and was the only person to apply for the job when it became vacant. Within a few weeks of starting work at the agency, Noor became aware that there are divisions within the staff between those who are see themselves as most competent and able to manage the complexity of the work, and those portrayed as 'slackers' or 'incompetent'. She is also aware that a number of staff are taking sick leave on a regular basis and that others are applying for positions elsewhere.

The issue recently came to a head when one staff member posted disparaging comments about a group of his colleagues on Facebook. This inadvertently came to the attention of one of this group who approached Noor to complain of bullying. It was also noticed by the agency's executive director, whose administrative assistant keeps a close eye on social media. She demanded Noor 'get her team into line' immediately. Although feeling intimidated by this reaction, Noor arranged an appointment with the executive director to talk through the issues relating to bullying, as well as workplace stress and work intensification within the team. It was agreed that, with the support of staff from the human resources department, Noor would meet with all staff individually to gain their feedback on team dynamics and their experience of the workplace. It was also agreed that the Facebook messages would be investigated in line with the organisation's workplace harassment policy, with the staff member who posted the comments potentially facing disciplinary action.

As a result of these initiatives, the team decides to argue for flexible work time and for consistency in the number of active cases team members need to deal with on a weekly basis. Some staff need to increase their work capacity in this regard but most staff have been overburdened by the volume and the difficulties of dealing with some clients. Another strategy the team wants to implement is good supervision arrangements for all staff, as well as processes for assigning complex cases to specialist professionals such as social workers.

PRACTICE EXAMPLE 8.1

One key strategy for social work in this area is to intervene as soon as possible in issues that affect staff well-being and health. How can 'unhealthy' stress in organisational systems be better managed? Having awareness of and responding to potential stressors can lead to better staff morale and greater understanding of internal work needs and pressures on staff. In effect, this prevents or cuts off the potential workload stressors. Such issues of stress and low morale in a workplace, while potentially related, need to be separated out from those of underperformance at work – keeping in mind that such underperformance itself can be caused by poor management practices.

  Reflective Questions

1   What are the factors that contribute to stress and bullying in the workplace in Practice Example 8.1? How can excessive stress and anxiety in social work services be reduced or overcome in staff development and supervision arrangements? Use Practice Example 8.1 to illustrate your response.
2   What factors can improve the workplace cultures and morale of human services? List your understanding of what can contribute to front-line workers' and professionals' well-being.

User and Staff Experiences

One of us (Wearing, 1998, 2001) has argued elsewhere that it is the experiential reality of clients and front-line staff that should be taken into account in adjusting or changing organisations to better meet social need or deal with identified social and personal risks. Front-line social workers are involved at 'the coalface' of programme delivery with their clients and families and in the 'on-the-ground' making of policy. They often have to make decisions based on their own discretion in their everyday individual or group work with these clients. As suggested, a key role for social work here is to identify, mediate and where possible reduce the stressors in the workplace. Some stress is normal and motivating; however, undue stress and work pressures will freeze a workforce and an organisation, and this unhealthy stress can quickly demoralise the work culture. The important perspective we provide here is one based on an existential and humanistic understanding of lived experience and the ways in which clients and staff give 'voice' to their concerns about specific services or practices.

What we outline in this chapter in terms of work practices and social work practice itself are experiential levels of reality in organisations. As illustrated in Chapter 1, one way of classifying social work interventions is to separate them into micro, mezzo and macro practices, though in reality these are not always easily or clearly separated. The better-known micro practices are those related to one-on-one work with individuals and groups, such as case management or counselling roles. Mezzo practice tends to be associated with team and organisational work, whereas macro practice occurs in 'organisational, community and policy arenas' (Netting et al., 1993: 3). This is a useful way of coming to terms with how clients and staff then experience different levels of reality in an organisation. We want to take a balanced approach to how organisational processes, procedures and compliance mechanisms can affect social work practices, depending on the nature of intervention and the ways in which such interventions challenge existing social, personal and community arrangements.

We agree with Netting et al. (1993: 123) when they claim that 'social workers with little or no idea of how organisations operate, or how they are influenced and changed by both outside and inside are likely to be severely limited in their effectiveness'. However, unlike their claim to macro practice as the key driver for changing the organisation, inside and out, we want to argue that all three areas of practice need to take account of the different levels of experience in organisations for a complete understanding of work in human service organisations. The three levels of social work intervention interact with the levels of experience in human service organisations. These folds of experiential reality help determine perceptions, relationships and knowledge frames in an organisation. Spiralling out from the everyday service encounter between front-line staff and client is the 'behind the scenes' work, such as staff meetings and other formal and informal gatherings, that helps to constitute office procedures, staff supervision (including social work supervision) and the organised hierarchy. In order to unfold these layers and interconnections between staff and clients, we need to understand how they are experienced by both staff and clients in different service settings. This analysis of organisational levels links to current public policy literature that examines in greater detail the external organisational and inter-organisational level of social and public policy making and service delivery (Hill, 2005; Wanna et al., 2010).

A setting we examine in this chapter is a large public housing estate located in the inner city of Sydney, Australia. The residents of this estate are among the poorest Australians on social and socio-economic indicators. Some of the unique features of human service organisations become apparent through this discussion, including their focus on clients who are serviced by these organisations using social welfare values, such as promoting human well-being and quality of life. There is a widely recognised policy trend and research literature that focuses on capacity building and the development of social capital or organisational intervention at all levels. This ranges from the individual through to the societal level in establishing, replenishing and embedding sound organisational cultures and structures in vulnerable, marginalised and disadvantaged communities (Bryan and Brown, 2015). Other examples provided in the chapter also demonstrate some of the power imbalances between social workers and their designated roles in organisations, their clients and other staff. Briefly these levels are:

- *Client and individual level*: this level and the group-networking level are primarily concerned with micro and mezzo experiences. This level includes both clients and staff such as front-line and professional workers who have unique and personal experience of the organisation. The meeting of the 'life-worlds' of these groups through interaction and social exchange in service provision requires a complex understanding of the everyday experiences and relationships of clients with service providers. Taking these perceptions and understandings of the client into the other four levels mentioned below is important in giving voice and choice to clients and their communities. The client's own participation and self-determination in such processes is also a desired objective of such social work practice.

- *Group and networking level*: this includes the sharing of information and co-constructions of knowledge about clients, their risks and their needs. Inter-professional and team collaboration can occur at this level to help the organisation identify risk and the needs of clients in such contexts. Important dimensions to the sharing of information and programme development are communication and interaction.
- *Intra-organisational level*: this level and the inter-organisational level are primarily concerned with mezzo and macro experiences that focus on groups and the wider community. At this level, the experience of reality is more general and diffuse. While all staff can be involved in the decision-making hierarchy, not all have control over the decisions and macro-interventions that are made on behalf of clients.
- *Inter-organisational level*: this is perhaps the most challenging and difficult area for understanding human service organisations, particularly in understanding how change and programme development and delivery in organisations can be enhanced and become more effective.
- *Community and society level*: in terms of contextualising social work practice in human service organisations, this is also a difficult level of experience. Community and societal attitudes, networks and forces impinge in complex ways on how a service is delivered, as well as on the use of strategic practices, such as empowerment, to enhance clients' lives, their well-being and the capacities of their communities for local social welfare.

Client and Individual Level

> Maintenance is slow. If it's a health problem like a bathroom you may get it done faster but if it's lighting – no it's very slow. We had a fire downstairs a few years ago and it blew up the fridge and it came straight up. We were promised that if they couldn't get it off the walls and roofs that they would come and paint – no such thing. They really botched it up. (41-year-old woman on disability pension)

This quote from a Sydney housing estate resident illustrates how the physical environment and services interact to create (or reduce) quality of life. This then impinges on the client's perceptions of service use, and the front line of organisations. The issues of organisational effectiveness and accountability are complicated when service users are included in change and innovation strategies. Social work ethics of self-determination and empowerment can be used to justify the service user or client being heard or having a say in how services are delivered. This, however, will require changes in certain processes and systems within and across human service organisations.

Human service organisations are primarily focused on the client at the individual level. Working in fine-detailed ways, one-on-one with clients, requires staff to exercise empathy and good communication skills. Skills in casework and case management require intensive training and practical experience. Professionally trained social workers bring skills in individual and group work, in administration and in community development. These skills and their knowledge base will not only enhance the well-being of clients but also contribute importantly to staff well-being and quality management processes. As this knowledge is programmatic and foundational in social work, it places the profession at the leading edge of human service organisations.

What skills and knowledge do competent social workers need to improve clients' experiences at the individual level of organisational work? Basic skills in communication and personal interaction will impact on the front-line worker–client interaction, the management of change, and potential conflicts within organisational teams. Qualified social workers need to develop considerable competence in change management skills derived from both university-based courses and their practice experience. In front-line relationships with clients, organisations not only need 'to have a good working understanding of the relationship and the expressed or implied contract from the very beginning, but they also need to establish time for review and renegotiation' (Egan, 1985: 170).

This level of experience involves the professional social worker in the 'live' learning of micro practice. Merighi et al. (2005) discuss the professional expertise needed for work with people with mental health needs, including knowledge, skill and approach. They argue that a skilled social worker's substantive knowledge is characterised by features such as 'recognizing multiple viewpoints and using an amalgam of information to create new knowledge' (2005: 716). Several illustrations are given by these authors of how social workers frame this knowledge and recast their skills as contextualised by the uncertainty and change in a person's life.

A key criterion for developing a better understanding of the experiences of social work clients is to take a wider perspective on their circumstances and background or to see 'the person-in-context' (Fook, Ryan and Hawkins, 2000). Merighi et al. (2005: 717) draw on experienced social workers' words to illustrate a 'wide lens' view of the client in context:

I have a natural inclination to work with families, and I actually have a personal philosophy that there is no such thing, no such person, as a person with a mental illness. There are only families with mental illness ... So that is actually my guiding philosophy, and it's how I work with most of the people I come in contact with.

Their most consistent finding was that the social workers were all 'articulating ideas about practice, reflecting upon their interventions, using theory appropriately and creatively, and engaging skilfully and ethically in practice' (Merighi et al., 2005: 722). How social work practice is then constrained by organisational capacities, compliance and values, given such expertise, is a key concern for reflective learning based on experience in social work. The degrees of individual motivation, competence, knowledge, skills, aptitude and capacity needed in such organisations are complex and multiple. Furthermore, there is a variety of roles, responsibilities and work relationships that will establish over time, which means a mixing of multi-professional skill bases with the organisational requirements of work.

Foundational skills at this level involve active listening and demonstrating respect for the views of the clients themselves. The exchange of information and views can start from these user interactions and be disseminated in various ways through the organisation. We can listen to clients' voices in relation to how they perceive both the services and the organisations that deliver these services. Understanding the point of view of clients also enables professionals and other service workers to develop appropriate and sensitive practice.

In the following example, there is a number of interventions that could be made by a social worker and sanctioned by the service organisation. There are also broader issues on this housing estate that affect the older residents:

> Somewhere to go for a cup of tea, somewhere to talk. Where they [the elderly] can be safe. They don't have to be in with a lot of young people, they don't want to be in with the rowdy teenagers. Teenagers should have their own kind of drop-in centre where the elderly should have theirs. If you are elderly you don't want to be around a lot of rowdy teenagers. (41-year-old woman on disability pension, long-term resident)

The social worker could mediate on behalf of the older residents with the young people and possibly bring the two parties – teenager and older resident – together to work on some of their differences in a mediating environment. On an individual level, the social worker might end up working with 'troubled' youth and families, or finding more emotional and personal support for older residents. There is a range of individual interventions that would be useful, such as ongoing meetings with both parties or work with the families of the young people that leads to new strategies for change around services or parenting. This is where a social worker's individual advocacy and skilful response to service users' needs can be invaluable. This could involve the social worker in complex processes of negotiating with his/her own organisation or networking with and lobbying service providers across a range of organisations, such as hospital systems, schools and community health agencies.

Once clients' needs and issues are identified, the personal history and biographic case record becomes part of the information bank of human services. How case records and other types of information are handled and communicated is crucial to the internal negotiations and interactions of the organisation, where factors such as social class, gender, 'race' and location can play their part in what information is shared or disseminated about clients. In this sharing, service organisations need to be aware of ethical issues of confidentiality and the monitoring and control of clients and their families (Wearing, 1998). In Britain, freedom-of-information legislation gives users the right to see their files, and this more open record sharing has raised ethical issues when information is used as evidence, say, in abuse and assault cases (Dalrymple and Burke, 1997: 139–40). Apart from the Freedom of Information Act 1999, which requires an application process to view files, no Federal Act exists in Australia to allow for the legislated sharing of client files with users themselves. Nonetheless, individual agencies do adopt the participatory framework more common in Britain and encourage clients to view their files and co-construct the information in them (see Wearing and Edwards (2003) for examples of user–provider sharing of client records).

Issues around how to improve the quality of practice and programmes at the front line and higher up in the organisation, and around the appointment of quality staff, play an important role in shaping organisational structures and governance. How often is it said as good management wisdom that 'If you understand all your staff from the bottom up and you have their respect you will be a good manager'? How often, however, does the reality fall short of this in practice? This is where information sharing and interpersonal communication establish channels for negotiation around who and what activities will be done in an agency or a bureaucracy. Worker empowerment is important on a daily basis for the staff's emotional and physical well-being. The literature in the area suggests that flexibility in human service employment, such as job-sharing, working from home and 'mental health' days, can parallel good practice in formal ways such as sanctioned continuing education and professional development (Turner and Shera, 2005: 87).

Group and Networking Level

As mentioned in Chapter 4, working in organisations at a team level creates new areas of stress. Team members are responsible for managing close group dynamics and negotiating issues of territory, career progression and equitable workloads. These issues are particularly challenging for workplaces involving a mix of professional, para-professional and non-qualified staff. Working on the ground in a housing estate, for example, with limited resources means that social workers need to be creative in their efforts to use organisational back-up and expertise. In many cases, this will mean going across organisations to 'poach' or network with social workers and other professionals in local hospitals, health centres, and so on. A creative use of these resources in cooperation with management can strengthen the advocacy and community development potential of organisational activity.

Staff changes can affect the quality and morale of the agencies, and organisational effectiveness (Riley, 2000). A key issue is how the internal capacity of the organisation, comprising both professionals and managers, is used to make new appointments. One way to go about this would be to use the creative ideas and knowledge of the team, and possibly clients, in making an appointment. Such a consultancy approach could help to match the team to the new appointment in terms of profile. In staff turnover and similar change situations, finding creative solutions and understanding the needs of the organisational culture in managing change would be part of a proactive intervention from both the team and management in cooperation.

The front line of service delivery involves workers and clients who interact in service encounters. It may also involve work relationships and friendships between colleagues, and sometimes, whether appropriately or not, between clients and staff. The mix of everyday interaction and decision making is rich in meaning and makes the organisational processes complex. How social workers manage their image and, in particular, how they create a work identity separate to others may be a priority. Pithouse (1987: 23–4) highlights these processes for social work in his study of an area social services office in England:

> The Area Office is a social world that provides both spatial and perceptual reference for the meaning of work ... The notion of 'world' emphasises aspects of negotiation, process, identity and communication ... Aware of their poor image in the eyes of related occupations the members defend themselves against a bruised and stigmatised identity. The sharing of stories, accounts and tales of deficiency in the would-be critics helps to repair a collective notion of competent practitioners. Through these group processes a social world is constructed to provide reference for the meaning of practice and a convivial setting for a sometimes embattled workforce.

At the level of the experience of the team and group networking across and within professional, managerial and other front-line occupations (including social workers), establishing the meaning of work and work identity becomes a complex and fluid process. We have emphasised that it is important for social work graduates and students to define and understand their own professional identities within the context of organisational cultures and change. Further, the strategic and tactical use of the self in encounters with management and other professionals forms an important part of personal defences that give a clear agenda for what such work can achieve in an organisation. In Chapter 9, we develop this argument further through the lens of learning and ethics as developing personal qualities and virtuous practices that encourage others in role modelling, among other things, leadership for human service organisations. Such insight into the strategic use of professional and personal identity should not be lost when working at the broader levels of intra-organisational and inter-organisational change to which we now turn.

Intra-organisational Level

This is the level at which management relates to professionals and to other senior staff in the organisation. Importantly, this level and the next link to the broader external context for policy making that sees the organisation as the key agency for the implementation of policy (Hill, 2005). At this level, the communication between front-line managers, in-line supervisors and managers and other agencies that affect internal decision making (including a management board and/or regulatory authority), all become important in the organisational reality and hierarchy. There are limits to what management can do for staff in particular situations within organisations or for the organisational culture. However, it is usually recognised that good intra-organisational practice in human services involves the facilitation of change and sharing activities within the organisation.

Managers cannot 'empower' workers in the true sense of the word any more than the latter can 'empower' clients. What is possible, however, is for managers to utilise their power to bring changes and adaptations to the workplace which will make it more probable that workers will experience their professional selves as holding power. Managers can also encourage and promote participation in power-sharing activities and roles beyond the organisation to accelerate a sense of power (Turner and Shera, 2005: 91). We discuss client empowerment in the later section on the community and society level of experience.

We have largely been discussing clients' experience of service delivery, and yet it is also important to consider that of workers. Managers and workers can experience empowerment in realistic ways that give confidence to and enable workers. It is the complex networks of front-line staff and management that sometimes 'muddle through', and, at other times with clear cooperation, develop and enhance programme effectiveness for clients. The question here for practitioners is how managers, front-line staff and professionals relate to each other, and how they relate to clients. The question is also, at the intra-organisational level, how staff can achieve cooperation in doing so. The participatory framework suggested in previous chapters can enhance such relationships and also create a clear two-way communication process where front-line staff feel included in decision making and organisational tasks.

Harris (1998) describes some of the relationship processes between local managers, front-line staff and social workers in local authority social services. He suggests the idea of practitioners linking upwards with superiors/managers and sideways with other workers and para-professionals, and linking with social workers. Crucial to these processes is how social work and supervision relationships are defined by managers and how managers and social workers work together. In Harris's study,

> front-line managers neither came across as simply 'one of the workers' nor did any sense emerge of District Managers sharing goals with senior management. They emerge as people with their own objectives and priorities who are at a 'bottleneck', facing both ways: responsible for the implementation of Departmental policy in the pursuit of the organisation's legislative mandate and, at the same time, being exposed to the day-to-day pressures of front-line social workers. (Harris, 1998: 102)

In previous chapters, we have emphasised the importance and sustainability of worker participation in decision making, and of interdisciplinary and inter-agency work for social work. In being willing to work with others at the coalface of practice and create 'communities of practice' and collaboration between organisations, the social worker can become more effective in helping organisations to learn. Through the use of participatory tools, such as empowerment evaluation, front-line workers can document their practice and use this to inform management of the importance of practice at the coalface. Organisations do not operate in isolation and both internal and external activities can all provide a healthy and fluid environment that encourages and motivates the workforce. Cooperation between staff at the level of intra-organisational experience can foster inter-organisational cooperation and vice versa. Wearing (1998) argues elsewhere that a crucial part of this cooperation in and across service organisations is network communication in inter-agency meetings, community meetings and community forums in local areas. This can mitigate the unhealthy potential for inter-organisational rivalry over clients and, especially, for competitively tendered contracts in an area. It can also mitigate unhealthy conflict and tensions within organisations over what voices of change can help to drive change in service delivery.

Making connections with other professionals and gaining the support of the organisation and the network of providers can help to direct and manage intra-organisational change. Gursansky et al. (2003: 116), for example, mention both professional and organisational support as crucial in overcoming what they call 'habitually inward-looking practice' in case management. If no agency-based professional team is established, then setting up a group of disparate case managers can pool resources and lobby for changes, notably in gaining greater user control of services. In gaining organisational support, plans from such a group could link workers' activities with client goals and be compatible with the organisation's enterprise and funding (Gursansky et al., 2003: 116). Such strategies of team building among workers and professionals in and across organisations also offer collectivised hope and can improve morale, particularly in periods of scarce and decreasing resources for many human service agencies. The next section discusses inter-organisational concerns, noting especially community development and partnership issues that can be strong elements of inter-collaboration between local service organisations in social welfare systems.

Inter-organisational Level

An illustration of inter-organisational cooperation can be found in a community development project carried out during the late 1990s and early 2000s in one of the socio-economically poorest suburbs in Australia, a suburb called Claymore on the south-western tip of Sydney. This project, known as the 'Animation Project', was established by the Catholic-based St Vincent de Paul Society to 'animate' or enliven the processes necessary to re-build community supports and relationships in an economically depressed area. The society's approach was modelled on the conscientisation work it had used in communities and villages in India and that was developed by Paulo Freire (1972) in Central America. The project linked direct service organisations and residents of the suburb to create greater community cohesion and feelings of safety in an area otherwise known for vandalism and unsafe public space. The community development workers who worked on the project say that it made a substantial and noticeable difference to the personal and social lifestyles of those who lived on the estate. The key worker said: 'Claymore is an example of what kinds of changes are possible with the support of a number of organisations working in a way that respects and supports people at a local level' (Paul Power, quoted in Kerjean, 2002).

The Animation Project and other community development initiatives have changed residents' attitudes and the local social and physical environments of housing estate areas in Sydney. The style of partnership emphasised in these initiatives has been local, democratic and participatory, and has some parallels with housing initiatives in Europe (see Geddes, 2000). What can the social work profession provide in relation to inter-organisational strategies and broader community development issues? Local community projects such as the Animation Project also demonstrate a need for community development and social action, undertaken either as professional social work or community work. The idea of advocacy networks as involving social actors, from individual activists and service users to corporate and church-based organisations in social change strategies, is one example of how social work can work with broader justice and global human rights concerns (Keck and Sikkink, 1999).

In considering inter-organisational experience and strategies for intervention, certain modes of collective action supported by the social work profession need to be taken with and on behalf of oppressed and vulnerable groups. The emerging policy context in the UK and Australia, which emphasises partnership arrangements between the state and local community groups who are self-motivated by a social justice ethos, has led to new calls for community-work-trained social workers. This new climate for community involvement and development raises the issue of styles of community development training and professionalisation (Geoghegan and Powell, 2006; Turner and Shera, 2005). There is also a converging skills literature between social work and social development as a starting point in understanding new organisational forms and initiatives in social welfare (see e.g. Keck and Sikkink, 1999).

Part of the practice base for organisational social work is working on documents and submissions that enable new funding arrangements for a service, or advocating changes for client groups of that service. This professional activity is invaluable across organisations in a number of ways: feeding in inputs that bring about programme and possibly funding changes; informing the funders and other providers of services about client needs; and encouraging the service to look towards policy and programme change and keep ahead of developments in order to tender for funding. Such work can be fraught with time- and energy-consuming issues for social workers on the ground. Here a worker in a front-line service area vents her frustration:

> In the last submission I wrote [the department] actually called me up and said 'You've been putting your work plans in for the same thing for the last three years. Are you not going to change it?' I said 'Well, not until people's needs change!' And they actually pulled up the fact that not many of the workers from my centre attend meetings ... They're bullshit meetings basically and we don't have time. I put interagency meetings as my goals and they said 'Why don't you attend them?' I said 'Because we just don't have enough hours in the day to attend them'. Not unless they want to provide us with extra funding. (Professional worker in a small Australian non-profit organisation, cited in Meagher and Healy, 2003: 45)

One of the challenges for both front-line and professional staff working in small and large human service organisations today is that they are often regulated by funding agencies and larger organisations. Daily activities revolve around new accounting, auditing and accountability frameworks that are about creating relationships with funding organisations. We have mentioned that modes of both social work supervision and work supervision have changed because of the pressures from work intensification and more general managerial measures. Also, information sharing across agencies and professional cultures is an issue of inter-organisational collaboration and partnership. In British health and social care, there are some agreed safeguards and legislation on information sharing. Despite policy developments to facilitate such sharing, the reality of collaboration falls short, with some professionals, such as doctors, apparently recalcitrant about sharing information with social services. Thus, a fuller model that respects information sharing behaviour is restricted by inter-professional and inter-organisational cultures (Richardson and Asthana, 2006: 665–6).

What, then, of the voice of users at the inter-organisational level of experience? On the Waterloo housing estate in Sydney, residents expressed views on how service organisations can be interlinked. They saw the wider spectrum of services – from human services to commercial services – as directly affecting their everyday needs, well-being and quality of life. The service users experienced a lack of options and choices in what services to access and whether these services were even available. This seems particularly the case where the needs of disadvantaged and economically vulnerable clients are not met by local infrastructures of human and health services, as well as other services such as local shopping malls or commercial banks:

> There has to be more places for people to go, I don't mean elderly people or young people, just people. People who want to go to a club or go somewhere and do something whether it be play chess or talk to somebody, there just doesn't seem to be a place around here to do that. You can go to a café and drink coffee but you can't sit there for hours and hours ... There doesn't seem to be a community centre you know. It needs some sort of community centre where you can centralize a lot of things that people want to do – library services, social workers, op shops, lamington fairs. (42-year-old man with a physical disability (in a wheelchair), long-term resident)

This quote from a physically disabled man indicates how the lack of a local sense of 'place' can militate against well-being. Other examples can be drawn from the hierarchy of organisations where managers in the new partnership arrangements try to inform and establish links with local communities and networks of service provider organisations.

Winkworth (2005: 82) has argued in the area of employment services that Centrelink, Australia's social security office, has resources and organisational capacities including front-line staff to 'work with other services and community groups to create employment pathways'. In her study, she asked Centrelink managers about their role in partnerships. This role was largely described as 'intermediary' between individuals and community groups. The following quote from a manager illustrates this:

> My role would be more along the lines of providing policy information and putting that information in a context that the community can relate to so they can actually see the benefits ... you know we have a pretty good understanding of our community, where they are coming from, what their concerns are, what

their fears are. And I think that puts us in a very good position. A relationship of trust is always the first step in building partnership. (Quoted in Winkworth, 2005: 91)

In Britain, there have been partnerships and collaborative efforts in areas such as employment programmes and urban planning. These can be partnerships between organisations on a large scale, with the need for trust, good communication and strong organisational capacities to bring about change such as urban renewal. Williams (2006), for example, assessed the impact of collaborative partnerships between private and public sector organisations on the renewal of Manchester city centre from 1997 to 2001 after the bombing of the city centre by terrorists in 1996 (1200 properties and 43 streets were damaged). A partnership formed between the city council, emergency services, property landowners and property leaseholders, and a task force was set up that developed 50 projects within one programme aimed at urban renewal. This urban renewal partnership was largely a success, when measured by physical and entrepreneurial standards, in encouraging successful marketing and investment in the city centre. The author, however, notes the equity issues in such a process and the need for regeneration of 'more disadvantaged neighbourhoods with a more holistic and less physically dominant programme management' (Williams, 2006: 205). It is important to consider investing in the renewal of local or community areas as opposed to a singular focus on disadvantage in these communities.

As shown in the example of the Claymore Animation Project, there is a good deal more to effective working across sectors or services, and initiating and activating change in local communities, than just government interventions and funding. These changes are not always visible and certainly not achievable in short-term and 'knee-jerk' resource or policy responses to so-called 'problem communities'. Some of the appropriate policy responses and inter-organisational strategies will be framed in the context of new partnership and collaborative arrangements. This can involve more critical responses via research and advocacy to government and non-government organisational interventions that make use of social work's professional skill base in the area. The linking up of organisations in such responses can create new issues for networking and avoiding overly formalised responses to a local community's needs and voice in the policy process. Here, again, the organisational structures and processes need to be sensitised to the experience and voice of clients and front-line staff, in particular, through clear channels of communication and information sharing across services and professionals. How will policy be made on the ground and who is being listened to as to the needs and wants of a local community or requested local resources? In this we can include the role and response of social work professionals in the necessary change process.

Community and Society Level

We now turn to the community and society level to finish our discussion of experiencing organisation in human services. At this level, staff and clients develop an understanding of how social, political and economic forces structure and influence the environment of the organisation. It is at this level that the organisation is directly shaped by such forces in which key social institutions such as the family, religion, the market economy or the state play an important part. In this sense, the capacities to empower clients to use services more effectively, and/or for staff to adopt more reflective and skilful approaches with clients, will depend on the societal and community environment. Anything less than strategic and careful development of community and societal capacity by professional social workers will not create such social empowerment:

> Empowerment is connected to the process of developing the consumer's capabilities, to their ability to improve their skills in acquiring resources … And it is more important than whether they (the consumers) acquire the resources or not … I would say that my job as a social worker empowering consumers is to provide tools, and my question is how my consumers research the resources, rather than if s/he now has it. (Social worker, quoted in Boehm and Staples, 2002: 453–4)

Can the efforts of professionals and other staff in human service organisations empower clients? As suggested earlier, 'empowerment' has different meanings in the management and the professional social work literature. In social work, empowerment usually means realigning personal or social resources that can include both emotional and material assistance to the client. Harris (1997: 33) takes a critical perspective on the use of the term, arguing that in social work empowerment is seen in an anti-oppressive approach as a politicising process for clients or from within liberational frameworks as ambiguously tied to professional knowledge and power that can be both constraining and liberating. According to Harris, a key point on the use of the term in social work is that:

> Power is interactional: to understand it we must comprehend the behaviour of the powerless as well as the powerful … Social workers talk about empowering others, but if power is intrinsic to social work and social workers are carriers not progenitors of power it is not necessarily theirs to surrender, or even share. (Harris, 1997: 29)

This is a more critical and perhaps cynical view of power in social work. Nevertheless, this view helps us to 'sharpen up' how social work is implicitly involved in power relations with clients and others, so that social work itself cannot claim that it is not a part of the social and economic system or machinery that creates oppression and domination. In the management literature, empowerment can refer to staff's own empowerment to work harder or produce more for a company or organisation. In this literature, there is often little regard for empowering consumers or clients of the organisation, for which there is little bottom line in terms of profit maximising unless they are part of the social welfare system where codes of practice and conduct require such regard in variable and limited ways (see Chapters 7 and 9; Wilson et al., 2008). Empowerment is therefore an issue in social work education and practice, and managerial perspectives on this can serve to further confuse the issue.

It is difficult to argue that services today and the organisations that deliver these services are involved in empowering clients in the way social work might define this. If, however, we move away from a fixed understanding of giving resources to views that embody relationships and networking in organisations – linking up and communicating certain awareness to vulnerable and disadvantaged groups – perhaps, then, empowerment starts to take on a different meaning. Starkey (2003: 273, 280–1) argues that the literature on empowerment in social work and human services can be divided into two conceptual categories: the consumerist perspective, commonly found in health care, which focuses on the user's voice; and the liberational perspective, common to social work, that focuses on oppression and social justice. This also reflects the divide in service user participation arguments, as suggested in Chapters 5 and 7. The consumerist view is dominant in professional practice and in human service restructuring strategies. However, the use of the liberational view by social work has sought to move beyond consumerist ideology in genuine and sometimes successful attempts to link clients into research processes and outcomes. It has also striven to listen to the needs, wants and desires of communities and individuals and to directly support service user movements such as survivor groups of mental health consumers (Strier and Binyamin, 2010). Aspects of this support include: developing clients' capacity to control and choose dimensions of their quality of life; showing respect for clients in that they are listened to and their self-respect is enhanced; enabling them to be open about their trauma or health concerns; involving them in groups and in the community; contributing to and helping others; and providing information and education to clients (Aronson and Smith, 2010; Beresford and Croft, 2004; Croft and Beresford, 1997; Starkey, 2003).

There are important questions for social policy and social work that emerge from the discussion around empowerment and service users. What impact have the privatisation, contracting out and associated managerial strategies of market-oriented governments in Britain and Australia had on the possibilities for client empowerment? The shift in Britain and Australia to contracted services and policy frameworks has created a new era of complex organisational forms in human services – often with difficult, overlapping or competing boundaries that enhance elements of chaos, resistance and power struggles within and across these organisations.

Some lessons for social work practice can be learned and modelled from the American experience, especially since the contracted model of service delivery has dominated human service delivery in that country for the last 20 or more years. Gibelman (2005: 467) has, for example, emphasised the need for social work research and practice in the USA to be more aware of workforce changes. To this we can add the need to understand how privatisation, global shifts in the use and capacities of human service labour and new managerial techniques in service delivery have combined. Studies of female managers in Canada have shown that social service and social work managers can find space in the recent managerial and performance shifts in organisations to insert social justice and equity concerns. Nonetheless, they also show that notions of the public service as a progressive social force are on the wane (Aronson and Smith, 2010). This combination of forces brought to bear in human service organisations has constrained change and created, in some contradictory ways, the possibilities for change and empowerment of clients and staff. Such factors have also set new social policy arrangements and social work's labour process within these arrangements.

Further problems are raised in concentrated areas of low-income families and social security recipients. What happens when culturally diverse clients come into contact with predominantly white and 'middle-class' human service organisations? Kossak (2005) looks at the role of trust in relationships between client and social worker in culturally relevant service delivery in the USA. In her study, this need for trust of service providers was predominantly gendered towards African-American men's experience of the service. Women clients, however, were more concerned to value the 'accomplishments, availability and caring attitudes of workers' (2005: 192).

PRACTICE
EXAMPLE 8.2

Developing collaborative partnerships in disadvantaged urban neighbourhoods

Brightley is a small city of around 50,000 people that in the last 15 years has seen the loss of several key businesses, local services such as banking and shopping facilities and, subsequently, sources for local employment. The local social service office and Brightley City Council, along with several commercial operators and property developers, are interested in creating a partnership to bring about urban change and renewal in the area. There is a significant number of the Brightley community who are aged and/or living on social security benefits, and are socio-economically disadvantaged. Social work has a key role to play in assessing the needs of disadvantaged people in the area and the ways in which private–public partnerships can enhance quality of life and well-being. If social workers are going to initiate a task force and partnership group, how would they go about this? What would be the focus of their concerns? Williams (2006: 197) lists the flexible framework developed for the renewal of the city of Manchester by partnership during 1997–2001, and this informs some of Brightley Council's thinking about urban renewal in the local area. Some criteria for Manchester's renewal included:

● restoration and enhancement of the retail core;
● stimulation and diversification of the city's economic base;
● development of an integrated transport strategy;
● creation of a quality core city fit for the twenty-first century;
● creation of a living city by increasing its residential population; and
● coordination, delivery and promotion of the rebuilding programme.

The task for social workers and city planners is to ensure that the commercial benefits gained in the process also have community benefits that enhance the well-being of disadvantaged members of the community. It is decided between planners and social workers that a separate 'community development enterprise' or social enterprise to the collaborative partnership will be set up. A social or community development enterprise is a business run not for profit but to deliver benefits to the community. This would help to ensure that such benefits from the collaborative partnership might flow to the community through increases in social capital. Social capital is defined as combining six elements in a community focus: the stock of trust; reciprocity and mutuality; shared social norms; shared commitment and belonging; informal and formal social networks; and effective information channels (Pearce, 2003: 74–5). Importantly, the community development enterprise would build a community-led common vision for social and economic action through a series of community futures workshops. This vision would be based on the following principles:

- that local development should be community led;
- that it should involve all community stakeholders: residents, local business and industry, the public sector, and church and voluntary organisations;
- that developing a common understanding of the nature of a community and its problems will lead to a common vision, which in turn will lead to a common purpose;
- that community development should be based on an equality of partnership between stakeholders;
- that discussion about local development should lead to practical plans for action; and
- that development should embrace, connect with and tackle social, economic and environmental issues. (Pearce, 2003: 88)

There are several outstanding examples in the literature where organisational effectiveness in enhancing social capital using community development strategies has been shown. Effective strategies have been identified in child welfare agency collaborations and in terms of enhancing workforce mental well-being through inter-organisational collaboration and programme innovation (Cheung and Young, 2015; Claiborne, Auerbach and Zeitlin, 2015; David, 2013). All such strategies can add to the social capital and capacity building of human services and the communities they serve.

In the Brightley practice example, partnerships and collaborative arrangements can work by linking up human service organisations with disadvantaged and economically depressed neighbourhoods. Practices such as information sharing, inter-organisational networking and other collaborative work, based in these partnerships, will benefit clients. Further, service users have a major role in these partnerships in providing their views on community needs and appropriate service responses. These are, in fact, some of the key working tools that the OECD suggests in its work on citizen participation in making public policy (OECD, 2001). Social workers can use their group and networking skills at this level of intra-organisational experience to foster and develop such arrangements. The capacity for inter-organisational collaboration will depend on the ability and willingness of senior management to provide resources and planning to manage partnerships. This organisational context and practice is also key to how policy processes are followed through beyond their initial formulation to achieve certain social outcomes. Even at this level, the explicit recognition of values in organisational aims, mission and guidelines for practice and the ethical dimensions of professional social work remain core to how effective are capacity building and the positive learning nurturing of staff within the organisation and in assisting clients. The effectiveness of organisational objectives and policy can then be called into question if specified outcomes are not met or are not, in a real sense, accountable to consumers and the objectives of the programme or policy (Hill, 2005).

Reflective Questions

1   How can social workers adjust their practice so that they are more responsive to the participation of service users and the experiences they have when encountering human service organisations?
2   Using Practice Example 8.2, what are the tensions for service users in forming these kinds of partnerships? What can be done to improve their experience of collaboration?

Conclusion

Organisations that create, innovate and plan are more suited to change, including resource changes, than those that do not (Hill, 2005; Jaskyte and Dressler, 2005). While change from within the organisation is desirable, it is, however, more likely that external bodies such as funding agencies or social and economic policy agendas of a country, or even local demands, will determine directions for change or whether existing structures are maintained (Lune and Oberstein, 2001). Change itself is counter-posed to organisational order and stability. The order created in an organisational team or unit or in the organisation in general is a result of individual and inter-subjective action (Strati, 2000: 94–8). As we have seen in this chapter, including clients' and front-line staff's own experiences and perceptions in decision making can enable dynamic and useful change in organisations.

This chapter has shown that both clients' and workers' experience and their realities are fundamental to how social work can understand organisational ethos, purpose and change in the current period of social service delivery. We have also shown that practice requires relearning and change within strategies of enrichment of organisational cultures that will enable the capacity building of all staff. Part of social workers' role in this is to use their expertise to develop the skills, values and knowledge base of any human service organisation and culture. They also have a responsibility to make this matter in a world of social difference and the larger social inequalities faced in contemporary societies, including those across borders and within developing countries (Stanley and Lincoln, 2015). Drawing on inspirational, rational and empirical material in the social sciences, human services and social work, we find both challenges to social work as a profession and ways of moving forward in changing organisational structures. The next chapter will take further the active approach to social work education, practice and learning we have advocated throughout this book by concentrating on the centrality and fine detail of ethical challenges for practice in organisations.

In Chapter 2, we described social work as inextricably linked to work in organisations, particularly the complex formal organisations that Max Weber described as public 'bureaucracy'. We need to ask, to what extent is social work involved in bureaucratic and potentially authoritarian processes? Or has the profession now shifted to a nuanced and humane approach to organisational practice? In our final chapter, we discuss the humanising agenda of social work in organisations, particularly in its focus on ethical, active and reflexive learning.

9 Active and Ethical Practice

In this chapter we overview

- moving beyond bureaucratic and managerialist modes of operating;
- professional ethics in organisations, including ethical decision making and virtue ethics;
- active social work that uses a spontaneous, situated and practical ethics for organisational practice;
- leadership and initiative in change cultures;
- an active, relationship-based and critical reflexive approach to professional learning and organisational practice.

Introduction

Rather than providing a settled and unproblematic conclusion, we see our discussion as contributing to ongoing, active, relationship-based and reflexive learning in and about human service organisations. Having fixed or rigid prescriptions for organisational practice will not work because organisations and their environments are constantly changing. This means that the development and nurturing of a competent skill development with a knowledge base is crucial to practice and involves a continual learning process. Additionally, the situations social workers confront are frequently indeterminate and contingent on their specific contexts. Sometimes social workers are confronted with 'wicked problems', which are difficult to define and where there is a lack of clarity as to the best course of action (Head and Alford, 2015). As indicated in earlier chapters, there is a difference between theoretical and academic knowledge, and practical 'knowing': insight and deep intuition forming practice wisdom. This theory–practice split is highlighted by the debates and issues raised by evidence-based practice in social work. Recent authors on this debate have emphasised not what is known for social work practice, but *how* it is known and *for whom* (Blom, 2009), and, importantly, how qualitative research and knowledge, including what has been called the relational, conversational and 'narrative turn' in social work (Riessman and Quinney, 2005), can be integrated into this framework (Gould, 2010).

Much of social work involves uncertain and intangible knowledge that relies on a worker's relationships with others and reflection with clients over time. Holding the diversity of the knowledge base in social work, including both the more determinate academic knowledges and the indeterminate, intuitive and practical knowledge, can not only bring about less reductionist views of practice and clients, but also encourage more holistic, creative, reflexive and lateral approaches to an 'active' (rather than reactive) practice (cf. Ruch, 2005). Thus, social workers need to develop ways of working and learning flexibly within organisations, balancing commitments to society, to the profession, to the organisation, and to service users and communities. We call this active practice in moving with change, and it can be counter-posed to 'defensive' or 'negative' practice. Social workers also need to be aware of the social context for organisations and the social constraints imposed on social workers and other staff by work in organisations. In this regard, we have highlighted issues such as values, norms, discourses and culture as an important focus for understanding organisational change and for the management of this change.

Beyond Bureaucracy and Managerialism: Networking and Learning Organisations

'Buck passing' and 'red tape' are part and parcel of large formal organisations in the health and human services. These large organisations continue to contain many of the characteristics described by Weber's (1971 [1922]) bureaucracy ideal type. Nonetheless, many human service organisations today are smaller in size and have a flatter and less hierarchical structure than the traditional bureaucracy. What is clear is that all forms of organisational change over time and require creative and innovative thinking to navigate through or around the difficult and sometimes impassable problems they create. In earlier chapters, we acknowledged the front-line experience of working in such organisations – referred to by Lipsky (1980) as street-level bureaucracy – which, in its most damaging form, can categorise service users as objects of service to be managed, ignored, patronised, and worse. McKevitt (1999) identifies professional decision making as crucial to equitable and effective service delivery by the core public services. Studies in the USA highlight the impact of neo-liberal reform on the everyday realities of service use (Lurie and Riccucci, 2003). We argue, therefore, that much of social work practice in human service organisations should be about humanising the dehumanising aspects of these bureaucratic machines. In part, this involves exposing the human elements in organisational and management systems and structures. Crucially, it also involves enabling clients to assert their own humanity and agency within these organisations, by, for example, making advocacy and complaints mechanisms easily available.

How are changes to the social welfare system impacting on professional work in these organisations? As discussed earlier in this book, we must be particularly concerned with the impact of neo-liberal and managerialist reforms, such as contracting out and service restructuring. These reforms have affected social work's capacity to deal with and learn from organisational change (Dominelli, 2002; Webb, 2006). However, while the social work profession has become partly captive to these neo-liberal and managerialist practices, it has still been able to assert some autonomy and control over workplace activities. Thus, assertions of the conservatism of the profession in light of this are potentially misleading. As Dominelli (2002: 148–52) argues, strategic alliances in and across professions, front-line staff and clients ensure stronger networks that are robust in the face of managerial change and the neo-liberal privatisation of the welfare state. However, writers such as Dominelli (2002) and Webb (2006) also alert social work to the 'short-termism' of managerial agendas that can trade off effective services for economic efficiencies, in pursuit of budget cuts and the ideological drive for 'competitive advantage' in service delivery. These are agendas that arguably further corrode networking, cooperation, partnership and mutual respect between provider organisations in human services.

Interestingly, Egan (1985) foreshadowed some of these shifts in human service work, particularly the need to shift from inflexible and bureaucratic organisational structures and cultures to more flexible modes of working. He argues that hierarchical organisational forms *qua* bureaucracies have failed, and that networking is the new participatory mode of decision making (cf. Payne, 2000). This approach may transform leadership and management:

> The failure of various kinds of hierarchies to solve social problems has given impetus to networking. An example in human services is the rapid growth of self-help groups. Networks provide what hierarchies cannot – horizontal links ... As networking becomes more valued in the organization a different style of management emerges, one that encourages autonomy and participatory decision making ... Network-based approaches to authority, control and decision making are not displacing the pyramid with its claim of command and control, but they are helping to humanize organizations and make them more effective and efficient. (Egan, 1985: 208–9)

Today, social workers are required to be organisational networkers *par excellence* in attempting to 'run ahead' of too much organisational formality and economic efficiency. Nonetheless, there are key challenges. For example, excessive risk management and accountability documentation and rigid client information systems, in particular, seem to create a hyper-bureaucracy rather than one freer of formality. This also raises the thorny question of how social work will integrate its theory and practice in organisational contexts (Raeymaeckers and Dierckx, 2013; Thompson, 2000; Wearing, 2016).

Networking is also essential between organisations and within their local communities. However, the extent to which human service organisations are embedded within their local cultures and communities varies considerably. The way local relations are constituted within the organisation may enable particular workers to operate with some autonomy and discretionary control. For example, if workers live in the area they can develop local knowledge about the people who live there and the services that are used. They could also develop stronger biases for or against clients in the area based on their subjective knowledge of local cultures. Lune and Oberstein (2001), in a study of three HIV/AIDS organisations in New York City, show how the relations in which organisations are embedded can determine constraints and opportunities for organisational change, learning and growth.

Networking within and across organisations stimulates an openness in learning from others, which in turn may facilitate intra- and inter-organisational change, information sharing and resource building. Kramer (2010: 134–5) has recently emphasised the importance in organisational work of communication topic networks – both formal and informal – in creating various kinds of relationships with work colleagues and clients. These networks provide both resources and information to members. As identified in organisational research, Kramer lists such networks and their properties:

- a task network assists in getting work done;
- a social network provides friendship relationships;
- an authority network has responsibility and delineates rewards and punishments;
- an innovative network promotes new ideas and opportunities; and
- a political network, both formally and informally, influences resource allocation.

In reliance on these networks, workers can develop relationships that have varying positive outcomes, such as increased effectiveness, positive work attitudes and behaviour, and shared understandings of structures and stress management. We have also emphasised in this book a deeper investigation by practitioners as organisational agents into the less visible traditions of social work theory and practice for working in organisations. Psychoanalytic, existential and humanist traditions in social work that engage an awareness of organisational theory and practice have been more visible in recent years through, for example, the influence of the Tavistock Institute and the *Journal of Social Work Practice*. The strong traditions of existentialism and humanism are enjoying somewhat of a renaissance (Miller, 2012; Tajima, 2014; Thompson, 1992) in social work education. A relational perspective that focuses on 'the being' of clients and of all staff who work with social work professionals can encourage more holistic respect of others and a sense of, what Carl Rogers called, 'positive regard' (Miller, 2012: 31–2; Rogers, 1961) in a human service workplace.

The enhancement of these positive attitudes and behaviours is one crucial ingredient for building trust in the networks of providers and among professional colleagues. Social workers are immersed and trained in such traditions and can use these to good effect in organisational contexts. The degree of involvement in different networks will also reflect whether a worker will have high or low involvement in their job and varying degrees of job satisfaction. It is important to remember that social workers are not the only ones who use networking in organisations or service delivery, but they are well trained interpersonally to create network relationships, especially for new staff and those who feel they are marginalised in an organisation.

The concept of 'communities of practice', discussed in Chapter 4, is grounded in the idea that networks of people naturally form around common interests and concerns (Wenger et al., 2002). By engaging with each other and exploring possible solutions to key problems, a spiral of learning emerges, which improves confidence and competence. These networks or communities are a crucial resource for organisations in times of organisational change. Facilitating such networks is one strategy an organisation can take in becoming a learning organisation. Other strategies that encourage organisational learning include:

- critical reflection;
- embedding critical reflection within organisations;
- encouraging participation by all stakeholders;
- service user involvement; and
- addressing managerial practice and analysing its effectiveness in advancing general and organisational policy. (Baldwin, 2004: 174–5)

In order for social workers to play a part in humanising the organisations they work in and with, there is a need to imagine and implement locally sensitive, participatory and user-friendly programmes. Social work practice is located within and across varied organisational and community contexts. From our perspective, much is to be gained, within modern service organisations, by a shift from depoliticised bureaucratic work to new forms of political, policy and advocacy networking. This is not a managerialist form of networking, whereby predetermined organisational goals are achieved through carefully controlled collaborative strategies. Rather, it is a networking that relies on a plurality of actors who take collective action and embark on a journey together. For Folgheraiter (2004: 163), this involves a reflexivity in shared learning – exploring indeterminate ad hoc solutions – 'as they undertake courses of action unknown to them at the outset'. We regard this reflexivity as being willing to act spontaneously in response to new organisational mandates and formal structures from a value stance that includes doing the least harm, while upholding justice and compassion for others.

It is important for social work to remember that much of its effectiveness has been based in anti-bureaucratic and humane approaches that assist clients in their negotiation of large organisations. For us, it is essential that social work values inform the ways in which we work flexibly across organisations and communities, and the ways in which we stimulate organisational learning. Putting social work values into practice requires an awareness of ethical issues and dilemmas, and a capacity to negotiate these in the everyday life of the organisation.

 Reflective Questions

1   What might be some challenges for social workers in their attempts to 'run ahead' of bureaucratic processes?
2   Consider an organisation you know something about. What opportunities are there for increasing intra- and inter-organisational networking? How could increasing networking assist in increasing knowledge and learning within the organisation?

Professional Ethics in Organisations

Ethical Judgement and Decision Making

The professions, such as social work, are involved in a reflective understanding of their own and others' 'right conduct', and, in this sense, their self-integrity. In human service organisations, professional ethics can be distinguished from morals in that they are informed in part by formal codes of ethics and training in ethical decision making (Beauchamp and Childress, 2001; Lonne et al., 2004; Yeung et al., 2010). Ethical practice within organisations is also informed by organisational protocols and practice standards (Hughes, 2016). Thus, like other professionals, social workers reason, make judgements and take action on the basis of their knowledge and expertise, both as professionals and as organisational operators. They are also inevitably constrained by the limits of this knowledge and expertise, as well as by the potential for conflict between their dual professional and organisational responsibilities.

Spaces are required in social work education, research and practice to enable reflective practice and time (Ruch, 2002) to allow practitioners to come to terms with self-managing and performance-based practice within the current managerial and neo-liberal political climate. Notably, we have emphasised that this climate has core elements of increased efficiencies and increased resource pressure that often result in work intensification, undue occupational stress and a general tendency to 'overwork'. We have argued earlier in this book that managerialist and technocratic ideology appear to have undermined social work values in some organisational settings. Thus, as recognised in codes of ethics (e.g. Australian Association of Social Workers, 2010; British Association of Social Workers, 2012), negotiating the tensions between organisational and professional responsibilities is an increasingly explicit script for practice in human service organisations.

Research and scholarship on professional ethics make a useful distinction between normative and applied ethics, which can help us to understand these tensions within and between professional and organisational responsibilities.

Normative ethics focuses on determining right and wrong courses of action. It includes consequentialist ethics (e.g. utilitarianism), which suggests that right behaviour should be determined by what the outcomes of that behaviour might be. Normative ethics also includes deontological ethics, which focuses on individual duty regardless of the consequences. Codes of ethics invariably reflect a deontological position in the way they set out the principles for practice to which professionals are obliged to conform. The commonly expressed values of social work derive from normative biomedical ethical frameworks (e.g. as developed by Beauchamp and Childress, 2001). They include:

- respect for persons;
- social justice;
- professional integrity. (AASW, 2010: 12–13)

These values help the social work profession frame and focus on broader professional issues, such as maintaining integrity and competence in the face of change, external organisational pressures, and possible conflicts among funders, providers and users of services.

However, codes of ethics can only act as guides to ethical conduct in our everyday practice in organisations. Beyond these, we apply our own assumptions, world views, histories and experiences to any particular situation we encounter.

Applied ethics is interested in everyday ethical practice: how we negotiate and resolve ethical conflicts and dilemmas in real situations. From this position, it is possible to recognise that in some situations there may be no clearly identifiable right course of action. The actions we claim to be virtuous and right may not be the ones we are able to choose and follow through with. Organisational contexts increase this moral complexity because the competing interests within and without the organisation – such as those of clients, staff, volunteers, funding bodies, managers – are often difficult to accommodate.

In complex organisations, the mix of interactions and communications means that it is sometimes hard to decipher how decisions in difficult situations are made, and how ethical reasoning comes into play. Figure 9.1 provides an outline of how judgement and reasoning can be used in making ethical decisions. What needs to be remembered is that in any social system there are supra systems that organise and constrain our actions in specific and micro social, economic and political contexts. There are also traditions and orthodoxy related to the history of the profession and a nation's

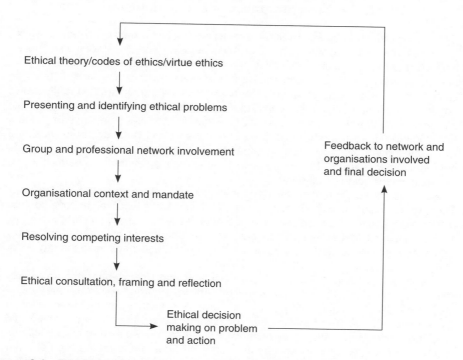

Figure 9.1   Ethical framing and decision making in organisational settings

history. The feedback model provided by Figure 9.1 on ethical decisions is designed to acknowledge and/or include diverse stakeholders in outcomes and at various points in the process. An awareness of possible outcomes and a sensitivity to democratic process and inclusiveness can help to make such decisions balanced, holistic and definite in their transparency. Transparency on who makes such ethical decisions, when and where, and in what kind of process is especially important for users.

A further issue involved in ethical judgement and decision making is the feelings experienced and the emotions expressed in the situation. Earlier in the book, we critiqued arguments that downplay or problematise the role of emotions in decision making and organisational change. For some, being a professional and being committed to professional ethics means being able to transcend emotion. For us, there is no doubt that it is important that social workers identify and set aside feelings of like and dislike when providing services equitably. However, setting aside emotion ignores an important source of information about the situation – our intuitive and psycho-physiological understanding – and threatens to result in unconscious emotional responses for which we are unaccountable. The challenge for professionals is to ensure that their emotional responses are 'other directed', in that they are used to better understand the service user's experiences (Hugman, 2005). In Practice Example 9.1, a team is faced with a complex family situation that requires careful and sensitive ethical decision making.

PRACTICE EXAMPLE 9.1

Practical ethics, organisational mandate and abuse

Zena, who is second-generation Sudanese, works in a family mediation centre, which, to assist in managing resources, has a policy of focusing workers' actions on a family's immediate presenting issues. Zena was recently referred a case involving a 15-year-old female, Mary, who has been accused of assaulting her father. Mary is the third child, with two male siblings, aged 17 and 18 years. All the children currently live at home with their parents. When Zena and a colleague visited the family, Mary's father threatened to charge her as he said that this was not the first time such an incident had occurred. Mary's mother appeared very passive and deferred to her husband when questioned. Zena arranged a separate meeting with Mary; however, she was not forthcoming in explaining her behaviour, other than to say that she hates her parents and wasn't going to cooperate.

Zena discussed the matter with her supervisor and colleagues in a team meeting. There was considerable discussion about the situation and what might have contributed to Mary's actions. Based on Zena's account of the interview with Mary's parents, some suspected that Mary's father may be a perpetrator of physical and possibly sexual abuse towards Mary and/or her mother, and this may have been the trigger for Mary's own behaviour.

In this case, a number of workers, Zena included, feel it is essential that the agency investigate more fully the possibility of wider abuse occurring within the family. The centre manager is reluctant to pursue this, given the agency's mandate to respond to presenting issues. The framing of the problem by the organisation's policies would preclude acting on this suggestion of the father's abuse, unless there is clear evidence of it having taken place. The workers are concerned that a referral to police or other agencies may not be responded to immediately given the lack of evidence.

Zena and her supervisor consult together and try to reframe the problem from a professional perspective rather than from an organisational one. An immediate decision and course of action might be to meet with the mother to find out further information and then to act to protect the mother and Mary if abuse is identified as being initiated by the father. Both decide that, in this instance, the most ethical response is to pursue this avenue, even though the action is not directly in line with the organisation's policy. They then take this to their manager and are able to convince her that this is the most appropriate ethical response in the unique situation.

In Practice Example 9.1, there is an emerging conflict between staff views and organisational policy. An ethical value which could focus organisational thinking is prevention of harm. Following the ethical framing process presented in Figure 9.1, it might also be possible to identify other values which support or possibly contradict the prevention of harm principle. One possible tension might be with the value of working competently within organisational systems and policies. An ethical problem has been identified and a decision needs to be made about whether or not to further investigate the possibility of wider domestic violence. Zena and her supervisor weigh up their professional responsibilities in light of this problem. They decide in this instance that the organisational policy is not facilitative of ethical professional practice and they take this view back to the centre manager. This results in an agreement to breach the policy in this instance; this might feasibly lead to a re-evaluation of the policy itself. A longer-term strategy may be for the workers to undergo professional development in ethical decision making. The complexity of the decision making in this instance demonstrates how ethical decisions and reflection can assist in organisational learning and embed new practices within an organisation.

The Active and Responsible Social Worker

Social work responsibility is a broader concept than that of professional accountability, as discussed in Chapter 7. It is about taking responsibility for professional actions in organisations and, more generally, in society. The ancient Greek philosopher Aristotle related responsibility to virtuous actions and irresponsibility to vice. Social work ethics can also be framed in this way: 'The role of the virtuous social worker is shown to be one that necessitates appropriate applications of intellectual and practical virtues such as justice, reflection, perception, judgement, bravery, prudence, liberality and temperance' (McBeath and Webb, 2002: 1015). While this approach – referred to as *virtue ethics* – is often framed as a normative ethical theory, McBeath and Webb recognise that these virtues can emerge in a less determinate and more interpretive and reflexive way in everyday practice. They argue that this is a counterpoint to the defensive style of practice that can emerge in organisations driven by economic, administrative and managerialist concerns, where being 'professional carries the ideas of closure, competency and control' (McBeath and Webb, 2002: 1016).

In organisational practice, we suggest that social work responsibility takes both passive and active forms (Bovens, 1998). As discussed in Chapter 7, passive responsibility relates to accountability for past action taken: 'To be accountable is to be in a position to give an explanation for one's actions – with reasons and justifications' (Shardlow, 1995: 67). Active responsibility relates to attempts to become more virtuous and more responsible in future action. Such action might arise, for example, from a commitment to anti-discriminatory, anti-oppressive and critical practice models. Inevitably, there are differences in the degree and form of responsibility that people can take in certain situations.

A child or teenager, for example, is unlikely to have the emotional and cognitive awareness to know how to act responsibly in all adult contexts. As Bovens (1998: 23) writes, 'there are many responsibilities which can differ according to context, the discourse and the views of the speaker'. These include responsibility as task (e.g. being responsible for doing something) and responsibility as capacity (e.g. a person with dementia being seen as responsible or not for their actions).

Being a responsible social worker is about pursuing virtuous actions as a professional, and discerning correct or appropriate actions. As discussed earlier, this may create tensions with organisational goals or duties. For example, social workers may find themselves at odds with management committees or CEOs over the right course of action in a specific situation. A key concern is how social workers can become more aware of the effects, including possible harm, they have on clients, colleagues and others. There is also a place for the human qualities and virtues that facilitate ethical decision making. Qualities such as courage, determination, honesty and respect could all be part of a professional ethic and identity.

Compassion, in particular, is one virtue that can emerge as a spontaneous emotion, and may, in the face of a bureaucratic encounter, serve to humanise the experience of service assessment or delivery: 'Professional ethics may (perhaps even must) attend to compassion because it involves the recognition of the person, or situation, in a way that demands a moral response' (Hugman, 2005: 66). This is not to forget that before the institutional welfare state of the twentieth century much charitable giving was, as Sennett (2003) argues about welfare history in the USA, based on 'sentimental compassion' or a compassion that blurs the difference between control and caring. An unconditional and spontaneous compassion is giving without sentimentality, and without the 'largesse' of institutionalised Christian or other faith-based ethics (Sennett, 2003: 127–40).

Increasingly, governments have been promoting new ways of regulating workers in the social and human services, including social workers. For some, the introduction of codes of practice and the registration of social work by government are seen as unnecessary intrusions into professional autonomy, which is already monitored – albeit infrequently and inconsistently – via codes of ethics. For others, however, these strategies provide clearer practice standards and extra levels of accountability needed to protect service users and maintain quality of service. Arguably, they also place social work on a par with other regulated professions, such as law and medicine, and add greater legitimacy to social work as a professional endeavour. From our perspective, they also provide a further touchstone for active responsibility: 'the realisation that one will or might be held to account, the passive side of responsibility, stimulates people to behave responsibly, the active side' (Bovens, 1998: 39).

Three contemporary strands of ethical theory, identified by Hugman (2005), illuminate strategies for social workers to act responsibly in the front line of organisational practice. First, a *pluralist approach* enables different normative stances on values and a flexible approach to the implementation of codes of ethics and practice standards. This can allow for some overlap between professional and organisational values, such as compassion, duty of care, recognition, respect and minimising harm. Reflecting on the ways in which ethical principles are variously applied in practice provides an opportunity to learn and improve practice. According to Hughes (2016), social workers need to guard against seeing themselves as heroic ethical warriors within organisations and look for opportunities to connect with the values of others in the organisation (and the organisation itself) and to negotiate ethical issues in a collaborative way.

Second, *discursive ethics* involves an open discussion of what is right and good. According to Hugman (2005: 137), a high level of generality can result from a discursive process that 'has the potential to enable all those who are participants in practice to speak and be heard'. We see this as a particularly important approach as it can bring social workers, managers, clients and communities together in conversations about practical matters that are of ethical concern. Such conversations are necessary where the work of human service organisations cuts across professional values and clients' interests, and where there are coercive statutory powers. For example, the removal of a child in an abuse situation from an Aboriginal or ethnic minority family requires discursive processes that acknowledge both general social justice concerns and the need to minimise harm in particular situations.

Third, recent developments in *feminist*, *postmodern* and *environmental ethics* provide new understandings of right and good practice. Each of these approaches has its own complexities of arguments. However, they have in common a concern with the contingencies of practice, which illuminates ethics as gendered, socially constructed and relative to partial truth claims (Hugman, 2005). These ideas parallel some of the 'upstream' metaphors of organisational theory discussed in Chapter 2.

These three approaches can inform more responsible social work practice in organisations, especially in terms of work with marginalised and disadvantaged clients and communities, such as black people and people with disabilities. Dominelli (2002: 44–7), for example, suggests that exclusionary processes are rooted in inequality and created in the service vocabulary of a 'them–us' dyad based on deepseated social divisions, including 'race', gender, sexual identity, age, disability, mental health and social class. These dyads inferiorise those who are 'one-down' and thus act to exclude 'the other'. Dominelli's (2002: 140–52) anti-oppressive approach to organisational change disrupts these dyads by encouraging negotiations and alliances across and within networks and services.

As suggested by research on network relationships in organisations, the stronger the involvement and commitment of a social worker to their job, the more they can encourage positive work outcomes for themselves and others, improve work attitudes and create more effective programme delivery. This may involve greater compliance with managerial agendas, but will also provide greater energy and enthusiasm for positive social outcomes and social justice for clients and their communities. This is, after all, the broader goal of the profession.

As Banks (2002) and Hugman (2005) argue, we cannot always do what we would prefer to do. Everyday organisational practice will always limit the extent to which social work values and aspirations can be fully realised. However, in striving to become more responsible, social workers can explain and account for their past actions, reflect on these and learn from their mistakes, and aim to better express social work virtues in the future. Our knowledge of social work virtues and ethical principles and dilemmas provides a basis for thinking through the possible ramifications of practice: the consequences of making one decision over another. Hugman's (2005) questioning approach is useful in this regard:

> It is the purpose of ethics to pose questions that challenge thought and action, that call attention to what is good and what is right. In this sense, ethics, whether as an ethos or as codified sets of principles, should be both unsettling and unsettled. Ethics is unsettling because consideration of ethics causes us constantly to examine the values and principles that are embodied in our own practices. This may place demands on us or present us with difficult choices. There are no easy formulae for ethical decision making. Ethics is also unsettled, because it necessarily remains unfinished. (Hugman, 2005: 160)

Active Leadership and Inclusive Change Cultures

One of the ways in which social workers can become more responsible is to exercise leadership within human service organisations. In Chapter 6, we noted that this may involve not just undertaking formal leadership roles, such as becoming a manager, but also exercising informal leadership capacity. Healy (2004) also highlights a potential role for social workers as practice leaders in the diversified human services labour market. Inevitably, though, social workers need to be able to work cooperatively and strategically with others who are in leadership roles, including non-social-work-qualified managers and other professionals. How they do this is particularly crucial in times of organisational change.

Organisational change is affected by a wide range of dynamics. Throughout this book, we have highlighted the impact of environmental change on organisational change. Research suggests that the funding of large non-profit organisations is particularly vulnerable in times of economic change (Berman et al., 2006), and thus managerialist strategies can be seen partly as a response to reducing social welfare budgets. Organisational change is also sensitive to internal relationships, emotions, interactions and processes. In times of organisational change, organisational culture – which comprises symbol systems, shared meanings, micro-cultures, subcultures and counter-cultures – sets the mood for decision making and influences communication processes and information sharing (Jones and May, 1992). Culture manifests as 'rituals, stories, humour, jargon, physical arrangements and formal structures and policies as well as informal norms and practices' (Martin, 2000: 55). For organisational change to be successful, organisational culture may also need to change. However, as discussed in Chapter 3, such a culture should facilitate debate and creativity, rather than try to impose a predetermined corporate culture on organisational members.

It would be interesting to observe closely the different leadership styles in human service organisations and see who advocates and who resists change. From a social work perspective, one concern might be how to move beyond top-down or Machiavellian styles and encourage collective and participatory action. As indicated in Chapter 7, performance management and resultant worker behaviour is in danger of using efficiency dividends and service outcomes to justify narrow, harsh and potentially dehumanising 'improvement' in organisational culture and work conditions. In a top-down or upwardly accountable service culture, senior management inevitably has a partial and limited view of the front-line reality and the world of the client. There are real dangers that people in these positions may reduce and stereotype individuals. Both front-line staff and clients have useful knowledge and skills and frequently have legitimate grievances with organisational processes and strategies. In social work, as suggested in Chapter 7, silencing such voices could not only be seen as oppressive, but also as reducing the range of valuable resources on which organisations can draw for their change initiatives. Social workers occupy unique positions in human service organisations. By engaging in and with organisational change strategies, they may be able to promote an inclusive, participatory and bottom-up change agenda.

Social workers can also become more aware of change strategies that introduce subtle coercive practices within the organisation. For example, as discussed in Chapter 4, computer-based client information systems can act as a social control mechanism through the surveillance of staff and clients (Beddoe, 2010). In the broader neo-liberal climate of advanced capitalism, we can argue that liquid surveillance as record keeping and the core of organisational memory is everywhere. The collection of data in formal and official organisational ways is a requirement of good monitoring systems in human and health service delivery. However, the collection and use of this data can also contribute to the felt and lived experience of clients and staff of an oppressive, anti-democratic, demonising and authoritarian societal climate of totalising security, particularly for the most vulnerable and disadvantaged in modern societies (Bauman and Lyon, 2013; Wearing, 2012). How this information and knowledge is transferred into decisions and action should be a key concern for social work for two reasons. First, we are aware that there are commonly particular groups within society – often among the most marginalised and powerless – that are subject to the heaviest surveillance and scrutiny. Second, we are also aware – for example, through the debates around evidence-based practice – that knowledge is often contestable and that it does not always feed easily into decision-making processes (see also Wearing and Hughes, 2014).

Thus, from our perspective, social work's orientation towards organisational change should reflect a wider social change agenda. That is, how we critique, engage with and lead organisational change should be informed by values such as social justice, empowerment and increased participation in society. This is not to imply that all organisational change should be large-scale: there is emancipatory potential in everyday practices (Healy, 2000). However, social work should take care not to promote such change in an overly deterministic and unreflexive manner. As Healy (2000: 61) argues, the 'liberatory claims of critical social workers are bound to be regarded with suspicion by those whose experience of welfare practices has been anything but liberatory!'

Learning for Active and Reflexive Practice

This last point highlights what, for social work, is an ongoing concern and dilemma: that in spite of our rhetoric and best intentions, sometimes social work exacerbates social injustice rather than ameliorates it. This concern strikes at the heart of social work values and our self-identity as a profession. It has given rise to critical practice in its many forms, such as anti-oppressive practice, radical social work and structural social work. Yet, these critical approaches are themselves not beyond their own critique in that there is the potential for them also to become hegemonic and dogmatic, just like orthodox or traditional social work (Healy, 2000). Additionally, for us this reflects the contingencies of the relationship between theory and practice in social work rather than seeing one as determining the other.

However, in critiquing the limits of and dilemmas in social work's social justice mandate, it is important not to throw the baby out with the bathwater. That is, we must recognise that social work is of society – especially the social work practised within the statutory realm – and that consequently it is unreasonable to expect the profession not to reflect something of the plurality of views and values present within society. Indeed, many of the core values of social work, such as respect for human dignity and individual freedom, are central values in western democracies. Similarly, we must also recognise that the difficulties faced by the profession in some areas do not negate the successes in other areas. From our position, a critical reflexive stance is essential when evaluating practice. Such an approach would learn from mistakes but also celebrate successes.

In organisational contexts, reflexivity involves an ongoing folding back of learning through experience and knowledge onto the organisation and its workers (Clarke, 2001; Egan and Kadushin, 2004). Crucially, it also involves the awareness that we are not outside our own critique and that we should subject ourselves, as organisational operators, as well as others, to ongoing scrutiny. A reflexive approach emphasises the contingencies of social work practice and its decision making, and the emergent nature of organisational change. It recognises that knowledge is contextual and contested, and that overly technical approaches to practice – 'how-to guides' – will inevitably be limited in the face of complex, multi-dimensional and often ambiguous practice situations. Reflexivity also involves a striving for double-loop learning, as conceptualised by Argyris and Schön (1978), where response to error comprises not a simple correction in line with existing objectives but a transformation of the underlying normative order of the organisation. The 2011 Munro Review of Child Protection, for example, gives social workers, as well as other workers, the opportunity to reflect on and learn from previous mistakes in child and family work. This is an exemplary model of organisational change and learning.

So how can social workers develop a reflexive approach to knowledge and learning in and about organisational practices? Certainly, one resource is the formal body of knowledge developed within social work and other disciplines as it relates to these different practices. This would incorporate knowledge that conforms to the principles of evidence-based and best practice. It would include research on service user experiences and expectations. For our purposes, it also includes the extensive body of theory from management and organisation studies, particularly the sociology of organisations. Another resource is the learning that the organisation itself obtains through its own systems (e.g. information management systems). Human service organisations increasingly rely on their own internal processes to generate information about how they are operating and how services are being delivered and received. The concept of the 'learning organisation' incorporates this sense that organisations can collect and draw on a wealth of information to inform their ongoing development, including making use of organisational memory so that staff turnover does not lead to 'reinventing the wheel' (Gould, 2000; Wearing, 2016).

Another resource for social workers in developing their knowledge of organisational practices is themselves and their colleagues. The concept of the 'reflective practitioner' (Schön, 1983) embodies the idea that practitioners are engaged in a constant learning process by engaging in action, applying knowledge as action takes place, reflecting on action taken, and planning and preparing for future action. Reflective practice requires the social worker to use their whole self in integrating knowledge and learning into their work (Miehls and Moffatt, 2000). Specific strategies can be adopted to facilitate reflection and to develop an awareness of practice within wider social and cultural contexts, including power inequalities. These include observations of practice, and drawing on reflective journals, reading, information sharing and discussion with colleagues, supervision and other professional development activities.

In engaging in these different strategies, we need to think critically about them, their relevance to the work at hand, and their impact on service users and communities. An important contribution from postmodern ideas is the notion that knowledge is not benign and that assertions of the 'truth' need to be unpacked and critiqued (Sellick et al., 2002). For us, this involves questioning not just the ways in which others construct knowledge and assert it as truth, but also the ways in which we ourselves do this. Sellick et al. (2002: 496–7) identify a series of questions on our sources of knowledge that are aimed to 'clarify where we speak from', that is, the values, interests and assumptions that are normally hidden:

- What frames of mind am I bringing to this situation?
- What am I taking to be the facts of the situation?
- Why did I orient to these particular facts rather than others?
- What am I not seeing in this situation?
- Would someone whose gender, social location, professional indoctrination or culture is different from mine orient differently to this situation?
- Where did I learn this 'way of looking'?
- Whose voice is being exercised in this knowledge? Is it mine or someone else's?
- What are the cultural, gender or epistemic bases implicit in this way of looking?
- Is my own experience represented in this knowledge?
- Is there some personal experience which is silenced by this knowledge?
- Do I recognise myself and my experience in this way of speaking my knowledge?

 Reflective Questions

1   Consider the times when you have felt frustrated by not having a 'how-to' guide to social work practice. What benefits might have been gained from such a guide (if it existed) and what might have been some of the limitations?
2   What are some strategies that help you learn best? How could these be used in a regular and structured way to facilitate reflective practice?

Reflexivity and organisational change

Dan, a social work-qualified case manager with a strong commitment to social justice, works at Covenant Care – a large provider of services to people with disabilities. Covenant is auspiced by a church group and articulates a Christian ethos. The agency facilitates consumer-directed (personalised) care via needs assessment, the development of care plans and the allocation of individual budgets through which people with disabilities (or their nominated representative) can purchase resources or services.

Dan has been working with Heather, a 19-year-old with Cerebral Palsy, who lives in a semi-independent group home with other young adults with disabilities. Since moving out of her parents' home two years ago, and feeling more independent, Heather has become more open about her decision to transition from male to female (she was previously known as Paul). Heather recently expressed to Dan her frustration at having to explain to staff and other residents about her identity and her decision to transition. She has experienced both negative and supportive responses from others, but generally feels concerned about the Christian environment in which she lives. Dan is aware that the organisation has no policies or programmes affirming lesbian, gay, bisexual and transgender (LGBT) identities. There is also little understanding of what resources transgender people might need and how an individual budget may be used to access these resources. Heather wants to receive hormone treatment and meet up with other transgender young people, as well as access social opportunities with a view to meeting someone for a romantic relationship.

Heather's situation spurs Dan to take up the issue of LGBT rights with Covenant's CEO who facilitates discussions with senior staff and the board of directors. She involves Dan in the discussions. There is much debate, with some feeling positive about this initiative and others feeling that a formal policy on LGBT issues would undermine the organisation's Christian ethos. As a starting point, the CEO decides to collaborate with a local LGBT community organisation to provide training to staff on LGBT awareness, although Dan worries that this will not be enough to change the culture of the organisation. He approaches Heather to see if she would be prepared to be involved in the training – to provide a service user perspective – and she is horrified about the idea of being 'paraded' around in this way and treated as a 'freak show'.

Heather's response leads Dan to question his own motives for the change process he sought to initiate. He wonders if his commitment to social justice and a desire to see change take place has led him to lose focus on his client's experience and the understanding and compassion she requires. Following reflection, he talks with Heather about his mistakes and seeks to regain her trust. He also accesses literature on organisational change to help him consider the ways in which he can work within the agency to build support for a culture change process. The experience leaves Dan feeling less certain about his own capacities and world view, and more aware of the impact of himself on others.

Conclusion

Active, relational, reflexive and ethical social work practice in organisations confronts the indeterminacies of organisational work. According to Folgheraiter (2004: 133), social work practice is like an 'adventurous journey' where what matters 'is not the certainty of where one is going but the achievement of good arriving'. A good arriving comes from not just having good intentions. We must take action and, in doing so, be prepared to make mistakes and be held to account for these mistakes. A critical reflexive approach allows for different possibilities within action and recognises that mistakes will be made. But what is important is to learn from these experiences. It is not a panacea, nor is it a justification for inaction. There are very significant social welfare policy and broader political agendas that social work needs to be aware of and involved in. This is essential in the quest for greater social equality and equity within social and organisational systems. Further examination is needed of how practice strategies and advocacy can bring this about (see Hughes and Wilson, 2016; Raeymaeckers and Dierckx, 2013; Thompson, 2011).

Of course, social workers are not alone on their 'adventurous journey'. We have fellow travellers – service users – who are not so dissimilar to or separate from ourselves (Healy, 2000). (Indeed, it is not hard to imagine that many, if not most, social workers may, at some point in their lives, become a user of social work services.) Parton and O'Byrne (2000: 76–8) frame social work reflexivity as workers and users engaging in co-construction and co-dialogue. This establishes a relationship view of social work as working with other staff and with clients: a relationship approach emphasises deep listening and unconditional positive regard for others and seeks to realign and re-think structures internal to the organisation and in social structures of society as the external environment. For example, Rao, Kellhear and Miller (2015) examined the important issue of realigning cultures within human service organisations to facilitate new positive gender norms, including the acceptance and support of women's leadership. This is one illustration of how deep structures might need to be shifted in terms of social work hierarchies and the organisations we find ourselves working in. While it is important not to ignore our own authority – such as that accorded by our organisational or statutory role – so too is it important not to ignore the authority service users have, particularly in relation to their own lives and stories. A networked and open teamwork approach to practice (e.g. Folgheraiter, 2004; Payne, 2000) acknowledges the relationships between social workers, other workers and service users as crucial in achieving a good arriving.

In this book, we have sought to explore some of the tensions involved in social work practice in contemporary human service organisations. We have striven to achieve a balance between a critical and a practical approach. We recognise that social workers operate within managerialist and bureaucratic organisations and we acknowledge that they will need to engage with neo-liberal agendas regularly in their day-to-day work. Nonetheless, there are many opportunities for social workers to influence these organisations in line with social work values and their awareness of the needs and rights of clients and communities. Being an effective social worker in human service organisations means maintaining responsibilities to the organisation and its management, to the profession, to clients and communities, and to wider society.

These various commitments and the strategies that flow from them cannot be handled in a guidebook fashion. Each chapter of this book makes a case for the teaching and learning of crucial dimensions to good practice in social work in the context of organisations. This has included the dimensions of reflection, knowledge, theory, skills, technical understanding, values, evidence, accountability, experience, responsibility and learning. We have suggested that a way of integrating this material is to develop and nurture a practical ethics for negotiating the dilemmas involved in everyday practice in social work. This would make use of codes of ethics and codes of practice, but would not implement them in an overly deterministic manner. We have also argued, in this chapter and throughout the book, that a critical reflexive approach is best suited to developing a sustained critique around social justice issues and to integrating a wide range of knowledge into organisational practice. Importantly, social work itself would not be beyond the boundaries of this critique.

References

Ager, W., Dow, J. and Gee, M. (2005) 'Grassroots networks: a model for promoting the influence of service users and carers in social work education', *Social Work Education*, 24(4): 467–76.

Al-Amoudi, I. and Willmott, H. (2011) 'Where constructionism and critical realism converge: interrogating the domain of epistemological relativism', *Organizational Studies*, 32: 27–46.

Alexander, J.C. and Smith, P. (1996) 'Social science and salvation: risk society as mythical discourse', *Zeitschrift fur Soziologie*, 25(4): 251–62.

Alkandry, M.G. and Tower, L.E. (2011) 'Covert pay discrimination: how authority predicts pay differences between women and men', *Public Administration Review*, 71(5): 740–50.

Alston, M. and Bowles, W. (2003) *Research for Social Workers*, 2nd edn. Sydney: Allen and Unwin.

Alvesson, M. and Skoldberg, K. (2012) *Reflexive Methodology*, 2nd edn. London: Sage.

Andrews, K.R. (1971) *The Concept of Corporate Strategy*. Homewood, IL: Irwin.

Antonacopoulou, E.P. and Gabriel, Y. (2001) 'Emotion, learning and organizational change: towards an integration of psychoanalytic and other perspectives', *Journal of Organizational Change Management*, 14(5): 435–51.

Argyris, C. and Schön, D. (1978) *Organizational Learning: A Theory of Action Perspective*. Reading, MA: Addison-Wesley.

Arnstein, S. (1969) 'A ladder of citizen participation', *Journal of the American Institute of Planners*, 35(4): 216–23.

Aronson, J. and Smith, K. (2010) 'Managing restructured social services', *British Journal of Social Work*, 40: 530–47.

Australian Association of Social Workers (AASW) (2010) *Code of Ethics*. Canberra: AASW.

Australian Institute of Health and Welfare (AIHW) (2011) *Australia's Welfare 2011*. Canberra: AGPS.

Avakian, S. and Roberts, J. (2012) 'Whistleblowers in organisations: prophets at work', *Journal of Business Ethics*, 110: 71–84.

Avby, G., Nilsen, P. and Ellstrom, P. (2015) 'Knowledge use and learning in everyday social work practice: a study in child investigation work', *Child and Family Social Work*, 24(40): 1–11.

Baker, S., Warburton, J., Hodgkin, S. and Pascal, J. (2014) 'Reimagining the relationship between social work and information communication technology in the network society', *Australian Social Work*, 67(4): 467–78.

Baldry, E., Green, S. and Thorpe, K. (2006) 'Urban Australian Aboriginal peoples' experience of human services', *International Social Work*, 49(3): 364–75.

Baldwin, M. (2004) 'Conclusions: optimism and the art of the possible', in N. Gould and M. Baldwin (eds), *Social Work, Critical Reflection and the Learning Organization*. Aldershot: Ashgate.

Bamford, T. (1990) *The Future of Social Work*. Houndmills: Macmillan.

Banks, S. (2002) 'Professional values and accountabilities', in R. Adams, L. Dominelli and M. Payne (eds), *Critical Practice in Social Work*. London: Palgrave Macmillan. pp. 28–45.

Banks, S. (2004) *Ethics, Accountability and the Social Professions*. Basingstoke: Palgrave Macmillan.

Banks, S. (2010) 'Integrity in professional life: issues of conduct, commitment and capacity', *British Journal of Social Work*, 40: 2168–84.

Barak, M., Nissly, J.A. and Levin, A. (2001) 'Antecedents to retention and turnover among child welfare, social work, and other human service employees: what can we learn from past research?', *Social Service Review*, 75(4): 625–61.

Bargal, D. (2000) 'The manager as leader', in R.J. Patti (ed.), *The Handbook of Social Welfare Management*. Thousand Oaks, CA: Sage.

Barile, A.L. and Durso, F.T. (2002) 'Computer-mediated communication in collaborative writing', *Computers in Human Behavior*, 18: 173–90.

Barraket, J. (2008) 'Social enterprise and governance: implications for the Australian third sector', in J. Barraket (ed.), *Strategic Issues for the Not-for-Profit Sector*. Kensington, NSW: UNSW Press.

Bartunek, J.M. and Woodman, R.W. (2015) 'Beyond Lewin: toward a temporal approximation of organization development and change', *Annual Review of Organizational Psychology and Organizational Behavior*, 2(1): 157–82.

Bauman, Z. (2000) *Liquid Modernity*. Cambridge: Polity Press.

Bauman, Z. and Lyon, D. (2013) *Liquid Surveillance*. Cambridge: Polity Press.

Beauchamp, T.L. and Childress, J.F. (2001) *Principles of Biomedical Ethics*, 5th edn. New York: Oxford University Press.

Beck, U. (1992) *Risk Society: Towards a New Modernity*. London: Sage.

Beckett, C. and Horner, N. (2016) *Essential Theory for Social Work Practice*, 2nd edn. London: Sage.

Beddoe, L. (2010) 'Surveillance or reflection: professional supervision in "the risk society"', *British Journal of Social Work*, 40(4): 1279–96.

Beeson, I. and Davis, C. (2000) 'Emergence and accomplishment in organizational change', *Journal of Organizational Change Management*, 13(2): 178–89.

Begum, N. (2006) *Doing It for Themselves: Participation and Black and Minority Ethnic Service Users*. Bristol: Social Care Institute for Excellence (SCIE) and the Race Equality Unit (REU).

Bell, E. and Taylor, S. (2011) 'Beyond letting go and moving on: new perspectives on organizational death, loss and grief', *Scandinavian Journal of Management*, 27: 1–10.

Bellinger, A. and Elliott, T. (2011) 'What are you looking at? The potential of appreciative inquiry as a research approach for social work', *British Journal of Social Work*, 41(4): 708–25.

Bennett, S. (1999) *White Politics and Black Australians*. Sydney: Allen and Unwin.

Beresford, P. (2000) 'Service users' knowledges and social work theory: conflict or collaboration?', *British Journal of Social Work*, 30: 489–503.

Beresford, P. and Croft, S. (2004) 'Service users and practitioners reunited: the key component of social work reform', *British Journal of Social Work*, 34: 53–68.

Beresford, P. and Evans, C. (1999) 'Research and empowerment', *British Journal of Social Work*, 29: 671–7.

Berger, P. and Luckmann, T. (1966) *The Social Construction of Reality: A Treatise in the Sociology of Knowledge*. Harmondsworth: Penguin Books.

Berman, E.M. (1998) *Productivity in Public and Nonprofit Organizations*. Thousand Oaks, CA: Sage.

Berman, G., Brooks, R. and Murphy, J. (2006) 'Funding the non-profit welfare sector: explaining changing funding sources 1960–1999', *Economic Papers*, 25(1): 83–99.

Berthold, S.M. and Fischman, Y. (2014) 'Social work with trauma survivors: collaboration with interpreters', *Social Work*, 59(2): 103–10.

Bessarab, D. (2000) 'Working with Aboriginal families: a cultural approach', in W. Weeks and M. Quinn (eds), *Issues Facing Australian Families: Human Services Respond*. French's Forest, NSW: Pearson Education.

Bhabha, H.K. (1994) *The Location of Culture*. London: Routledge.

Bhaskar, R. (1991) *Philosophy and the Idea of Freedom*. Oxford: Blackwell.

Bill, B.T. and Zabrana, R.E. (2009) 'Critical thinking about inequality: an emerging lens', in B.T. Dill and R.E. Zambrana (eds), *Emerging Intersections: Race, Class and Gender in Theory, Policy and Practice*. New Brunswick, NJ: Rutgers University Press.

Bion, W. (1978) *Four Discussions with W.R. Bion*. Strathtay, Scotland: Clunie Press.

Bisman, C. (2004) 'Social work values: the moral core of the profession', *British Journal of Social Work*, 34: 109–23.

Blom, B. (2009) 'Knowing and un-knowing? That is the question in the era of evidence-based social work practice', *Journal of Social Work*, 9: 158–77.

Boehm, A. and Staples, L.H. (2002) 'The functions of the social worker in empowering: the voices of consumers and professionals', *Social Work*, 47(4): 449–60.

Bourgeois, L.J. (1980) 'Strategy and environment: a conceptual integration', *Academy of Management Review*, 5: 25–39.

Bovens, M. (1998) *The Quest for Responsibility*. Cambridge: Cambridge University Press.

Bradley, G. (2003) 'Administrative justice and charging for long-term care', *British Journal of Social Work*, 33: 641–57.

Bradley, G. and Höjer, S. (2009) 'Supervision reviewed: reflections on two different social work models in England and Sweden', *European Journal of Social Work*, 12(1): 71–85.

Brewis, J. (2001) 'Telling it like it is? Gender, language and organizational theory', in R. Westwood and S. Lindstead (eds), *The Language of Organizations*. London: Sage.

Briskman, L. (2003) 'Indigenous Australians: towards a postcolonial social work', in J. Allan, B. Pease and L. Briskman (eds), *Critical Social Work*. Sydney: Allen and Unwin.

British Association of Social Workers (BASW) (2012) *The Code of Ethics for Social Work: Statement of Principles*. Birmingham: BASW.

Broadhurst, K., Hall, C., Wastell, D., White, S. and Pithouse, A. (2010) 'Risk, instrumentalism and the humane project in social work: identifying the informal logics of risk management in children's statutory services', *British Journal of Social Work*, 40: 1046–64.

Brody, R. and Nair, M.D. (2014) *Effectively Managing and Leading Human Service Organizations*, 4th edn. Thousand Oaks, CA: Sage.

Bryan, T.K. and Brown, C.H. (2015) 'The individual group, organizational and community outcomes of capacity-building programs in human service nonprofit organizations: implications for theory and practice', *Human Service Organizations: Management, Leadership & Governance*, 39: 426–43.

Bryman, A. (1992) *Charisma and Leadership in Organizations*. London: Sage.

Bryman, A. (1999) 'Leadership in organizations', in S.R. Clegg, C. Hardy and W.R. Nord (eds), *Managing Organizations: Current Issues*. London: Sage.

Buchbinder, E. and Eisikovits, Z. (2008) 'Collaborative discourse: the case of police and social work relationships in intimate violence intervention in Israel', *Journal of Social Service Research*, 34(4): 1–13.

Burke, P. (1999) 'Social services staff: risks they face and their dangerousness to others', in P. Parsloe (ed.), *Risk Assessment in Social Care and Social Work*. London: Jessica Kingsley.

Burnes, B. (2004) 'Kurt Lewin and complexity theories: back to the future?', *Journal of Change Management*, 4(4): 309–25.

Burnes, B. (2005) 'Complexity theories and organizational change', *International Journal of Management Reviews*, 7(2): 73–90.

Burnett, R. and Appleton, C. (2004) 'Joined-up services to tackle youth crime: a case study in England', *British Journal of Criminology*, 44(1): 34–54.

Burrell, G. and Morgan, G. (1979) *Sociological Paradigms and Organizational Analysis*. London: Heinemann.

Burton, J. and van den Broek, D. (2009) 'Accountable and countable: information management systems and the bureaucratisation of social work', *British Journal of Social Work*, 39: 1326–42.

Busse, S. (2009) 'Supervision between critical reflection and practical action', *Journal of Social Work Practice*, 23(2): 159–73.

Butcher, D. and Atkinson, S. (2001) 'Stealth, secrecy and subversion: the language of change', *Journal of Organizational Change Management*, 14(6): 554–69.

By, R.T., Oswick, C. and Burnes, B. (2014) 'Looking back and looking forward: some reflections on journal developments and trends in organizational change discourse', *Journal of Change Management*, 14(1): 1–7.

Carey, M. (2015) 'The fragmentation of social work and social care: some ramifications and a critique', *British Journal of Social Work*, 45(8): 2406–22.

Carmen, J.G. (2010) 'The accountability movement: what's wrong with this theory of change?', *Nonprofit and Voluntary Sector Quarterly*, 39(2): 256–74.

Carr, A. (2001) 'Understanding emotion and emotionality in a process of change', *Journal of Organizational Change Management*, 14(5): 421–34.

Carr, S. (2004) *Has Service User Participation Made a Difference to Social Care Services?* Bristol: Social Care Institute for Excellence (SCIE) and the Race Equality Unit (REU).

Carrilio, T.E. (2008) 'Accountability, evidence, and the use of information systems in social service programs', *Journal of Social Work*, 8(2): 135–48.

Carson, E., Chung, D. and Evans, T. (2015) 'Complexities of discretion in social services in the third sector', *European Journal of Social Work*, 18(2): 167–84.

Casey, C. (2004) 'Contested rationalities, contested organizations: feminist and postmodern visions', *Journal of Organizational Change Management*, 17(3): 302–14.

Chenoweth, L. and Clements, N. (2011) 'Participation opportunities for adults with intellectual disabilities provided by disability services in one Australian state', *Journal of Policy and Practice in Intellectual Disabilities*, 8(3): 172–82.

Cherniss, C. (1995) *Beyond Burnout: Helping Teachers, Nurses, Therapists and Lawyers Recover from Stress and Disillusionment.* New York: Routledge.

Cheung, C. and Young, J. (2015) 'Enhancing job performance and mental health through organizational nurturing culture', *Human Service Organizations: Management, Leadership & Governance*, 39: 251–69.

Chia, R. (1996) *Organizational Analysis and Deconstructive Practice.* Berlin: Walter de Gruyter.

Chia, R. (2002) 'On organizational becoming: rethinking organizational change', *Organization Science*, 13(5): 567–82.

Claiborne, N., Auerbach, C. and Zeitlin, W. (2015) 'Organizational climate factors of successful and not successful implementation of workforce innovations in voluntary child welfare agencies', *Human Service Organizations: Management, Leadership & Governance*, 39: 69–80.

Clarke, J. and Newman, J. (1997) *The Managerial State.* London: Sage.

Clarke, N. (2001) 'The impact of in-service training within social services', *British Journal of Social Work*, 31: 757–74.

Clayton, J., Donovan, C. and Merchant, J. (2015) 'Emotions of austerity: care and commitment in public service delivery in the north east of England', *Emotion, Space and Society*, 14: 24–32.

Clegg, S. (1989) *Frameworks of Power.* London: Sage.

Clegg, S., Kornberger, M. and Pitsi, T. (2008) *Managing and Organizations.* Los Angeles, CA: Sage.

Clyde, The Lord (1992) *Report of the Inquiry into the Removal of Children from Orkney in February 1991, HoC. 195.* London: HMSO.

Coffey, M., Lindsey, D. and Tattersall, A. (2004) 'Stress in social services: mental wellbeing, constraints and job satisfaction', *British Journal of Social Work*, 34: 735–46.

Cohen, B. (1999) 'Intervention and supervision in strengths-based social work practice', *Families in Society*, 80(5): 460–6.

Cohen, S. (1985) *Visions of Social Control: Crime, Punishment and Classification*. Cambridge: Polity Press.

Collins, S. (2001) 'Bullying in social work organisations', *Practice*, 13(3): 29–43.

Condliffe, P. (2012) *Conflict Management: A Practical Guide*, 4th edn. Chatswood, NSW: LexisNexis.

Connolly, M. and Harms, L. (2012) *Social Work from Theory to Practice*. Melbourne: Cambridge University Press.

Cooperrider, D.L. and Whitney, D. (2005) *Appreciative Inquiry: A Positive Revolution in Change*. San Francisco, CA: Berrett-Koehler.

Corbett, D. (1991) *Public Sector Management*. Sydney: Allen and Unwin.

Coulshed, V. and Mullender, A. (2001) *Management in Social Work*, 2nd edn. Houndmills: Palgrave.

Cousins, C. (2004) 'Becoming a social work supervisor: a significant role transition', *Australian Social Work*, 57(2): 175–85.

Crevani, L., Lindgren, M. and Packendorff, J. (2010) 'Leadership, not leaders: on the study of leadership as practices and interactions', *Scandinavian Journal of Management*, 26: 77–86.

Croft, S. and Beresford, P. (1990) *From Paternalism to Participation: Involving People in Social Services*. London: Open Services Project.

Croft, S. and Beresford, P. (1997) 'Service user perspectives', in M. Davies (ed.), *The Blackwell Companion to Social Work*. Oxford: Blackwell.

Crook, S., Pakulski, J. and Waters, M. (1992) *Postmodernization*. London: Sage.

Crozier, M. (1964) *The Bureaucratic Phenomenon*. London: Tavistock.

Cuff, E.C. and Payne, G.C.F. (1984) *Perspectives in Sociology*. London: Allen and Unwin.

Dachler, H.P. and Hosking, D. (2013) 'The primacy of relations in socially constructed organizational realities', in D. Hosking, H.P. Dachler and K.J. Gergen (eds), *Management and Organization: Relational Alternatives to Individualism*. Aldershot: Avebury.

Dalrymple, J. and Burke, B. (1997) *Anti-oppressive Practice: Social Care and the Law*. Buckingham: Open University Press.

D'Amour, D. and Oandasan, I. (2005) 'Interprofessionality as the field of interprofessional practice and interprofessional education: an emerging concept', *Journal of Interprofessional Care*, Supplement 1: 8–20.

Darlington, Y., Feeney, J.A. and Rixon, K. (2004) 'Complexity, conflict and uncertainty: issues in collaboration between child protection and mental health services', *Children and Youth Services Review*, 26: 1175–92.

David, B. (2013) 'Social network analysis: applied tool to enhance effective collaboration between child protection organisations by revealing and strengthening work relationships', *European Journal of Mental Health*, 8: 3–28.

Davis, A. (1998) 'Risk work and mental health', in H. Kemshall and J. Pritchard (eds), *Good Practice in Risk Assessment and Risk Management*. London: Jessica Kingsley.

Dawson, P. (2014) 'The processual perspective: studying change in organisations', in H. Hasan (ed.), *Being Practical with Theory: A Window into Business Research*. Wollongong, NSW: THEORI.

Dean, H. (2000) 'Managing risk by controlling behaviour: social security administration and the erosion of citizenship', in P. Taylor-Gooby (ed.), *Risk, Trust and Welfare*. London: Macmillan.

De Bortoli, L. and Dolan, M. (2015) 'Decision making in social work with families and children: developing decision-aids compatible with cognition', *British Journal of Social Work*, 45(7): 2142–60.

Dent, E.B. and Goldberg, S.G. (1999) 'Challenging "resistance to change"', *Journal of Applied Behavioral Science*, 35(1): 25–41.

Doherty, B., Eccleston, R., Hansen, E., Kristen, N. and Churchill, B. (2015) 'Building evaluation capacity in micro community organisations: more burden than benefit?', *Evaluation Journal of Australasia*, 15(4): 29–37.

Dolgoff, R., Harrington, D. and Loewenberg, F.M. (2012) *Ethical Decisions for Social Work Practice*, 9th edn. Belmont, CA: Brooks/Cole.

Dominelli, L. (1997) *Anti-racist Social Work: A Challenge for White Practitioners and Educators*, 2nd edn. London: Macmillan.

Dominelli, L. (1998) 'Anti-oppressive practice in context', in R. Adams, L. Dominelli and M. Payne (eds), *Social Work, Themes, Issues and Critical Debates*. London: Macmillan.

Dominelli, L. (2002) *Anti-oppressive Social Work Theory and Practice*. London: Palgrave.

Donaldson, L. (1986) *In Defence of Organization Theory: A Reply to the Critics*. Melbourne: Cambridge University Press.

Duff, C. (2003) 'The importance of culture and context: rethinking risk and risk management in young drug using populations', *Health, Risk and Society*, 5(3): 285–99.

Dunoon, D. (2002) 'Rethinking leadership for the public sector', *Australian Journal of Public Administration*, 61(3): 3–18.

Dwyer, S. (2007) 'The emotional impact of social work practice', *Journal of Social Work Practice*, 21(1): 49–60.

Eagly, A.H. and Carli, L.L. (2007) 'Women and the labyrinth of leadership', *Harvard Business Review*, 85: 63–71.

Ebrahim, A. (2005) 'Accountability myopia: losing sight of organizational learning', *Nonprofit and Voluntary Sector Quarterly*, 34(1): 56–87.

Ebrahim, A., Battilana, J. and Mair, J. (2014) 'The governance of social enterprise: mission drift and accountability challenges in hybrid organisations', *Research in Organisational Behaviour*, 34: 81–100.

Egan, G. (1985) *Change Agent Skills in Helping and Human Service Settings*. Monterey, CA: Brooks/Cole.

Egan, G. (2014) *The Skilled Helper: A Problem-Management and Opportunity-Development Approach to Helping*, 10th edn. Belmont, CA: Brooks/Cole, Cengage Learning.

Egan, M. and Kadushin, G. (2004) 'Job satisfaction of home health social workers in the environment of cost containment', *Health and Social Work*, 29(4): 287–96.

Egan, R. (2012) 'Australian social work supervision practice in 2007', *Australian Social Work*, 65(2): 171–84.

Ellis, K. (2011) '"Street-level bureaucracy" revisited: the changing face of frontline discretion in adult social care in England', *Social Policy and Administration*, 45(3): 221–44.

Elrod, P.D. and Tippett, D.D. (2002) 'The "death valley" of change', *Journal of Organizational Change Management*, 15(3): 273–91.

Erikson, E. (1968) *Identity: Youth and Crisis*. London: Faber and Faber.

Etzioni, A. (ed.) (1969) *The Semi-professions and Their Organization: Teachers, Nurses, Social Workers*. New York: Free Press.

Evans, D. (2010) 'Aspiring to leadership … a woman's world? An example of developments in France', *Cross Cultural Management*, 17(4): 347–67.

Evans, T. (2013) 'Organisational rules and discretion in adult social work', *British Journal of Social Work*, 43(4): 739–58.

Evans, T. and Harris, J. (2004) 'Street-level bureaucracy, social work and the (exaggerated) death of discretion', *British Journal of Social Work*, 34: 871–95.

Farmakopoulou, N. (2002) 'What lies underneath? An inter-organizational analysis of collaboration between education and social work', *British Journal of Social Work*, 32: 1051–66.

Fawcett, B., Goodwin, S., Meagher, G. and Phillips, R. (2010) *Social Policy for Social Change*. London: Palgrave.

Ferguson, I. and Lavalette, M. (2013) 'Crisis, austerity and the future(s) of social work in the UK', *Critical and Radical Social Work*, 1(1): 95–110.

Ferguson, K.E. (1984) *The Feminist Case Against Bureaucracy*. Philadelphia, PA: Temple University Press.

Fetterman, D.M., Kaftarian, S. and Wandersman, A. (eds) (1996) *Empowerment Evaluation: Knowledge and Tools for Self Assessment and Accountability*. Thousand Oaks, CA: Sage.

Fieldler, F.E. (1993) 'The leadership situation and the black box in contingency theories', in M.M. Chemers and R. Ayman (eds), *Leadership Theory and Research: Perspectives and Directions*. New York: Academic Press.

Finger, M. and Brand, S.B. (1999) 'The concept of the "learning organization" applied to the transformation of the public sector', in M. Easterby-Smith, L. Araujo and J. Burgoyne (eds), *Organizational Learning and the Learning Organization*. London: Sage.

Fisher, E.A. (2009) 'Motivation and leadership in social work management: a review of theories and related studies', *Administration in Social Work*, 33: 347–67.

Fisher, R., Ury, W. and Patton, B. (1991) *Getting to YES: Negotiating Agreements Without Giving In*, 2nd edn. New York: Penguin Books.

Fitze, M. (2006) 'Discourse and participation in ESL face-to-face and written electronic conferences', *Language Learning and Technology*, 10(1): 67–86.

Folgheraiter, F. (2004) *Relational Social Work: Toward Networking and Societal Practices*. London: Jessica Kingsley.

Fook, J. (2002) *Social Work: Critical Theory and Practice*. London: Sage.

Fook, J., Ryan, M. and Hawkins, L. (2000) *Professional Expertise: Practice, Theory and Education for Working in Uncertainty*. London: Whiting and Birch.

Frawley-O'Dea, M.G. and Sarnat, J.E. (2001) *The Supervisory Relationship: A Contemporary Psychodynamic Approach*. New York: Guilford Press.

Freire, P. (1972) *Cultural Action for Freedom*. Harmondsworth: Penguin Books.

French, R. (2001) '"Negative capability": managing the confusing uncertainties of change', *Journal of Organizational Change Management*, 14(5): 480–92.

Frenkel, M. and Shenhav, V. (2006) 'From binarism back to hybridity: a postcolonial reading of management and organization studies', *Organization Studies*, 27: 855–76.

Gaertner, D. (2011) '"The climax of reconciliation": transgression, apology, forgiveness and the body in conflict resolution', *Bioethical Inquiry*, 8: 245–56.

Garrett, P.M. (2005) 'Social work's "electronic turn": notes on the deployment of information and communication technologies in social work with children and families', *Critical Social Policy*, 25(4): 529–53.

Garrow, E. and Hasenfeld, Y. (2010) 'Theoretical approaches to human service organizations', in Y. Hasenfeld (ed.), *Human Services as Complex Organizations*, 2nd edn. Thousand Oaks, CA: Sage.

Gatley, S., Lessem, R. and Altman, Y. (eds) (1996) *Comparative Management: A Transcultural Odyssey*. London: McGraw Hill.

Geddes, M. (2000) 'Tackling social exclusion in the European Union? The limits of the new orthodoxy of local partnership', *International Journal of Urban and Regional Research*, 24(4): 782–800.

Gellis, Z.V. (2001) 'Social work perceptions of transformational and transactional leadership in health care', *Social Work Research*, 25(1): 17–25.

Geoghegan, M. and Powell, F. (2006) 'Community development, partnership governance and dilemmas of professionalization: profiling and assessing the case of Ireland', *British Journal of Social Work*, 36: 845–61.

Gibbs, L. and Gambrill, E. (2002) 'Evidence-based practice: counterarguments to objections', *Research on Social Work Practice*, 12(3): 452–76.

Gibelman, M. (2005) 'Social workers for rent: the contingency human services labor force', *Families in Society*, 86(4): 457–69.

Giddens, A. (1990) *The Consequences of Modernity*. Cambridge: Polity Press.

Gillard, S.G., Edwards, C., Gibson, S.L., Owen, K. and Wright, C. (2013) 'Introducing peer worker roles into UK mental health service teams: a qualitative analysis of the organisational benefits and challenges', *BMC Health Services Research*, 13(188) [online]. Available at: http://bmchealthservres.biomedcentral.com/articles/10.1186/1472-6963-13-188

Gillingham, P. (2016) 'Technology configuring the user: implications for the redesign of electronic information systems in social work', *British Journal of Social Work*, 46(2): 323–38.

Gilroy, P. (1997) 'Diaspora and the detours of identity', in K. Woodward (ed.), *Identity and Difference*. London: Sage.

Glaister, K.W. and Falshaw, J.R. (1999) 'Strategic planning: still going strong?', *Long Range Planning*, 32(1): 107–16.

Gould, N. (2000) 'Becoming a learning organization: a social work example', *Social Work Education*, 19(6): 585–96.

Gould, N. (2010) 'Integrating qualitative evidence in practice guideline development', *Qualitative Social Work*, 9: 93–109.

Gould, N. and Baldwin, M. (eds) (2004) *Social Work, Critical Reflection and the Learning Organization*. Aldershot: Ashgate.

Gray, I., Parker, J. and Immins, T. (2008) 'Leading communities of practice in social work: groupwork or management?', *Groupwork*, 18(2): 26–40.

Gray, M. and Schubert, L. (2016) '"Do something, change something": feminist leadership in social work', in S. Wendt and N. Moulding (eds), *Contemporary Feminisms in Social Work Practice*. Abingdon: Routledge.

Greenslade, L., McAuliffe, D. and Chenoweth, L. (2015) 'Social workers' experiences of covert workplace activism', *Australian Social Work*, 68(4): 422–37.

Gregory, M. and Holloway, M. (2005) 'Language and the shaping of social work', *British Journal of Social Work*, 35: 37–53.

Grint, K. and Holt, C. (2011) 'Leading questions: if "total place", "big society" and local leadership are the answers: what's the question?', *Leadership*, 7(1): 85–98.

Gross, E. and Etzioni, A. (1985) *Organizations in Society*. Englewood Cliffs, NJ: Prentice Hall.

Grunwald, K. and Thierch, H. (2009) 'The concept of the "lifeworld orientation" for social work and social care', *Journal of Social Work Practice*, 23(2): 131–46.

Gunawardena, C.N., Hermans, M.B., Sanchez, D., Richmond, C., Bohley, M. and Tuttle, R. (2009) 'A theoretical framework for building online communities of practice with social networking tools', *Educational Media International*, 46(1): 3–16.

Gursansky, D., Harvey, J. and Kennedy, R. (2003) *Case Management: Policy, Practice and Professional Business*. Sydney: Allen and Unwin.

Hair, H.J. and O'Donoghue, K. (2009) 'Culturally relevant, socially just social work supervision: becoming visible through a social constructionist lens', *Journal of Ethnic and Cultural Diversity in Social Work*, 18: 70–88.

Hampton, G., Buggy, M., Graves, J., McCann, L. and Irwin, J. (2016) 'Grappling with realities: policy and practice in HIV social work', *Australian Social Work*, 1–12.

Hancock, P. and Tyler, P. (2001) *Work, Postmodernism and Organization*. London: Sage.

Harris, J. (1998) *Managing State Social Work: Front-line Management and the Labour Process*. Aldershot: Ashgate.

Harris, N. (1987) 'Defensive social work', *British Journal of Social Work*, 17: 61–9.

Harris, R. (1997) 'Power', in M. Davies (ed.), *The Blackwell Companion to Social Work*. Oxford: Blackwell.

Hassard, J. (1995) *Sociology and Organizational Theory: Positivism, Paradigms and Postmodernity*. Cambridge: Cambridge University Press.

Hatch, M.J. (1997) *Organization Theory: Modern, Symbolic, and Postmodern Perspectives*. New York: Oxford University Press.

Hatch, M.J. and Cunliffe, A.L. (2013) *Organization Theory: Modern, Symbolic, and Postmodern Perspectives*, 3rd edn. Oxford: Oxford University Press.

Head, B.W. and Alford, J. (2015) 'Wicked problems: implications for public policy and management', *Administration & Society*, 47(6): 711–39.

Health and Care Professions Council (2012) *Standards of Proficiency: Social Workers in England*. London: Health and Care Professions Council.

Healy, K. (1998) 'Participation and child protection: the importance of context', *British Journal of Social Work*, 28: 897–914.

Healy, K. (2000) *Social Work Practices*. London: Sage.

Healy, K. (2002) 'Managing human services in a market environment: what role for social workers?', *British Journal of Social Work*, 32: 527–40.

Healy, K. (2004) 'Social workers in the new human services marketplace: trends, challenges and responses', *Australian Social Work*, 57(2): 103–14.

Healy, K. and Meagher, G. (2004) 'The reprofessionalization of social work: collaborative approaches for achieving professional recognition', *British Journal of Social Work*, 34: 243–60.

Healy, L. (2007) 'Universalism and cultural relativism in social work ethics', *International Social Work*, 50(1): 11–26.

Held, D. and McGrew, A. (2000) 'The great globalization debate: an introduction', in D. Held and A. McGrew (eds), *The Global Transformations Reader*. Cambridge: Polity Press.

Higgins, J.M. and McAllaster, C. (2004) 'If you want strategic change, don't forget to change your cultural artifacts', *Journal of Change Management*, 4(1): 63–73.

Hill, M. (2005) *The Public Policy Process*. London: Pearson Longman.

Hill, T. and Westbrook, R. (1997) 'SWOT analysis: it's time for a product recall', *Long Range Planning*, 30(1): 46–52.

Hochschild, A.R. (1983) *The Managed Heart: Commercialization of Human Feeling*. Berkeley, CA: University of California Press.

Hodson, R. (2001) *Dignity at Work*. Cambridge: Cambridge University Press.

Hodson, R. and Sullivan, T.A. (1995) *The Social Organization of Work*, 2nd edn. Belmont, CA: Wadsworth.

Hoggett, P. and Miller, C. (2000) 'Working with emotions in community organizations', *Community Development Journal*, 35(4): 352–64.

Holosko, M. (2009) 'Social work leadership: identifying core attributes', *Journal of Human Behavior in the Social Environment*, 19(4): 448–59.

Honey, P. and Mumford, A. (1986) *The Manual of Learning Styles*. Maidenhead: Ardingly House.

Hoogvelt, A. (1997) *Globalization and the Postcolonial World: The New Political Economy of Development*. Houndmills: Macmillan.

hooks, b. (1996) *Killing Rage: Ending Racism*. Harmondsworth: Penguin Books.

Hough, G. (1999) 'The organization of social work in the customer culture', in B. Pease and J. Fook (eds), *Transforming Social Work Practice: Postmodern Critical Reflections*. London: Routledge.

Houston, S. (2001) 'Transcending the fissure in risk theory: critical realism and child welfare', *Child and Family Social Work*, 6: 219–28.

Howard, M.O. and Jensen, J.M. (1999) 'Clinical practice guidelines: should social work develop them?', *Research on Social Work Practice*, 9(3): 283–301.

Hudson, B. (2002) 'Interprofessionality in health and social care: the Achilles' heel of partnership', *Journal of Interprofessional Care*, 16(1): 7–17.

Hughes, L. (2004) 'Women and management: Catholic sisters in late nineteenth century Sydney', *Advances in Social Work and Welfare Education*, 6(1): 16–29.

Hughes, L. (2010) 'Catholic sisters and Australian social welfare history', *Australasian Catholic Record*, 87(1): 30–46.

Hughes, M. (2016) 'Ethics in organisations', in R. Hugman and J. Carter (eds), *Ethics in Social Work*. London: Palgrave Macmillan.

Hughes, M. and Heycox, K. (2010) *Older People, Ageing and Social Work: Knowledge for Practice*. Sydney: Allen and Unwin.

Hughes, M. and Wilson, J. (2016) 'Advocacy: an overarching approach', in E. Moore (ed.), *Case Management for Community Practice*, 2nd edn. Melbourne: Oxford University Press.

Hughes, O. (1994) *Public Management and Administration*. Melbourne: Macmillan.

Hugman, R. (2001) 'Post-welfare social work? Reconsidering post-modernism, post-Fordism and social work education', *Social Work Education*, 20(3): 321–33.

Hugman, R. (2005) *New Approaches in Ethics for the Caring Professions*. Houndmills: Palgrave Macmillan.

Humphries, B. (2004) 'An unacceptable role for social work: implementing immigration policy', *British Journal of Social Work*, 34: 93–107.

Ife, J. (1997) *Rethinking Social Work*. Melbourne: Longman.

Ingram, R. (2013) 'Emotions, social work practice and supervision: an uneasy alliance?', *Journal of Social Work Practice*, 27(1): 5–19.

Irvine, R., Kerridge, I., McPhee, J. and Freeman, S. (2002) 'Interprofessionalism and ethics: consensus or clash of cultures?', *Journal of Interprofessional Care*, 16(3): 199–210.

Iszatt-White, M. (2009) 'Leadership as emotional labour: the effortful accomplishment of valuing practices', *Leadership*, 5(4): 447–67.

IText Working Group, Geisler, C., Bazerman, C., Doheny-Farina, S., Gurak, L., Haas, C., et al. (2001) 'IText: future directions for research on the relationship between information technology and writing', *Journal of Business and Technical Communication*, 15(3): 269–308.

Itzhaky, H. (2000) 'The secret in supervision: an integral part of the social worker's professional development', *Families in Society*, 81(5): 529–37.

Jamous, H. and Peloile, B. (1970) 'Professions or self-perpetuating systems? Changes in the French university hospital system', in J.A. Jackson (ed.), *Professions and Professionalization*. Cambridge: Cambridge University Press.

Jamrozik, A. and Nocella, L. (1998) *The Sociology of Social Problems: Theoretical Perspectives and Methods of Intervention*. Cambridge: Cambridge University Press.

Jaskyte, K. and Dressler, W.W. (2005) 'Organizational culture and innovation in nonprofit human service organizations', *Administration in Social Work*, 29(2): 23–41.

Jones, A. and May, J. (1992) *Working in Human Service Organizations: A Critical Introduction*. Melbourne: Longman.

Jones, M. (2000) 'Hope and despair at the front line: observations on integrity and change in the human services', *International Social Work*, 43(3): 365–80.

Kadushin, A. (1968) 'Games people play in supervision', *Social Work*, 13: 23–32.

Kadushin, A. (1976) *Supervision in Social Work*. New York: Columbia University Press.

Kafka, F. (1984 [1925]) *The Trial*. London: Penguin Books.

Kanter, R.M. (1983) *The Change Masters*. New York: Simon and Schuster.

Kanter, R.M., Stein, B.A. and Jick, T.D. (1992) *The Challenge of Organizational Change*. New York: Free Press.

Kark, R. (2004) 'The transformational leader: who is (s)he? A feminist perspective', *Journal of Organizational Change Management*, 17(2): 160–76.

Katz, D. and Kahn, R.L. (1966) *The Social Psychology of Organizations*. New York: John Wiley and Sons.

Keck, M.E. and Sikkink, K. (1999) 'Transnational advocacy networks in international and regional politics', *International Social Science Journal*, 51(159): 89–101.

Kemshall, H. (1998) 'Enhancing risk decision making through critical path analysis', *Social Work Education*, 17(4): 419–34.

Kemshall, H. (2000) 'Conflicting knowledges on risk: the case of risk knowledge in the probation service', *Health, Risk and Society*, 2(2): 143–58.

Kemshall, H. (2002) *Risk, Social Policy and Welfare*. Buckingham: Open University Press.

Kemshall, H. (2010) 'Risk rationalities in contemporary social work policy and practice', *British Journal of Social Work*, 40: 1247–62.

Kerjean, M. (2002) 'Saving Claymore: Caritas plan helped residents reclaim suburb', *The Catholic Weekly*, August. Available at: www.catholicweekly.com.au/02/aug/18/24.html (accessed 1 October 2006).

Kerka, S. (1995) 'The learning organization: myths and realities', *Eric Clearinghouse*. Available at: www.eric.ed.gov/PDFS/ED388802.pdf

Kersten, A. (2001) 'Organizing for powerlessness: a critical perspective on psychodynamics and dysfunctionality', *Journal of Organizational Change Management*, 14(5): 452–67.

Kettner, P., Moroney, R. and Martin, L. (2013) *Designing and Managing Programs: An Effectiveness-Based Approach*, 4th edn. Los Angeles, CA: Sage.

Kharicha, K., Iliffe, S., Levin, E., Davey, B. and Fleming, C. (2005) 'Tearing down the Berlin wall: social workers' perspectives on joint working with general practice', *Family Practice*, 22: 399–405.

Kharicha, K., Levin, E., Iliffe, S. and Davey, B. (2004) 'Social work, general practice and evidence-based policy in the collaborative care of older people: current problems and future possibilities', *Health and Social Care in the Community*, 12(2): 134–41.

Kimball, E. and Kim, J. (2013) 'Virtual boundaries: ethical considerations for use of social media in social work', *Social Work*, 58(2): 185–8.

King, S., Carson, E. and Papatraianou, L.H. (2016) 'Self-managed supervision', *Australian Social Work*. DOI: 10.1080/0312407X.2015.1134608.

Kirton, D., Feast, J. and Goddard, J. (2011) 'The use of discretion in a "Cinderella" service: data protection and access to child-care files for post-care adults', *British Journal of Social Work*, 41: 912–30.

Kish-Gephart, J.J., Detert, J.R., Treviño, L.K. and Edmondson, A.C. (2009) 'Silenced by fear: the nature, sources, and consequences of fear at work', *Research in Organizational Behavior*, 29: 163–93.

Klarner, P., Todnem, R. and Diefenbach, T. (2011) 'Employee emotions during organizational change: towards a new research agenda', *Scandinavian Journal of Management*, 27: 332–40.

Knowles, M. (1990) *The Adult Learner: A Neglected Species*, 4th edn. Houston, TX: Gulf Publishing.

Ko, R. and Choo, R. (2015) *Cloud Security Ecosystem*. Waltham, MA: Elsevier Science.

Kolb, D.A. (1984) *Experiential Learning*. Englewood Cliffs, NJ: Prentice Hall.

Korinek, A.W. and Kimball, T.G. (2003) 'Managing and resolving conflict in the supervisory system', *Contemporary Family Therapy*, 25(3): 295–310.

Kossak, S.N. (2005) 'Exploring the elements of culturally relevant service delivery', *Families in Society*, 86(2): 189–95.

Kotter, J.P. (1990) *A Force for Change: How Leadership Differs from Management*. New York: Free Press.

Kotter, J.P. (1995) 'Leading change: why transformation efforts fail', *Harvard Business Review*, 73(2): 59–67.

Kouzes, J. and Posner, B. (2005) 'Leading in cynical times', *Journal of Management Inquiry*, 14(4): 357–64.

Kouzes, J.M. and Posner, B.Z. (2012) *The Leadership Challenge: How to Make Extraordinary Things Happen in Organizations*, 5th edn. San Francisco, CA: John Wiley & Sons.

Kramer, M.W. (2010) *Organizational Socialization: Joining and Leaving Organizations*. Malden, MA: Polity Press.

Kubler-Ross, E. (1969) *On Death and Dying*. New York: Touchstone.

Larner, G. (2004) 'Family therapy and the politics of evidence', *Journal of Family Therapy*, 26: 17–39.

Latif, S., Tariq, R., Tariq, S. and Latif, R. (2015) 'Designing an assistive learning aid for writing acquisition: a challenge for children with dyslexia', in C. Sik-Lanyi, E. Hoogerwerf, K. Miesenberger and P. Cudd (eds), *Assistive Technology: Building Bridges*. Amsterdam: IOS Press.

Lawler, J. (2007) 'Leadership in social work: a case of caveat emptor?', *British Journal of Social Work*, 37: 123–41.

Lazarus, R.S. and Folkman, S. (1984) *Stress, Appraisal, and Coping*. New York: Springer.

Lazzari, M.M., Colarossi, L. and Collins, K.S. (2009) 'Feminists in social work: where have all the leaders gone?', *Affilia: Journal of Women and Social Work*, 24(4): 348–59.

Leipzig, R.M., Hyer, K., Ek, K., Wallenstein, S., Vezina, M.L., Fairchild, S., et al. (2002) 'Attitudes toward working on interdisciplinary healthcare teams: a comparison by discipline', *Journal of American Geriatrics Society*, 50(6): 1141–8.

Lens, V. (2004) 'Principled negotiation: a new tool for case advocacy', *Social Work*, 49(3): 506–13.

Levin, L., Goor, Y. and Tayri, M.T. (2013) 'Agency advocacy and organisational development: a feasible policy practice alliance', *British Journal of Social Work*, 43: 522–41.

Lewin, K. (1947) 'Frontiers in group dynamics: I. Concept, method and reality in social sciences – social equilibria and social change', *Human Relations*, 1(1): 5–41.

Lewin, K. (1951) *Field Theory in Social Science*. New York: Harper and Row.

Lewis, S. and Crook, W.P. (2001) 'Shifting sands: an AIDS service organization adapts to a changing environment', *Administration in Social Work*, 25(2): 1–20.

Lietz, C., Hayes, M., Cronin, T. and Julien-Chinn, F. (2014) 'Supporting family-centered practice through supervision: an evaluation of strengths-based supervision', *Families in Society: The Journal of Contemporary Social Services*, 95(4): 227–35.

Lipsky, M. (1980) *Street-level Bureaucracy: Dilemmas of the Individual in Public Services*. New York: Russell Sage.

Longoria, R.A. (2005) 'Is inter-organizational collaboration always a good thing?', *Journal of Sociology and Social Welfare*, 32(3): 123–39.

Lonne, B., McDonald, C. and Fox, T. (2004) 'Ethical practice in contemporary human service', *Journal of Social Work*, 4(3): 345–67.

Ludema, J., Cooperrider, D. and Barrett, F. (2001) 'Appreciative inquiry: the power of the unconditional positive question', in P. Reason and H. Bradbury-Huang (eds), *The Handbook of Action Research: Participative Inquiry and Practice*. London: Sage.

Lukes, S. (1974) *Power: A Radical View*. London: Macmillan.

Lune, H. and Oberstein, H. (2001) 'Embedded systems', *Voluntas*, 12(1): 17–33.

Lurie, I. and Riccucci, N.M. (2003) 'Changing the culture of welfare offices: from vision to the front lines', *Administration and Society*, 34(6): 653–77.

Lymbery, M. (2004) 'Responding to crisis: the changing nature of welfare organizations', in M. Lymbery and S. Butler (eds), *Social Work Ideals and Practice Realities*. Basingstoke: Palgrave Macmillan.

Lymbery, M. (2006) 'United we stand? Partnership working in health and social care and the role of social work in services for older people', *British Journal of Social Work*, 36: 1119–34.

Lymbery, M. and Butler, S. (2004) 'Social work ideals and practice realities: an introduction', in M. Lymbery and S. Butler (eds), *Social Work Ideals and Practice Realities*. Basingstoke: Palgrave Macmillan.

Lyotard, J.F. (1984) *The Postmodern Condition: A Report on Knowledge*. Minneapolis, MN: University of Minneapolis Press.

McAlearney, A.S., Hefner, J.L., Sieck, C.J. and Huerta, T.R. (2015) 'The journey through grief: insights from a qualitative study of electronic health record implementation', *Health Services Research*, 50(2): 462–88.

McAuliffe, D. (2005) 'Putting ethics on the organizational agenda: the social work ethics audit on trial', *Australian Social Work*, 58(4): 357–69.

McBeath, G. and Webb, S.A. (2002) 'Virtue ethics and social work: being lucky, realistic, and not doing one's duty', *British Journal of Social Work*, 32: 1015–36.

McDonald, C. (2006) *Challenging Social Work: The Context of Practice*. Basingstoke: Palgrave.

McDonald, C. and Chenoweth, L. (2009) 'Leadership: a crucial ingredient in unstable times', *Social Work and Society*, 7(1): 102–12.

McDonald, C., Marston, G. and Buckley, A. (2003) 'Risk technology in Australia: the role of the Job Seeker Classification Instrument in employment services', *Critical Social Policy*, 23(4): 498–525.

Macdonald, G. (1999) 'Evidence-based social care: wheels off the runway?', *Public Money and Management*, 19(1): 25–32.

Macdonald, I., Burke, C. and Stewart, K. (2005) *Systems Leadership: Creating Positive Organisations*. London: Gower.

McKevitt, D. (1999) *Managing Core Public Services*. Malden, MA: Blackwell.

McLaughlin, H. (2004) 'Partnerships: panacea or pretence?', *Journal of Interprofessional Care*, 18(2): 103–13.

McWilliam, C.L., Coleman, S., Melito, C., Sweetland, D., Saidak, J., Smit, J., et al. (2003) 'Building empowering partnerships for inter-professional care', *Journal of Interprofessional Care*, 17(4): 363–76.

Management Improvement Advisory Committee (MIAC) (1991) *Accountability in the Commonwealth Public Sector*. Canberra: Australian Government Publishing Service.

Manela, R.W. and Moxley, D.P. (2002) 'Best practices as agency-based knowledge', *Administration in Social Work*, 26(4): 1–23.

Manthorpe, J., Cornes, M., O'Halloran, S. and Joly, L. (2015) 'Multiple exclusion homelessness: the prevention role of social work', *British Journal of Social Work*, 45: 587–99.

Manthorpe, J., Moriarty, J., Hussein, S., Stevens, M. and Sharpe, E. (2015) 'Content and purpose of supervision in social work practice in England: views of newly qualified social workers, managers and directors', *British Journal of Social Work*, 45(1): 52–68.

Mantle, G. and Critchley, A. (2004) 'Social work and child-centred family court mediation', *British Journal of Social Work*, 34: 1161–72.

Manz, C.C. and Sims, H.P. (1989) *SuperLeadership: Leading Others to Lead Themselves*. New York: Prentice Hall.

Manz, C.C. and Sims, H.P. (1991) 'SuperLeadership: beyond the myth of heroic leadership', *Organizational Dynamics*, 19(4): 18–35.

Marsh, P. and Doel, M. (2004) *The Task Centred Book*. London: Routledge.

Martin, E.W. (1992) 'Human service organizations: an Australian perspective', *Social Policy and Administration*, 26(4): 320–35.

Martin, M.W. (2000) *Meaningful Work: Rethinking Professional Ethics*. New York: Oxford University Press.

Mary, N.L. (2005) 'Transformational leadership in human service organizations', *Administration in Social Work*, 29(2): 105–18.

Mattison, M. (2000) 'Ethical decision making: the person in the process', *Social Work*, 45(3): 201–12.

Maynard, B.R. (2010) 'Social service organizations in the era of evidence-based practice', *Journal of Social Work*, 10(3): 301–16.

Meagher, G. and Healy, K. (2003) 'Caring, controlling, contracting and counting: government and non-profits in community services', *Australian Journal of Public Administration*, 62(3): 40–51.

Meagher, G. and Parton, N. (2004) 'Modernising social work and the ethics of care', *Social Work and Society*, 2(1): 10–27.

Medley, B.C. and Akan, O.H. (2008) 'Creating positive change in community organizations: a case for rediscovering Lewin', *Nonprofit Management and Leadership*, 18(4): 485–96.

Melville, R. (2008) '"Token participation" to "engaged participation": lessons learnt and challenges ahead for Australian not-for-profits', in J. Barraket (ed.), *Strategic Issues for the Not-for-Profit Sector*. Kensington, NSW: UNSW Press.

Merighi, J.R., Ryan, M., Renoulf, N. and Healy, B. (2005) 'Reassessing a theory of professional expertise: a cross-national investigation of expert mental health social workers', *British Journal of Social Work*, 35: 709–25.

Merton, R. (1957) *Social Theory and Social Structure*. New York: Free Press.

Meyer, S. (2004) 'Organizational response to conflict: future conflict and work outcomes', *Social Work Research*, 28(3): 183–90.

Miehls, D. and Moffatt, K. (2000) 'Constructing social work identity based on the reflexive self', *British Journal of Social Work*, 30: 339–48.

Miller, L. (2012) *Counselling Skills for Social Work*, 2nd edn. London: Sage.

Miller, R., Freeman, T., Davidson, D. and Glasby, J. (2015) *An Adult Social Care Compendium of Approaches and Tools for Organisational Change*. Birmingham: University of Birmingham and Middlesex University.

Miller, S.J., Hickson, D.J. and Wilson, D.C. (1996) 'Decision making in organizations', in S. Clegg, C. Hardy and W. Nord (eds), *The SAGE Handbook of Organization Studies*. Thousand Oaks, CA: Sage.

Mills, C.W. (1977) [1959] *The Sociological Imagination*. Harmondsworth: Penguin Books.

Milner, J., Myers, S. and O'Byrne, P. (2015) *Assessment in Social Work*. London: Palgrave.

Mishna, F., Bogo, M., Root, J., Sawyer, J.-L. and Khoury-Kassabri, M. (2012) '"It just crept in": the digital age and implications for social work practice', *Clinical Social Work Journal*, 40(3): 277–86.

Mizrahi, T. and Abramson, J.S. (2000) 'Collaboration between social workers and physicians: perspectives on a shared case', *Social Work in Health Care*, 31(3): 1–24.

Mizrahi, T. and Rosenthal, B.B. (2001) 'Complexities of coalition building: leaders' successes, strategies, struggles, and solutions', *Social Work*, 46(1): 63–78.

Morgan, G. (2006) *Images of Organization*. Thousand Oaks, CA: Sage.

Morrison, T. (2001) *Staff Supervision in Social Care: Making a Real Difference for Staff and Service Users*. Brighton: Pavilion.

Morrison, T. (2007) 'Emotional intelligence, emotion and social work: context, characteristics, complications and contribution', *British Journal of Social Work*, 37(2): 245–63.

Moxley, D.P. and Manela, R.W. (2000) 'Agency-based evaluation and organizational change in the human services', *Families in Society*, 81(3): 316–27.

Mulroy, E.A. (2004) 'Theoretical perspectives on the social environment to guide management and community practice: an organization-in-environment approach', *Administration in Social Work*, 28(1): 77–96.

Munro, E. (1996) 'Avoidable and unavoidable mistakes in child protection work', *British Journal of Social Work*, 26: 793–808.

Munro, E. (1998) 'Improving social workers' knowledge base in child protection work', *British Journal of Social Work*, 28: 89–105.

Munro, E. (2004) 'The impact of the audit on social work practice', *British Journal of Social Work*, 34: 1075–95.

Munro, E. (2005) 'A systems approach to investigating child abuse deaths', *British Journal of Social Work*, 35: 531–46.

Munro, E. (2008) 'Lessons from research on decision making', in D. Lindsey and A. Shlonsky (eds), *Child Welfare Research: Advances for Practice and Policy*. Oxford: Oxford University Press.

Munro, E. (2011) *The Munro Review of Child Protection: Final Report – A Child-Centred System*. London: The Stationery Office.

Munro, E. and Hubbard, A. (2011) 'A systems approach to evaluating organisational change in children's social care', *British Journal of Social Work*, 41(4): 726–43.

Murphy, A. and McDonald, J. (2004) 'Power, status and marginalization: rural social workers and evidence-based practice in multidisciplinary teams', *Australian Social Work*, 57(2): 127–36.

Naccarato, T. (2010) 'Child welfare informatics: a proposed subspecialty for social work', *Children and Youth Services Review*, 32(12): 1729–34.

National Audit Office (NAO) (2010) *Reorganising Central Government*. London: NAO.

Netting, F.E. and O'Connor, M.K. (2005) 'Lady boards of managers: subjugated legacies of governance and administration', *Afflia: Journal of Women and Social Work*, 20(4): 448–64.

Netting, F.E., Kettner, P.M. and McMurtry, S.L. (1993) *Social Work Macro Practice*. New York: Longman.

Netting, F.E., Nelson, H.W., Borders, K. and Huber, R. (2004) 'Volunteer and paid staff relationships: implications for social work administration', *Administration in Social Work*, 28(3/4): 69–89.

Neuman, W.L. and Kreuger, L.W. (2003) *Social Work Research Methods: Qualitative and Quantitative Approaches*. Boston, MA: Pearson Education.

New South Wales Family and Community Services (2013) *Code of Ethical Conduct*. Sydney: Family and Community Services.

Noble, C. and Irwin, J. (2009) 'Social work supervision: an exploration of the current challenges in a rapidly changing social, economic and political environment', *Journal of Social Work*, 9(3): 345–58.

Noordegraaf, M. (2007) 'From "pure" to "hybrid" professionalism: present-day professionalism in ambiguous public domains', *Administration and Society*, 39(6): 761–85.

Northouse, P.G. (2009) *Leadership: Theory and Practice*, 5th edn. Thousand Oaks, CA: Sage.

O'Brien, M. (2011) 'Equality and fairness: linking social justice and social work practice', *Journal of Social Work*, 11(2): 143–58.

O'Connor, I., Hughes, M., Turney, D., Wilson, J. and Setterlund, D. (2006) *Social Work and Social Care Practice*. London: Sage.

O'Connor, I., Wilson, J., Setterlund, D. and Hughes, M. (2008) *Social Work and Human Service Practice*, 5th edn. French's Forest, NSW: Pearson Education Australia.

Organisation for Economic Co-operation and Development (OECD) (2001) *Citizens as Partners: OECD Handbook on Information, Consultation and Public Participation in Policy-making*. Paris: OECD.

Osborne, D. and Gaebler, T. (1992) *Reinventing Government*. New York: Penguin Books.

Osborne, S.P. and Brown, K. (2005) *Managing Change and Innovation in Public Service Organizations*. Abingdon: Routledge.

Ospina, S., Diaz, W. and O'Sullivan, J.S. (2002) 'Negotiating accountability: managerial lessons from identity-based nonprofit organizations', *Nonprofit and Voluntary Sector Quarterly*, 31(1): 5–31.

Oswick, C., Grant, D., Michelson, G. and Wailes, N. (2005) 'Looking forwards: discursive directions in organizational change', *Journal of Organizational Change Management*, 18(4): 383–90.

Page, M.L. (2011) 'Gender mainstreaming: hidden leadership?', *Gender, Work and Organization*, 18(3): 318–36.

Parker, C. (2015) 'Practicing conflict resolution and cultural responsiveness within interdisciplinary contexts: a study of community service practitioners', *Conflict Resolution Quarterly*, 32(3): 325–57.

Parker-Oliver, D., Bronstein, L.R. and Kurzejeski, L. (2005) 'Examining variables related to successful collaboration on the hospice team', *Health and Social Work*, 30(4): 279–86.

Parlevliet, M. (2009) *Rethinking Conflict Transformation from a Human Rights Perspective*. Berlin: Berghof Research Center for Constructive Conflict Management. Available at: http://edoc.vifapol.de/opus/volltexte/2011/2602/pdf/parlevliet_handbook.pdf

Parry, K. and Bryman, A. (2006) 'Leadership in organizations', in S.R. Clegg, W.R. Nord, C. Hardy and T. Lawrence (eds), *The Sage Handbook of Organization Studies*. Thousand Oaks, CA: Sage.

Parton, N. (1985) *The Politics of Child Abuse*. London: Macmillan.

Parton, N. and O'Byrne, N. (2000) *Constructive Social Work: Towards a New Practice*. Basingstoke: Palgrave Macmillan.

Patti, R.J. (1983) *Social Welfare Administration: Managing Social Programs in a Developmental Context*. Englewood Cliffs, NJ: Prentice Hall.

Payne, M. (1997) *Modern Social Work Theory: A Critical Introduction*, 2nd edn. Basingstoke: Macmillan.

Payne, M. (2000) *Teamwork in Multiprofessional Care*. Basingstoke: Macmillan.

Pearce, J. (2003) *Social Enterprise in Anytown*. London: Calouste Gulbenkian Foundation.

Pease, B. (2011) 'Men in social work: challenging or reproducing an unequal gender regime?', *Affilia: Journal of Women and Social Work*, 26(4): 406–18.

Perlman, D. and Takacs, G.J. (1990) 'The 10 stages of change', *Nursing Management*, 21(4): 33–8.

Perrons, D. (2000) 'Living with risk: labour market transformation, employment policies and social reproduction in the UK', *Economic and Industrial Democracy*, 21(3): 283–310.

Peters, T. and Waterman, R.H. (1982) *In Search of Excellence: Lessons from America's Best-run Companies*. London: Harper and Row.

Pincus, A. and Minahan, A. (1973) *Social Work Practice: Model and Method*. Itasca, IL: Peacock.

Pithouse, A. (1987) *Social Work: The Social Organization of an Invisible Trade*. Avebury: Gower.

Power, M. (1990) 'Modernism, postmodernism and organization', in J. Hassard and D. Pym (eds), *The Theory and Philosophy of Organizations: Critical Issues and New Perspectives*. London: Routledge.

Power, M. (1997) *The Audit Society: Rituals of Verification*. Oxford: Oxford University Press.

Qureshi, H. (2004) 'Evidence in policy and practice: what kinds of research designs?', *Journal of Social Work*, 4(1): 7–23.

Raeymaeckers, P. and Dierckx, D. (2013) 'To work or not to work? The role of the organisational context for social workers' perception of activation', *British Journal of Social Work*, 43: 1170–89.

Rank, M.G. and Hutchinson, W.S. (2000) 'An analysis of leadership within the social work profession', *Journal of Social Work Education*, 36(3): 487–502.

Rao, A., Kellhear, D. and Miller, C. (2015) 'No shortcuts to shifting deep structures in organisations', *IDS Bulletin*, 46(4): 82–91.

Ravi-Priya, K. (2012) 'Social constructionist approach to suffering and healing: juxtaposing Cassell, Gergen and Kleinman', *Psychological Studies*, 57(2): 211–23.

Rawls, J. (1971) *A Theory of Justice*. Cambridge, MA: Harvard University Press.

Ray, T., Clegg, S. and Gordon, R. (2004) 'A new look at dispersed leadership: power, knowledge and context', in J. Storey (ed.), *Leadership in Organizations: Current Issues and Key Trends*. London: Routledge.

Reamer, F.G. (2015) 'Clinical social work in a digital environment: ethical and risk-management challenges', *Clinical Social Work Journal*, 43(2): 120–32.

Reed, M. (1999) 'Organizational theorizing: a historically contested terrain', in S.R. Clegg and C. Hardy (eds), *Studying Organization*. London: Sage.

Reeves, S., Perrier, L., Goldman, J., Freeth, D. and Zwarenstein, M. (2013) 'Interprofessional education: effects on professional practice and healthcare outcomes (update)', *Cochrane Database of Systematic Reviews*, 28(3): CD002213.

Ren, H. and Gray, B. (2009) 'Repairing relationship conflict: how violation types and culture influence the effectiveness of restoration rituals', *The Academy of Management Review*, 34(1): 105–26.

Reynolds, H. (1999) *Why Weren't We Told?* Melbourne: Penguin Books.

Richardson, S. and Asthana, S. (2006) 'Inter-agency information sharing in health and social care services: the role of professional culture', *British Journal of Social Work*, 36: 657–69.

Ricoeur, P. (1978) *The Rule of Metaphor*. London: Routledge and Kegan Paul.

Riessman, C.K. and Quinney, L. (2005) 'Narrative in social work: a critical review', *Qualitative Social Work*, 4: 391–412.

Riley, P. (2000) 'Supervision of social service managers', in J. Pritchard (ed.), *Good Practice in Supervision*. London: Jessica Kingsley.

Ringel, S. (2001) 'In the shadow of death: relational paradigms in clinical supervision', *Clinical Social Work Journal*, 29(2): 171–9.

Robinson, G. (2003) 'Technicality and indeterminacy in probation practice: a case study', *British Journal of Social Work*, 33: 593–610.

Robinson, K. (2014) 'Voices from the front-line: social work with refugees and asylum seekers in Australia and the UK', *British Journal of Social Work*, 44: 1602–20.

Robinson, M. and Cottrell, D. (2005) 'Health professionals in multi-disciplinary and multi-agency teams: changing professional practice', *Journal of Interprofessional Care*, 19(6): 547–60.

Robotham, D. (2000) 'Postcolonialism and beyond', in G. Browning, A. Halcli and F. Webster (eds), *Understanding Contemporary Society: Theories of the Present*. London: Sage.

Roets, G., Roose, R., Schiettecat, T. and Vandenbroeck, M. (2016) 'Reconstructing the foundations of joined-up working: from organisational reform towards a joint engagement of child and family services', *British Journal of Social Work*, 46(2): 306–22.

Rogers, C. (1961) *On Becoming a Person: A Therapist's View of Psychotherapy*. Boston, MA: Houghton Mifflin Company.

Rojek, C., Peacock, G. and Collins, S. (1988) *Social Work and Received Ideas*. London: Routledge.

Rose, P. and Gidman, J. (2010) 'Evidence-based practice within values-based care', in J. McCarthy and P. Rose (eds), *Values-Based Health and Social Care: Beyond Evidence-Based Practice*. London: Sage.

Ross, W.H. and Conlon, D.E. (2000) 'Hybrid forms of third-party dispute resolution: theoretical implications of combining mediation and arbitration', *Academy of Management Review*, 25(2): 416–27.

Roy, A. (2010) *The Shape of the Beast*. London: Hamish Hamilton.

Ruch, G. (2002) 'From triangle to spiral: reflective practice in social work education, practice and research', *Social Work Education*, 21: 199–216.

Ruch, G. (2005) 'Relationship-based practice and reflective practice: holistic approaches to contemporary child care social work', *Child and Family Social Work*, 10: 111–23.

Ruch, G. (2012) 'Where have all the feelings gone? Developing reflective and relationship-based management in child-care social work', *British Journal of Social Work*, 42(7): 1315–32.

Ryan, T. (1998) 'Risk management and people with mental health problems', in H. Kemshall and J. Pritchard (eds), *Good Practice in Risk Assessment and Risk Management*. London: Jessica Kingsley.

Sackett, D.L., Rosenberg, W.M.C., Gray, J.A.M., Haynes, R.B. and Richardson, W.S. (1996) 'Evidence-based medicine: what it is and what it isn't', *British Medical Journal*, 312: 71–2.

Saleebey, D. (1992) *The Strengths Perspective in Social Work Practice*. New York: Longman.

Schalock, R.L., Lee, T., Verdugo, M., Swart, K., Claes, C., van Loon, J. and Lee, C.-S. (2014) 'An evidence-based approach to organization evaluation and change in human service organizations evaluation and program planning', *Evaluation and Program Planning*, 45: 110–18.

Schmid, H. (2004) 'Organization–environment relationships: theory for management practice in human service organizations', *Administration in Social Work*, 28(1): 97–113.

Scholz, S. (2010) *Feminism*. Oxford: Oneworld Guide.

Schön, D. (1983) *The Reflective Practitioner: How Professionals Think in Action*. New York: Basic Books.

Scott, D. (2005) 'Inter-organizational collaboration in family-centred practice: a framework for analysis and action', *Australian Social Work*, 58(2): 132–41.

Scott, D. and Swain, S. (2002) *Confronting Cruelty: Historical Perspectives on Child Protection in Australia*. Melbourne: Melbourne University Press.

Scott, R.W. (2002) *Organizations: Rational, Natural and Open Systems*, 5th edn. Englewood Cliffs, NJ: Prentice Hall.

Secker, J. and Hill, K. (2001) 'Broadening the partnerships: experiences of working across community agencies', *Journal of Interprofessional Care*, 15(4): 341–50.

Sellick, M.M., Delaney, R. and Brownlee, K. (2002) 'The deconstruction of professional knowledge: accountability without authority', *Families in Society*, 83(5/6): 493–8.

Senge, P. (1990) *The Fifth Discipline: The Art and Practice of the Learning Organization*. Milsons Point, NSW: Random House.

Sennett, R. (2003) *Respect: The Formation of Character in a World of Inequality*. London: Penguin Books.

Severson, M.M. (1998) 'Teaching mediation theory and skills in an interdisciplinary classroom', *Journal of Social Work Education*, 34(2): 185–94.

Severson, M.M. and Bankston, T.V. (1995) 'Social work and the pursuit of justice through mediation', *Social Work*, 40(5): 683–91.

Shapiro, M. (2000) 'Professions in the post-industrial labour market', in I. O'Connor, P. Smyth and J. Warburton (eds), *Contemporary Perspectives on Social Work and the Human Services: Challenges and Change*. Melbourne: Longman.

Shardlow, S. (1995) 'Confidentiality, accountability and the boundaries of client–worker relationships', in R. Hugman and D. Smith (eds), *Ethical Issues in Social Work*. London: Routledge.

Shaw, I. (2004) 'Evaluation for a learning organization?', in N. Gould and M. Baldwin (eds), *Social Work, Critical Reflection and the Learning Organization*. Aldershot: Ashgate.

Sheldon, B. (1998) 'Evidence based social services: prospects and problems', *Research, Policy and Planning*, 16(2): 16–18.

Sheppard, M. (1995) *Care Management and the New Social Work: A Critical Analysis*. London: Whiting and Birch.

Silverman, E. (2014) 'Organisational awareness: a missing generalist social work competency', *Social Work*, 60(1): 93–5.

Simon, H.A. (1957) *Models of Man*. New York: John Wiley.

Smith, M. (2007) 'Smoke without fire? Social workers' fears of threats and accusations', *Journal of Social Work Practice*, 21(3): 323–35.

Smith, M.K. (1998) 'Empowerment evaluation: theoretical and methodological considerations', *Evaluation and Program Planning*, 21: 255–61.

Smollan, R.K., Sayers, J.G. and Matheny, J.A. (2010) 'Emotional responses to the speed, frequency and timing of organizational change', *Time and Society*, 19(1): 28–53.

Spall, P. and Zetlin, D. (2004) 'Third sector in transition: a question of sustainability for community sector organizations and the sector?', *Australian Journal of Social Issues*, 39(3): 283–98.

Stack, S. (2003) 'Beyond performance indicators: a case study', *Australian Bulletin of Labour*, 29(2): 143–61.

Stanley, T. and Lincoln, H. (2015) 'Improving organisational culture: the practice gains', *Practice: Social Work in Action*, 28(3): 199–212.

Starkey, F. (2003) 'The "empowerment debate": consumerist, professional and liberational perspectives in health and social care', *Social Policy and Society*, 2(4): 273–84.

STARTTS (2004) *Working with Refugees: A Guide for Social Workers*. Sydney: New South Wales Service for the Treatment and Rehabilitation of Torture and Trauma Survivors.

Strati, A. (2000) *Theory and Method in Organizational Studies*. London: Sage.

Strier, R. and Binyamin, S. (2010) 'Developing anti-oppressive services for the poor: a theoretical and organizational rationale', *British Journal of Social Work*, 40: 1908–26.

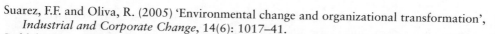

Suarez, F.F. and Oliva, R. (2005) 'Environmental change and organizational transformation', *Industrial and Corporate Change*, 14(6): 1017–41.

Suddaby, R. and Viale, T. (2011) 'Professionals and field-level change: institutional work and the professional project', *Current Sociology*, 59(4): 423–42.

Sveiby, K.E. (1997) *The New Organizational Wealth: Managing and Measuring Knowledge-based Assets*. San Francisco, CA: Berrett-Koehler.

Tafvelin, S., Hyvönen, U. and Westerberg, K. (2014) 'Transformational leadership in the social work context: the importance of leader continuity and co-worker support', *British Journal of Social Work*, 44(4): 886–904.

Tajima, H. (2014) 'Examination of the philosophical diversity of existential approaches in social work practice', *Japanese Journal of Social Welfare*, 54(5): 23–30.

Taylor, F.W. (1911) *The Principles of Scientific Management*. New York: Harper Bros.

Taylor, I., Sharland, E., Sebba, J., Le Riche, P., Keep, E. and Orr, D. (2006) *The Learning, Teaching and Assessment of Partnership Work in Social Work Education*. London: Social Care Institute for Excellence.

Telford, L. (1996) 'Selves in bunkers: organizational consequences of failing to verify alternative masculinities', in C. Cheng (ed.), *Masculinities in Organizations*. London: Sage.

Terry, D.J. and Jimmieson, N.L. (2003) 'A stress and coping approach to organizational change: evidence from three field studies', *Australian Psychologist*, 38(2): 92–101.

Thomas, J. (2004) 'Using "critical incident analysis" to promote critical reflection and holistic assessment', in N. Gould and M. Baldwin (eds), *Social Work, Critical Reflection and the Learning Organization*. Aldershot: Ashgate.

Thompson, N. (1992) *Existentialism and Social Work*. Aldershot: Avebury.

Thompson, N. (1993) *Anti-Discriminatory Practice*. London: Macmillan.

Thompson, N. (2000) *Theory and Practice in Human Services*, 2nd edn. Buckingham: Open University Press.

Thompson, N. (2003) *Promoting Equality: Challenging Discrimination and Oppression*. Basingstoke: Palgrave.

Thompson, N. (2011) *Promoting Equality: Challenging Discrimination and Oppression*, 3rd edn. Basingstoke: Palgrave Macmillan.

Thompson, N. (2015) *Understanding Social Work: Preparing for Practice*, 4th edn. London: Palgrave Macmillan.

Thompson, P. and McHugh, D. (2002) *Work Organizations*. Basingstoke: Palgrave.

Thylefors, I., Persson, O. and Hellstrom, D. (2005) 'Team types, perceived efficiency and team climate in Swedish cross-professional teamwork', *Journal of Interprofessional Care*, 19(2): 102–14.

Treen, J.W. (2015) 'Social media as technologies of accountability: explaining resistance to implementation within organisations', *American Behavioural Scientist*, 59(1): 53–74.

Trevithick, P. (2014) 'Humanising managerialism: reclaiming emotional reasoning, intuition, the relationship, and knowledge and skills in social work', *Journal of Social Work Practice*, 28(3): 287–311.

Tsang, E.W.K. (1997) 'Organizational learning and the learning organization: a dichotomy between descriptive and prescriptive research', *Human Relations*, 50(1): 73–89.

Turbett, C. (2004) 'A decade after Orkney: towards a practice model for social work in the remoter areas of Scotland', *British Journal of Social Work*, 34: 981–95.

Turner, L. and Shera, W. (2005) 'Empowerment in human service workers: beyond intra-organizational strategies', *Administration in Social Work*, 29(3): 79–94.

Urquhart, R. and Wearing, M. (2016) 'Organisational change in non-profit human services: reflections on a collaborative action research approach to working with child, youth and family organizations', in L. Rowell, C.D. Bruce, J.M. Shosh and M. Riel (eds), *The Palgrave International Handbook of Action Research*. New York: Palgrave Macmillan.

Usher, K., Woods, C., Casella, E., Glass, N., Wilson, R., Mayner, L., et al. (2014) 'Australian health professions student use of social media', *Collegian*, 21(2): 95–101.

van Breda, A.D. (2000) 'The practical value of strategic direction', *Administration in Social Work*, 24(3): 1–16.

van den Broek, D. (2003) 'Selling human services', *Australian Bulletin of Labour*, 29(3): 236–53.

Walker, P. (2002) 'Understanding accountability: theoretical models and their implications for social service organizations', *Social Policy and Administration*, 36: 62–75.

Wall, J.A., Stark, J.B. and Standifer, R.L. (2001) 'Mediation: a current review and theory development', *The Journal of Conflict Resolution*, 45(3): 370–91.

Wanna, J., Butcher, J. and Freyens, B. (2010) *Policy in Action: The Challenge of Service Delivery*. Sydney: UNSW Press.

Warren, E. and Toll, C. (1993) *The Stress Workbook: How Individuals, Teams and Organizations Can Balance Pressure and Performance*. London: Nicholas Brealey.

Wearing, M. (1998) *Working in Community Services: Management and Practice*. Sydney: Allen and Unwin.

Wearing, M. (2001) 'Risk, human services and contractualism', *Law in Context*, 18(2): 129–53.

Wearing, M. (2004) 'Medical dominance and the division of health care labour', in C. Grbich (ed.), *Health in Australia*, 3rd edn. Melbourne: Pearson Education.

Wearing, M. (2011) 'Strengthening youth citizenship and social inclusion practice: the Australian case', *Child and Youth Services Review*, 34(4): 534–40.

Wearing M. (2012) 'Demonizing non-white identities in the global security state: citizenship, social exclusion and racism in Australia', in D. Petty and C. MacFarland (eds), *Citizenship: Practices, Types and Challenges*. New York: Nova Science.

Wearing, M. (2016) 'Organisational and inter-organisational learning for case management', in E. Moore (ed.), *Case Management for Community Practice*, 2nd edn. Melbourne: Oxford University Press.

Wearing, M. and Edwards, M. (2003) *The Voice of Front-line Workers in Family Support Work: A Qualitative Study of Early Intervention in Child Abuse and Neglect*. Sydney: Uniting Care Burnside.

Wearing, M. and Hughes, M. (2014) 'On fluidity and flow in the networked space of human service organizations: understanding liquidity and organized welfare praxis', in J. Kociatkiewicz and M. Kostera (eds), *Liquid Organization: Zygmunt Bauman and Management Studies*. London: Routledge.

Wearing, S. and Wearing, M. (2006) '"Rereading the subjugating tourist" in neoliberalism: postcolonial otherness and the tourist experience', *Tourism Analysis*, 11(2): 143–65.

Webb, S. (2001) 'Some considerations on the validity of evidence-based practice in social work', *British Journal of Social Work*, 31: 57–79.

Webb, S. (2002) 'Evidence-based practice and decision analysis in social work', *Journal of Social Work*, 2(1): 45–63.

Webb, S.A. (2006) *Social Work in a Risk Society*. London: Palgrave.

Weber, M. (1971 [1922]) 'Power and bureaucracy', in K. Thompson and J. Tunstall (eds), *Sociological Perspectives*. Harmondsworth: Penguin Books.

Weeks, W. and Quinn, M. (eds) (2000) *Issues Facing Australian Families: Human Services Respond*. French's Forest, NSW: Pearson Education.

Welbourne, P., Harrison, G. and Ford, D. (2007) 'Social work in the UK and the global labour market: recruitment, practice and ethical considerations', *International Social Work*, 50(1): 27–40.

Weller, J.M. (2003) 'New therapeutics and AIDS activists' inventiveness: the history of a mutual aid and support centre for people living with AIDS', *Sciences Sociales et Santé*, 21(3): 37–70.

Wenger, E., McDermott, R. and Snyder, W.M. (2002) *Cultivating Communities of Practice: A Guide to Managing Knowledge*. Boston, MA: Harvard Business School Press.

Westwood, R. (2001) 'Appropriating the Other in discourses of comparative management', in R. Westwood and S. Linstead (eds), *The Language of Organization*. London: Sage.

Williams, G. (2006) 'Collaborative partnerships and urban change management: the renewal of Manchester city centre', *International Journal of Sociology and Social Policy*, 26(5/6): 194–206.

Willis, E. (2005) 'The variable impact of new public management and budget cuts on work intensification of nurses and doctors in one public hospital in South Australia between 1994 and 2000', *Australian Bulletin of Labour*, 31(3): 255–69.

Wilson, K., Ruch, G., Lymbery, M. and Cooper, A. (2008) *Social Work: An Introduction to Contemporary Practice*. London: Pearson Longman.

Winkworth, G. (2005) 'Public officials and collaboration: government service providers, local "communities" and pathways to employment', in M. Pawar (ed.), *Capacity Building for Participation: Social Workers' Thoughts and Reflections*. Wagga Wagga, NSW: Centre for Rural Social Research.

Winkworth, G. and Camilleri, P. (2004) 'Keeping the faith: the impact of human services restructuring on Catholic social welfare services', *Australian Journal of Social Issues*, 39(3): 315–28.

Wolin, S.S. (2004) *Politics and Vision*. Princeton, NJ: Princeton University Press.

Wood, J. (2008) *Report of the Special Commission of Inquiry into Child Protection Services in NSW*. Sydney: State of NSW.

Woodward, S. and Hendry, C. (2004) 'Leading and coping with change', *Journal of Change Management*, 4(2): 155–83.

Yeatman, A. (ed.) (1990) *Bureaucrats, Technocrats, Femocrats: Essays on the Contemporary Australian State*. Sydney: Allen and Unwin.

Yeung, K., Ho, A., Lo, M. and Chan, E. (2010) 'Social work ethical decision making in an inter-disciplinary context', *British Journal of Social Work*, 40: 1573–90.

Zell, D. (2003) 'Organizational change as a process of death, dying, and rebirth', *Journal of Applied Behavioral Science*, 39(1): 73–96.

Zifcak, S. (1994) *New Managerialism: Administrative Reform in Whitehall and Canberra*. Buckingham: Open University Press.

Zubrzycki, J. and Bennett, B. (2006) 'Aboriginal Australians', in W.H. Chui and J. Wilson (eds), *Social Work and Human Services: Best Practice*. Sydney: The Federation Press.

Index

Note: Page numbers in **bold** indicate practice examples and page numbers in *italics* refer to figures.